Learning Autonomy in Post-16 Education

D0076584

This book makes an important contribution to understanding the political, social and educational impact of assessment. Using a multi-layered approach, it offers a fascinating case study of how post-16 education systems are designed and debated inside policy-making processes. The author explores the complex factors that affect how teachers and students use formative assessment to achieve higher standards of educational attainment and more autonomous learning. She also explores the broader tensions at the heart of assessment policy.

Learning Autonomy in Post-16 Education is a comprehensive and authoritative account of policy and practice in post-16 assessment. The book weaves together new theoretical frameworks with evidence from research to offer a detailed picture of the diverse factors affecting the quality of formative assessment in further education.

The book will be of particular interest to teachers and practitioners across the post-16 sector on postgraduate and in-service professional development courses.

Dr Kathryn Ecclestone is a lecturer in post-compulsory education at the University of Newcastle.

Learning Autonomy in Post-16 Education

The politics and practice of formative assessment

Kathryn Ecclestone

London and New York

First published 2002 by RoutledgeFalmer
11 New Fetter Lane, London EC4P 4EE

Simultaneously published in the USA and Canada
by RoutledgeFalmer
29 West 35th Street, New York, NY 10001

RoutledgeFalmer is an imprint of the Taylor & Francis Group

© 2002 Kathryn Ecclestone

Typeset in Sabon by BC Typesetting, Bristol
Printed and bound in Great Britain by
TJ International Ltd, Padstow, Cornwall

British Library Cataloguing in Publication Data
A catalogue record for this book is available from the British Library

Library of Congress Cataloging in Publication Data
A catalogue record has been requested

ISBN 0–415–24740-3 (hbk)
ISBN 0–415–24741–1 (pbk)

Contents

Acknowledgements

It is difficult to write a book about the impact of formative assessment on learners' autonomy and motivation without reflecting on the social motivation and commitment to communities of practice and individuals that have underpinned this book and my own learning during the process of writing it.

I owe much to the teachers and students who let me share their experiences of assessment in vocational courses in further education colleges for this book. Friends who share a commitment to further education have also been crucial motivators. Les August, best friend, post-16 inspector and ex-senior manager in FE, is a brilliant role model. Sue Harrison probably does not realise how much our animated conversations over 15 years about pedagogy, assessment, dealing with students and colleagues have inspired me to be a better teacher, assessor and colleague. Jane Smedley, now at York College, is one of the best teachers and colleagues I worked with in further education. As one of a generation of ex-liberal studies teachers who went on to become college principals, the retirement of Alan Harrison from Mackworth College Derby reflects the loss to further education of managers who really care about the quality of education. I have also learned a lot about assessment and motivation from my good friend, Lynne Rybacki, and sister, Annie Barrett, whose primary school pupils are lucky to have them as assessors and teachers. And Julie Ecclestone is simply a great motivator, personally and professionally.

An academic community of practice, committed to robust critical but constructive scholarship is best exemplified by Frank Coffield who supervised the PhD that forms the basis for this book. His encouragement and feedback, insights about issues raised by the work, and the example set by his own research, all highlight the importance of professional apprenticeship. I am grateful to Professor Stephen Ball and Professor Patricia Broadfoot who examined the thesis and offered such good advice. I also owe much to feedback on various articles and sections of this book from Joanna Swann at King's College, Ann-Marie Bathmaker at Sheffield, Lorna Unwin at Leicester, John Field at Warwick, Christine Skelton and Mairtin Mac An Ghaill at Newcastle. They all combine the qualities of friendship, humour and high standards of scholarship with excellent formative feed-back. Such skills are a winning combination in academic networks.

Finally, the book owes much to a close friend, Debbie Thornton, principal of Harrogate College, who died at the age of 41 in September 2000, just as I submitted my PhD thesis for examination. Her interest in issues raised by the book, her professionalism, awe-inspiring output and pace of work, her brilliant sense of humour, and an unique ability to motivate colleagues and friends to strive beyond what they think they are capable of, are more inspiring than I can say.

List of abbreviations

BTEC:	Business and Technology Education Council
CPVE:	Certificate in Pre-Vocational Education
DES:	Department for Education and Science
DfE:	Department for Education
DfEE:	Department of Education and Employment
DfES:	Department for Education and Skills
FEFC:	Further Education Funding Council
FEDA:	Further Education Development Agency
FEU:	Further Education Unit
GNVQs:	General National Vocational Qualifications
LSCs:	Learning and Skills Council(s)
LSDA:	Learning and Skills Development Agency
MSC:	Manpower Services Commission
NCVQ:	National Council for Vocational Qualifications
NIACE:	National Institute of Adult and Continuing Education
QCA:	Qualifications and Curriculum Authority
TVEI:	Technical and Vocational Education Initiative
UDACE:	Unit for the Development of Adult and Continuing Education
UCAS:	Universities Careers and Admissions Service
YOP:	Youth Opportunities Programme
YTS:	Youth Training Scheme

Introduction

On a wet day in April 2000, I boarded a plane at Bordeaux, ready to spend the flight analysing students' interview transcripts from the research that underpins this book. With my head full of students' ideas about autonomy, motivation and formative assessment, I recognised immediately the airline steward welcoming us on to the plane, as Ruth, a catering student in the very first lesson of my full-time teaching career in further education at 9 o'clock on Friday 1 February 1985. Now 33, in charge of staff training for an airline at Stansted Airport (and with a private pilot's licence), she remembered me too and, during the flight, she recalled our 'People in Organisations' lessons in heartening detail, as well as the subsequent careers of her peers. 'College was the best time of my life,' she said, and, as music to the ears of a teacher, added 'I've just never stopped learning.'

Meeting Ruth at a pivotal moment in the research reminds me why the topic of this book is worthwhile. Of course, Ruth and the rest of her well-motivated, lively peer group knew nothing in 1985 of the political, social and educational significance of assessment initiatives that emerged during the 1970s and 1980s. But significantly, neither did I or many of my colleagues. Ruth and her peers represented a continuing stream of young people who chose actively to follow a vocational course in a further education (FE) college. Unlike many of the 69 per cent of 16 year olds for whom full-time education is now the only alternative to unemployment, low status employment schemes or poorly paid jobs, Ruth's enthusiastic first choice in 1985 was a BTEC National Diploma course in catering.[1] Yet, in parallel to mainstream vocational courses for Ruth and her peer group, youth unemployment schemes and other vocational initiatives, such as the Certificate of Vocational Education (CPVE) and the Technical Vocational Education Initiative (TVEI), brought a new 'type' of young person into FE colleges during the 1980s. And, alongside an influx of new students, those supervising work experience placements and life and social skills programmes on government-funded schemes for the unemployed began to move into FE colleges, forming a new professional strand in FE teaching, curriculum development and middle management.

Fifteen years after Ruth left FE, assessment policy and its impact on pedagogy and learning in post-16 education remains under-theorised and little understood. This book addresses this problem by exploring the changing relationship between the functions and formats of assessment systems and ideas about what counts as educational success in a society characterised increasingly by notions of 'risk' and 'crisis'. This introductory chapter sketches some of the background to issues raised by the book, outlines its theoretical rationale and describes the overall structure of the chapters that follow.

New forms of assessment

A combination of new students, new professionals and a series of vocational initiatives, have altered the assessment and pedagogical landscape in FE almost beyond recognition since my first lesson with Ruth in 1985. These changes reflect a political and professional will to motivate young people who might otherwise leave education. Leading directly to the introduction of General National Vocational Qualifications (GNVQs) in 1992, a focus on new approaches to formative and summative assessment in vocational education was partly a motivating device to encourage students to gain a credible qualification and partly a way of fostering 'independent' learning. Promoters of these new approaches to assessment in GNVQs also hoped they would gain political and professional parity of esteem with more traditional approaches. As this book shows, the transmogrification of GNVQs into Vocational A-levels dashed these hopes.

Vocational initiatives have formed part of a long-running response to a broader crisis of motivation amongst young people that began in the 1970s (see Hargreaves, 1989; Ainley, 1999) and to political demands for more work-related skills in general education courses. Current policy is reshaping notions of 'acceptable' assessment models, reflecting a shift from norm-referenced systems based on the enduring idea in the UK that assessment must select those learners with innate ability for limited places in education and good jobs. Instead, criterion-referenced and outcome-based systems claim to encourage people's potential, to make teachers and institutions more accountable to learners and other interest groups and to promote learner autonomy. In outcome-based models of assessment, such goals depend on giving people access to the outcomes and criteria. In theory at least, this not only encourages students to engage more actively with assessment but also makes evidence of achievement more flexible and therefore less dependent on formal structures and syllabi. Flexibility also makes accumulation and transfer of formal credit and certification possible, together with accreditation of prior achievement in formal learning programmes (see Jessup 1991; McNair, 1995).

The political and educational aims of assessment in these approaches resonate with growing interest amongst academic and policy-based researchers in the potential power of formative and diagnostic assessment to raise standards of attainment, to motivate learners and to make them more autonomous as learners. In part, such research builds upon initiatives such as Records of Achievement (see Broadfoot, 1986; Wolf, 1998). More broadly, research evidence also shows that better diagnosis of learners' needs and interests, reviewing achievement and involving learners actively in assessing the quality of their work, are all integral features of progressive, empowering assessment. A key interest in this research is the constructivist notion of creating 'communities of practice' between teachers and students based on developing shared understandings of criteria for quality (see Gipps 1994; Black and Wiliam 1998).

This book engages directly with aims in recent post-16 education policy that assessment models in vocational qualifications should motivate more learners to become autonomous whilst, simultaneously, achieving higher, more rigorous 'standards' of educational attainment. These goals produced intensive political intervention in the post-16 vocational curriculum through a series of initiatives during the 1980s and 1990s, culminating in GNVQs as 'the most extensive application of outcome-based assessment in the world' (Hillier, 1996). GNVQs were also the first time that features of portfolio-based assessment and records of achievement had been used on a mass scale in a mainstream qualification (Broadfoot, 1998; Wolf, 1998). Their re-launch as Vocational A-levels and Vocational GCSEs in September 2000, after eight years of controversial development inside policy processes, illustrates some of the intractable political and technical problems that beset assessment systems. Understanding these is especially important now that Vocational A-levels and Vocational GCSEs must meet dual aims of raising achievement and motivation amongst 14 and 16 year olds. It is also important because goals associated with outcome-based models are now more apparent in the assessment system of A-levels and in adult and higher education. The over-riding themes of the political and professional mantras that emanate from conference platforms and government documents are, therefore, the need to widen participation, raise achievement (for example, DfEE, 1999) and to motivate non-traditional learners in formal learning.

Yet, in parallel with interest in progressive possibilities for using particular forms of assessment to enhance learning, in advanced and developing countries alike, assessment is increasingly required to fulfil competing political, social and educational purposes (see Broadfoot, 1996). The book illustrates the extent to which some of these purposes clash in vocational qualifications, creating major contradictions in goals and practices for teachers and students having to implement them. Arguments in the book about the effects of contradictions on forms of autonomy and motivation in formal education programmes also have implications for other assessment systems, including those in the National Curriculum for schools and in higher education. More subtly, assessment models and the discourses that both underpin them and are produced by them are reshaping notions of autonomy and motivation, and through this, fundamental notions of educational success and aspiration.

A need for research

Research interest in the role of formative assessment in promoting learner autonomy has focused, so far at least, almost exclusively on the National Curriculum (Black and Wiliam, 1998). The same is true of case studies of assessment policy (see, for example, Black, 1995). There is therefore a dearth of evidence in post-compulsory education and FE colleges in particular about influences on teachers' and students' values, their dispositions towards learning and assessment practices in relation to developing autonomy and motivation. And, although there is growing evidence about organisational cultures and management practices in FE colleges (see, for example, Ainley and Bailey, 1997; Gleeson and Shain, 1999), we know little about how the macro levels of ideology, theories of learning and political conflict combine to affect policy-making around particular assessment models. Nor do we know much about how post-16 assessment policy and theory is interpreted at the meso level of institutional organisation, culture and ethos, and the micro level of interactions between teachers and students. Insights about these inter-locking spheres and levels of policy and practice are essential if research is to help qualification designers, teachers, curriculum managers and students in the post-compulsory sector to improve the links between formative assessment, autonomy and motivation.

In the light of these gaps in understanding about assessment policy and practice affecting FE colleges, this book focuses on research claims for formative assessment by attending to assessment policy design and its implementation at macro, meso and micro levels. It uses the over-arching theoretical device of analysing policy and everyday assessment practices in 'a policy trajectory' (Ball, 1997), drawing upon an in-depth theoretical and empirical study of assessment policy and practice in Advanced GNVQs. This aims to account for the ways in which a particular initiative evolves and is interpreted over time and at different levels. A policy trajectory may therefore help policy analysts, people inside policy and those on the receiving end of it to make sense of the 'seemingly tenuous connection between policy and practice' (Malen and Knapp, 1997: 419).

Analysis shows how new assessment models, the forms of regulation that underpin them, and assessment activities used by teachers and students, simultaneously reflect and construct notions of autonomy and motivation in post-compulsory education. One effect is that discourses surrounding autonomy, motivation and formative assessment are acquiring new meanings and losing others. Some discourses emerge through a uniform policy rhetoric where official documents, evaluation and inspection reports, development projects and subsequent amendments to an assessment model all combine to create certain themes for debate but subtly close down others.

Some themes are lost or gained in policy transmission and amendment and in conflicting themes of progressivism and empowerment in the vocational curriculum. In response to these shifts, it is pertinent to apply Frank Coffield's use of Wittgenstein's advice in relation to different meanings of a 'learning society' to discussion of motivation and autonomy in lifelong learning: 'sometimes an expression has to be withdrawn from language and sent for cleaning – then it can be put back into circulation' (Wittgenstein quoted by Coffield, 1997a: 454). In the vocational curriculum, this 'cleaning' is particularly apposite given that outcome-based assessment models have characterised policy initiatives since the 1980s: as Inge Bates argues, an outcome-based model is itself 'reconstructed in each terrain it passes, depending on the histories, purposes and meanings which actors bring to it' (Bates, 1998b: 43).

Research that hopes to address these shifting meanings and their implications has to locate an issue within a clear ideological, political and social context. A commitment to the complexity and richness of what Gerald Grace calls 'policy scholarship' (Grace, 1994) avoids the constraints of 'policy science' which focuses only upon 'the specifics of a particular set of policy initiatives' (Grace cited by Whitty and Edwards, 1994: 28). Without this commitment it is easy for researchers to over-simplify and over-rationalise policy directions and their underlying imperatives, and then to emphasise the technical aspects of their implementation. Using a theoretical framework informed by policy scholarship, the policy trajectory in this book explores four over-arching questions:

- How does the socio-economic and ideological context of policy for lifelong learning in the UK influence the types of motivation and autonomy seen as both desirable and realistic for post-16 students in general vocational education?
- What does a policy-based case study of the Advanced GNVQ assessment model show about policy design, development and implementation in the post-compulsory curriculum?
- What does a case study of implementing Advanced GNVQ assessment policy in FE colleges show about the impact of an outcome-based assessment model on students' autonomy and motivation and on formative assessment as a key to promoting motivation and autonomy?
- How can formative assessment in post-compulsory education be improved in order to enhance students' autonomy and motivation?

A need for multiple perspectives

The book is influenced by two academic traditions in education scholarship. The first is the type of 'policy sociology' pioneered in education research by Stephen Ball. His work encourages links between the layers of ideology, politics and policy-making, and practice, combined with critical reflexivity by researchers. The second influence is a small but growing literature on the sociology of assessment which combines analysis of the broader role of assessment and qualifications in post-industrial societies with close examination of assessment practices and activities (see, for example, Broadfoot, 1996).

In the current climate of educational research, Stephen Ball argues that policy scholarship is becoming increasingly elusive as 'policy entrepreneurship' lures researchers into mere proselytisations of acceptable solutions for turning practice into a mirror of policy intentions. This enhances the careers of those involved, including researchers themselves, and renders scholarship undesirable and even unacceptable (Ball, 1995). In the light of this argument, this book hopes to differentiate between specific policy-related effects and the complex variables that affect the day-to-day implementation of assessment policy in the FE sector at meso and micro levels. Striving for complexity highlights how policy is read, taken account of, or ignored and the effects of idiosyncratic micro-political factors in particular institutional settings (Ball, 1994).

Policy scholarship also address the problem of what C. Wright Mills calls 'historical provincialism: the assumption that the present is a sort of autonomous creation' (Mills, 1970: 151). Educational research that offers a timeless, ahistorical perspective tends to portray particular initiatives as uprooted from what went before and unaffected by other shifts in ideology and values in public policy. This leads to analyses dictated only by educational preoccupations and principles (Ball, 1997), making it important to examine the imperatives that give apparently disparate initiatives a general coherence.

In policy analysis, researchers also need to move beyond a neutral pluralist account that obscures complexities and power struggles in the vocational curriculum (Raggatt and Williams, 1999). This aim requires identifying connections between a structural context and political and organisational perspectives, competing interests and influences, and the effects on individuals and organisations of decisions made in different parts of the policy-making process. Interactionist analysis can explain how and why certain aspects of policy-making gain influence, or become expendable at various times. Tracking the different advocacy groups, experts and specialist knowledge that influence 'policy oriented learning' amongst key actors (Hulme, 1998) can illuminate avenues of influence. It is therefore useful to focus on what Ball (1994) calls 'policy as text', namely the representation of policy encoded in complex ways through political and organisational struggles, compromises and the ensuing public interpretations of policy intentions. Implementation and new interpretations by other actors and constituencies act as further decoders of policy texts. As Ball points out, attempts to present policy spread confusion as various mediators try to relate their understandings to particular contexts. It is therefore crucial to recognise that policy texts are not 'clear or closed or complete [but] the products of compromises at various stages (at points of initial influence, in the micro-politics of legislative formation, in the parliamentary process and in the politics and micropolitics of interest group articulation)' (1994: 16).

Like the National Curriculum, GNVQs generated a continuous deluge of texts during their eight year history. This book focuses on assessment speci-fications, guidance from NCVQ and QCA and awarding bodies to teachers, some minutes of policy meetings, commercial text books, guidance from agencies supporting policy development[2] and teachers' own translations of official specifications in schemes of work. These texts can all be seen as the 'cannibalised products of multiple (but circumscribed) influences and agendas' (Ball, 1994: 16).

It is also helpful to regard 'policy as discourse' (ibid). This illuminates how policy-makers and their intermediaries, such as inspectors, awarding bodies and curriculum support agencies, apply particular types of knowl-edge to perceived problems and then make teachers and students do the same. In debates about lifelong learning, for example, problems in assess-ment systems become problems of motivation, retention and attainment, poor 'human capital' and lack of parity of esteem between qualifications. As the policy case study shows in the book, new problems of 'rigour and consistency' in assessment came to dominate notions of 'parity'. Underlying these are stated problems of 'risks' associated with non-participation in, and low achievement of, formal qualifications. Such risks lead to demands for increased accountability and quality assurance. As this book highlights, policies are enacted and interpreted to solve particular problems but are already set within particular discursive frames (Ball, 1994).

Combining structural, interactionist and discourse analyses can therefore make sense of policies and their effects in different ways. Yet, as Malen and Knapp (1997) observe, there are no 'grand theories' for a researcher trying to construct an analytical model of policy and its impact on practice. A narrow focus on one initiative can overlook other influences and confirm prevailing assumptions amongst policy-makers, intermediaries and prac-titioners that gaps between policy and practice merely reflect failures in implementation. Researchers and policy-makers may claim that policy is so powerful that it is (variously) constraining, harmful and autocratic or empowering, transforming and innovative! Conversely, research might pre-sent policy as so easily sabotaged, undermined or ignored by teachers that it becomes submerged into the existing normative worlds of institutions and individuals (Malen and Knapp, 1977). It is therefore useful to adopt multiple perspectives in order to:

> encourage a comparative analysis of prominent perspectives in terms of their capacity to account for patterns of policy activity within and across settings; and they suggest 'avenues for influence', notably targets

and strategies actors might consider should they seek to affect policy developments.

(ibid.: 421)

This book adapts the analytical categories that Malen and Knapp's model offers. Briefly, rational perspectives emphasise apparently linear and orderly decision-making, traceable to individuals or key events and a discernible chronology in response to expressed problems. Political perspectives emphasise conflict and power battles over legitimate control and influence and over scarce recources. Normative dimensions appear over educational goals and notions of 'good' policy in response to these goals. Organisational perspectives reveal turf wars and struggles to preserve organisational cultures in a context of turmoil and political conflict. Last, symbolic perspectives illuminate underlying discourses and normative images of people, policy and practices. In summary, fieldwork for the book comprised:

- an in-depth policy analysis based on focused interviews with twenty-five key policy-makers involved in designing and implementing Advanced GNVQ assessment policy between 1991 and 2000 (see Appendix 1, at end of book)
- an intensive series over two years of observations of lessons, tutorials, post-observation and focused interviews and informal interviews with nine teachers and eighteen students in both year groups of Advanced GNVQ courses (Health and Social Care and Business) in two colleges in the north-east of England
- participant observation of marking students' work and agreeing grades with teachers (fifty assignments in total)
- two structured group discussions about formative assessment (one with the teacher sample, one with nine students), using a card sort activity based upon a typology of constructs of autonomy, motivation and formative assessment drawn from theoretical discussion in Chapter 2
- a questionnaire to seventy students within the eight cohorts covered by the study
- a questionnaire to thirty GNVQ course co-ordinators and 30 teachers in the same subjects in all FE and 6th form colleges in the north-east
- follow-up seminars with the nine teachers and four policy-based interviewees to discuss emerging findings
- follow-up interviews with four students progressing from GNVQ into higher education and employment in year three of the study.

Appendix 2 (at end of book) outlines the sequence and scope of fieldwork activities and the teacher and student samples.

Analysis was based on intensive, systematic 'open', 'selective' and 'axial' coding (Strauss, 1987; Strauss and Corbin, 1990). This grounds some ideas in the data and seeks discrepancies, rich detail and lateral connections.

It also enables *in vivo* codes to arise from language used by participants, for local meanings to be connected with broader concerns and for categories to be distilled into central themes for follow-up sampling. Additional ways of not taking the apparent 'reality' of transcripts and fieldwork notes at face value were to quantify themes or ideas, to look for silence or absence of issues or, conversely, to see if a particularly strong emphasis given by participants might really signify the opposite case.

Despite my recognition of a need for complexity and richness, making analysis accessible to readers almost invariably involves 'second order constructs and categories which can rigidify, simplify and reify the actual interpretations, perspectives and meanings held by teachers and pupils' (Ball, 1981: xiii). Public accounts are therefore only ever an approximation of reality even when researchers aim for analytical integrity in line with their aims and values, to account for complexity and reflexivity, and to be accessible to different audiences. And, as Ball *et al.* remind education researchers, not only are interviews the most fleeting and elusive glance at the complex, contradictory lives of participants in a study, but researchers invariably exercise choice over what they show and omit (Ball *et al.*, 2000). There is therefore a constant struggle over representation and a long-running criticism about how qualitative researchers use data, such as selective quotes to support pre-conceived and partisan ideas. I have therefore aimed not to use quotes as self-evident justifications or because, like journalism, they happen to tell a good story. But nor have I adopted a detailed, narrative approach, partly because of the size of my sample and the space available for analysis, but also because the study did not aim for a 'grounded' ethnographic approach.

Instead, the book aims to 'tell a story' through participants' accounts and my own observations. As the rationale here shows, it emerges from a commitment to striving for policy scholarship within a framework of structural, interactionist and discursive perspectives. Draft accounts have been discussed as extensively as possible with all participants in attempts to enhance validity and authenticity. However, to minimise embarrassment noted by participants when I produced exact quotes with dialect and hesitations intact, I have edited quotes to remove repetition, confusing phrasing, half-finished thoughts or a diversion from the main point, indicated by '. . .' in the text. Although researchers polish their own writing until they appear as articulate as possible and never (or rarely) write in dialect or slang, this presentation raises unresolved dilemmas about the imposition of the researcher's voice (see also discussion in Coffield *et al.*, 1986 and Ball *et al.*, 2000).

Further problems are caused by using the various labels, discussed later in the book, about students' motivation and attitudes to learning, policymakers' and teachers' educational beliefs and their responses to policy and to students as organising categories. It is easy, for example, to construct categories that students might resist or challenge or to avoid the need to create dialogue with research 'subjects' which, according to Joe Harkin (1999) merely confirms the prevailing lack of voice and dialogue already experienced by many college students. It is also tempting to create negative stereotypes of policy-makers in contrast to much more empathetic ones for teachers and students or to present what Ball calls a form of 'golden ageism' about policy (Ball, 1997). Categories can easily lead from useful analytical tools to fixed 'essentialising' identities for participants. Since researchers write up their accounts in particular ways, they need to show as often as possible their own reflexive awareness of representation, general-isations about participants' responses and motives, the limitations of inter-views and problems in taking accounts back.

Lastly, notwithstanding an aim to address complexity in education policy and its effects, achieving this task is affected by new uncertainties in ideo-logical and political positions. Some stances taken in research, such as that of critical policy analyst, imply an increasingly uncomfortable moral highground:

> Policy research is always in some degree both reactive and parasitic. Careers and reputations are made as our research flourishes on the rotting remains of the Keynsian Welfare State. Both those inside the policy discourse and those whose professional identities are established through antagonism to the discourse benefit from the uncertainties and tragedies of reform.
>
> (Ball, 1997: 258)

And a more salutary and compelling dilemma lurks behind goals for critical analysis:

> Critical researchers, apparently safely ensconced in the moral high-ground, nonetheless make a livelihood trading in the artefacts of misery and broken dreams of practitioners. None of us remains untainted by the incentives and disciplines of the new moral economy.
>
> (ibid.: 258)

The structure of the book

The book's structure follows five levels of analysis. At the macro level of ideology, Chapter 1 explores how political imperatives to motivate more people for lifelong learning cannot be isolated from a climate of deep-seated pessimism about a risk-filled future. An important aim in this chapter is to relate ideas about people's motivation for education, and the types of autonomy that learners might develop through it, to an emerging ideology of risk aversion. This simultaneously arises from, and fuels, concerns about the effects of what Ulrich Beck has portrayed as a 'risk society' (Beck, 1992) with new definitions of 'risk' and new ways to regulate them.

When education is both portrayed and accepted as a major inoculation against certain risks, non-participation itself becomes a focus of increasingly moralistic judgements about the risk that individuals cause to themselves and to their communities.

At the macro level of beliefs, theories and practices in relation to knowledge and learning, all assessment systems, to greater and lesser extents, offer teachers oblique and contradictory messages about using formative assessment to raise achievement. Chapter 2 explores tensions between constructivist notions of 'assessment communities' and enduring behaviourist perspectives about motivation. The chapter offers a theoretical typology that connects different types of individual and social motivation and autonomy with particular formative assessment practices. The typology therefore enables some empirical purchase on these attributes during fieldwork and sets the scene for analysis of policy developments and confusing, ambiguous messages over an eight-year period about autonomy and motivation offered to students and teachers in Advanced GNVQs.

At the macro level of policy-making, Chapter 3 uses empirical data to explore perceptions amongst ministers, civil servants, designers of the GNVQ assessment model, inspectors and representatives of external constituencies about policy developments and rationales for repeated change to assessment in GNVQs over eight years between 1992 and 2000. It also explores constructs of autonomy, motivation and formative assessment amongst the policy-based interviewees. Analysis of the political tensions over 'standards' in assessment that beset these constructs forms the backdrop to conflicting messages about the aims of GNVQ assessment that students and teachers had to deal with in implementing the assessment model.

Moving to the meso level of institutional cultures and organisation, Chapter 4 highlights how vocational initiatives during the 1980s affected professional perspectives on students' autonomy within different educational traditions in FE. It also shows how these initiatives paved the way for new forms of political intervention in FE colleges, culminating in the strong forms of regulation used in GNVQs to standardise assessment between centres. Repeated political interventions have contributed to the incursion of new targets, and forms of regulation and top-down restructuring in FE alongside unprecedented upheaval in conditions of service in FE colleges. The chapter concludes by describing the two college fieldwork sites and the samples of teachers and students.

At the micro level of interactions within learning groups in GNVQs, Chapter 5 explores motivation amongst students and teachers in the two colleges in relation to maintaining their goals in Advanced GNVQ over two years of the course. It analyses how different factors, both GNVQ-related and external to the assessment model, affected these goals. Chapter 6 relates goals for motivation to the ways in which students and teaches constructed autonomy during the two-year course. It analyses the diverse pressures on images of autonomy and the 'formal, non-formal and informal learning' activities (Eraut *et al.*, 1999) associated with developing, but also constraining, autonomy.

Merging the implications of macro, meso and micro analysis in previous chapters, Chapter 7 then explores how teachers and students viewed assessment practices in relation to motivation and autonomy. It proposes that the diverse pressures affecting the formative assessment practices that teachers and students adopted created a 'comfort zone' within which to work. Different factors at macro, meso and micro level therefore began to shape images of good students and teachers and also new forms of professionalism amongst teachers in the FE colleges in this study.

Finally, Chapter 8 synthesises analysis and arguments emerging throughout the book to evaluate the possibility that policy and practice in post-16 vocational education have created 'assessment regimes' rather than mere assessment models and, in turn, 'assessment careers' as a powerful strand in what Bloomer (1997) has called 'post-16 learning careers'. The chapter examines the prognosis for improving formative assessment practices in colleges and offers recommendations for different constituencies involved in designing, evaluating and implementing assessment regimes. It also offers practical considerations for other policy analysts and constituencies wishing to research assessment policy or to try and influence it. The concluding section suggests some broader implications of arguments developed in the book for expectations about the types of autonomy and motivation that might be possible, or desirable, in lifelong learning.

Summary

Two aims motivated me to write this book. One is a desire to use the intentions, design and implementation of an influential assessment policy in the post-compulsory sector as a case study and to go beyond academic fault-finding in order to offer a more rational basis for improving the links between assessment and learning. This is, ultimately, a modernist mission, resting on a belief (or perhaps a futile hope) that rational argument might persuade qualification designers, teachers and researchers of drawbacks to existing formative assessment policy and practices. A deeper commitment lies behind these goals, namely to promote forms of learning and assessment that are genuinely empowering, inspiring and motivating for students and teachers alike. Implicit in this aim is a fear that lifelong participation in formal learning for many people could end up as a series of instrumental, individualistic and self-regulating experiences, rather than being transforming, social and intrinsically motivating.

All five levels of evaluation in this book reveal, in various ways, different meanings of 'autonomy' and explicit and implicit expectations about learners' motivation amongst different agencies and constituencies in post-16 education. Indeed, the idea that 'autonomy' should be a focus of learning has taken on many of the characteristics of what Ball (1995) calls a 'mantric affirmation of belief'. A multi-layered analysis of the impact of assessment policy on motivation and autonomy might prevent progressive goals for formative assessment from becoming a mere 'technology' where practices are divorced from social and educational aims and become, instead, impoverished ends in a compliant, ultimately meaningless, pursuit of performance targets.

1 Learning in a risk society: empowerment, care or control?*

Introduction

Political demands for strategies to motivate more people for lifelong learning come at a time when profound doubts about globalisation and technological progress foster discourses of 'crisis', 'social polarisation' and 'social transformation' in education policy throughout Europe and in New Zealand, the United States and Australia. In particular, growing concern about 'a risk society' encourages new definitions and regulation of social, economic and personal 'risk' that require new social and political responses. These movements reflect a profound loss of confidence in Enlightenment ideas of rational 'truth', scientific and social progress and technological innovation (Beck, 1992) alongside increasing scepticism about both the possibility and desirability of education as a key to scientifically progressive and humane knowledge for the 'good of all'.

Concerns about the future sanction new forms of political intervention and patterns of influence in education structures, curriculum content and assessment systems. These aim to secure pedagogic and institutional change alongside broader adherence to new national, transnational and economic structures, across the European Union (see Field, 2000; Brine, 1995; Sultana, 1995). In the UK, powerful rhetorics of empowerment, motivation and access to useful qualifications accompany political intervention in the scope and format of assessment systems. There is a growing homogeneity in assessment models, accompanying rhetoric and forms of political intervention in the National Curriculum, post-14 vocational and general curricula, work-based training, parts of adult and community education and higher education. In part, this responds to what Habermas has portrayed as a 'crisis of legitimation' in advanced capitalist societies. Following this analysis, Andy Hargreaves argues that assessment systems are a crucial mechanism for securing social consent amongst young people who are no longer guaranteed jobs in return for compliance in education. Assessment

* Parts of this chapter are reproduced with permission from Blackwell Science (see Ecclestone, 1999).

systems must therefore, simultaneously, motivate people to achieve in formal education, legitimise the rationing of jobs and education and provide an alternative to 'obedience for qualifications leading to jobs' (Hargreaves, 1989: 111), for adults and young people alike.

This chapter explores how notions of autonomy and motivation implicit and explicit in our images of educational success and aspirations are affected by these broader themes and discourses. The first section engages critically with themes of motivation and autonomy in current debates about lifelong learning. The following section offers a critique of concerns about participation in lifelong learning and relates these to a new ideology of 'risk aversion'. Discussion here is therefore a precursor to discussion in Chapter 2 of the different types of motivation and autonomy that formal learning programmes might develop.

Rationales for lifelong learning

Across Europe, concerns about lifelong learning are embroiled in fears about competitiveness, innovations in technology and capitalist globalisation. Preceding the European Year of Lifelong Learning in 1996, the Delors White Paper, 'Growth, Competitiveness and Employment' proposed that 'human resource development – and hence, education, training and participation – is the key in maintaining European competitiveness, which in turn, is essential to economic and social well-being across the Community' (Chisholm, 1997: 43). European concerns parallel the pessimistic invocations of looming disaster, lack of options, and a common stake in bending before the economic whirlwind, routinely cited in British policy papers from the 1970s. For example: 'If we lack skills, we lose out. The economy, the performance of every business and the prosperity of every citizen suffer. We have no choice. We must all invest in learning for the future' (Stuart, 1997: 67).

In response to such problems, education is now portrayed in policy initiatives as the most important route to social and economic well-being and the key to workforce development (see, for example, National Skills Task Force, 2001).

Political and professional discourses embedded in consensus about the purposes of lifelong learning are suffused with themes of democracy, anti-elitism, social cohesion, inclusiveness and economic prosperity. Across the European Union, such discourses shift social policy goals from 'equal opportunities' to 'inclusion' within existing social formations (see also Brine, 1995; Sultana, 1995). Yet, notwithstanding espoused commitments to diverse purposes for lifelong learning, policy concentrates on economic competitiveness, where horizons for social change are reduced to connecting state education with participation in vocationally relevant qualifications and hopes for economic prosperity. This view is epitomised in the British Labour government's view that 'education is the best economic policy we have' (Tony Blair in DfEE, 1998), and that 'education *is* social justice' (Blair cited by Ainley, 1999: 23).

Such moves reflect a wider move from left and right wing politics to what Avis calls a 'modernising settlement' (1998) amongst many academics, policy-makers, employers' organisations and teachers. This elides liberal, modernising and social justice perspectives and promotes changes to institutional structures, qualifications and funding formulae as ways to erode divisions in a mass post-compulsory system (see, for example, Hodgson and Spours, 1997). At the same time, there is a growing consensus that community-based, informal and formal activities are 'purposeful' if they provide a springboard into formal, accredited learning or training at work. This leads to an increasingly prevalent view that young people and adults who do not participate in purposeful learning are 'at risk' of marginalisation, disenfranchisement and exclusion. One effect is the growing political and professional convergence between education initiatives and welfare and youth service initiatives designed to combat these dangers (Bullen *et al.*, 2000; Colley, 2000). New initiatives and further top-down restructuring of post-16 education and training structures, introduced in 2001, reveal both the government's determination to merge education and welfare policy and to maintain the state's growing hold over it by diverting funding from Local Education Authorities and Social Services through quangos and other state agencies. In some areas, there is growing interest in the 'full service school' where welfare, leisure and educational services emanate from one centre.

The consensus emerging from attempts to motivate more people for lifelong learning and to portray it as a form of welfare, is to make dissent from eliding participation in formal learning with employment and social inclusion extremely difficult. Increasing deference to contradictory demands from employers' organisations, particularly large companies, at all levels of curriculum design and implementation mean, for example, that it is easier to look at technical barriers to non-participation in formal learning, or apparent lack of motivation amongst potential learners, than more intractable structural barriers. Despite a record of poor investment in training amongst British firms, the 'needs' of employers are cited regularly as a driving force for educational change. There is also a powerful but littleheard argument which proposes that lack of investment in education and training, and low prices, monopolies and low wages, are rational strategies by some elements of capital in a competitive, rapidly stratifying global economy (Keep and Mayhew, 1998). Some employers, therefore, do not want, or need, highly skilled workers, a problem that is particularly prevalent in the North East where my research study took place (Jones, 2001).

Current images of problems with motivation and autonomy for learning, together with qualifications skewed to work-related skills and attitudes obscure these important detractions from consensus about the 'needs of the economy'. They also reinforce images of highly skilled, adaptable, problem-solving team workers moving autonomously between jobs and using evidence of educational achievement to gain them. Such images reinterpret broader notions of personal and social development as transferable 'skills' and generic competences for employment and overlook how many employers' recruitment practices still rely on traditional qualifications from the 'best' education institutions (Coffield, 1997b).

One response to these tensions is to support technical reforms to qualification systems in order to erode academic and vocational divisions and to secure the interests of diverse groups (see, for example, Hodgson and Spours, 1997). However, as Avis points out, the idea that policy can somehow be 'ideology-free' ignores social conflict and differentiation, 'as if these can be wished away or at least ameliorated through successful economic and educational strategies' (1998: 260). More broadly, current political emphasis on 'education as social justice' and 'parity of esteem' between qualification systems signals a lowering of expectations that equality of opportunity is a viable rationale for better assessment systems. A climate therefore exists where once-contested goals that education should encourage cultural vibrancy, equal opportunities, citizenship, social cohesion, the benefits of scientific progress and creating modern workforces have mutated into a new form of liberal vocationalism. This climate masks social inequality and moves policy from 'training without jobs' to 'learning without jobs', where 'like actors "resting", no-one would ever be unemployed, but only "learning"' (Ainley, 1999: 176). And, despite technical reforms to qualification systems, 'finely tuned differentiation' and growing segregation increasingly characterise educational and career destinations and aspirations (see also Hargreaves, 1989; Coffield and Williamson, 1997; Ball *et al.*, 2000).

Alongside the repeated waves of technical change that have characterised the post-16 sector over the past twenty years is a political emphasis on lifelong learning as an investment in 'human capital', namely the skills, motivation and achievement that individuals and society invest in to improve economic prosperity. This notion emphasises the importance of human beings as another capital investment:

> Just as physical capital is created by changes in materials to form tools that facilitate production, human capital is created by changes in persons that bring about skills and capabilities that make them able to act in new ways.
>
> (Coleman, cited by Schuller and Field, 1998: 227)

From the perspective of human capital, modular curriculum structures and outcome-based assessment systems equate learning with pursuit of vocationally relevant qualifications by self-interested individuals in a competitive labour market. Autonomy is therefore synonymous with self-interest and unfettered movement around the job and education market.

From this perspective, learning becomes 'commodified as a private good and a national resource' (Macrae *et al.*, 1997: 500) and assessment is an individualistic process of accumulating purposeful and measurable achievements, perhaps recorded in lifelong learning portfolios.

Emphasis on human capital leads to increased political concern with how returns on investment in education and training are distributed and paid for. For some critics, this enables problems of unemployment, job insecurity and continuous training to be 'privatised and handed over to individuals to solve' (Coffield, 1999a: 65). Human capital also provides 'an intellectual and moral escape mechanism from unpleasant social and political difficulties' (Balogh and Steeten quoted by Schuller, 1997: 117) and allows politicians to assert that fragmentation in social structures is produced by (uncontrollable) global forces and the (manageable) failings of a low skilled workforce (Macrae *et al.*, 1997). These perspectives produce a stream of largely unchallenged rhetoric that successful education systems create successful economies, an argument untainted by capitalist crises during the 1990s in Japan and Germany, not to mention Korea, Indonesia, Malaysia and Thailand.

Despite injunctions that education must prepare people for a post-Fordist world, many post-16 learners face unemployment, low status training, low wages and part-time, temporary work as alternatives to FE or university. As Ball *et al.* (2000) point out, the 'lived realities' of local job markets have a profound effect on young people's motivation for the education and training opportunities on offer, creating new conditions for 're-establishing and re-legitimating' social divisions. These realities cannot, therefore, be divorced from people's chances of becoming autonomous either inside formal programmes or outside them. Instead, job markets are far from the idealised opportunities portrayed by a post-Fordist, high skills rhetoric. James Avis, for example, argues that this rhetoric overestimates the extent of post-Fordist practices and overlooks how post-Fordist settings, such as Nissan in the UK, can be oppressive for workers (Avis, 1996). At the same time, many companies expect their highly skilled workers to be loyal and flexible but abandon their skilled workers as soon as the economic going gets tough (Coffield, 1999b). In the UK, the demise in June 2000 of BMW and the Rover Group, threats in 2001 by Nissan to relocate production to France and the closing of more steel plants in January 2001, show that even the productive, skilled and motivated workforces of Nissan and the steel industries are not immune from the vagaries of capitalism. The Rover example is particularly salutary given the proud boasts of its managing director about workers' development as a powerful tool for creating a learning organisation and, following current rhetoric, for profitability (see Coffield, 2000a).

In a climate of uncertainty about globalisation, there are corresponding concerns about the risk of marginalisation and growing inequality and the way that human capital obscures socio-economic barriers to monetary and cultural capital. But, more contentiously, these concerns mask profoundly difficult questions about how far lifelong participation in formal learning can really counter capitalist imperatives to relocate and restructure for profit. Instead, discourses of access and participation in 'learning' quickly become blame for non-participation and failure to succeed in employment (Coffield, 1999b; Edwards, 1997). In addition, many adults experience such pressure to update and retrain that lifelong learning becomes virtually compulsory (Tight, 1998a), a trend also evident in parts of Europe (Coffield, 1999a).

Importantly for discussion of motivation in the next chapter, human capital encourages educators and policy-makers alike to promote self-interest and instrumental motivation based on credentialism. This consolidates cultural dispositions in the UK to narrow expectations of occupational relevance and reward in education and training:

> The people who reject education and training and the people who accept its value in the production of credentials – and feel they are owed the chance to earn those credentials – all feel they must be compensated for putting up with education and training if they have to undergo it.
>
> (Fevre *et al.*, 1999: 19)

Credential inflation, where people chase qualifications that offer progression and status, bears out the prevalence of this motive (Wolf, 1997b; Hickox and Moore, 1995). Although technical incentives such as credit-based, modular assessment and individual learning accounts make accreditation more accessible, merely making people willing to pay as purchasers of (or speculators in) qualifications, while their underlying attitude is unchanged, does not make them 'buyers of the substance of education and training' (Fevre *et al.*, 1999). Instead, tightly prescribed, over-loaded curricula encourage an ethos of 'getting students through' (Eraut, 1997) or lead teachers to manipulate the criteria (Field, 1991).

A new ideology of 'risk'

Despite the caveats and dissenting perspectives outlined above, criticism of profound inequality in a deep, but largely undiscussed, and well-obscured capitalist crisis (see Hill *et al.*, 1999; Ainley, 1999) is not a feature of mainstream debates about lifelong learning. Nevertheless, a number of alternative themes arise from concerns to counter instrumental compliance in education and to offer a broader liberal rationale for lifelong learning. In particular, social capital theorists show that communal and social interests inspire a good deal of learning, engendering commitments to 'the features of social life – networks, norms and trust – that enable participants to act together more effectively to pursue shared objectives' (Putnam cited by

Schuller and Field, 1998: 228). Interest in promoting social capital requires better understanding of these links and networks and also of the factors in specific communities, including organisations, that enhance voluntary, mutual acceptance of obligations. The social motivation that underpins social capital is based, according to Fevre *et al.* (1999), on a desire to gain skills and knowledge, not from self-interest but from social commitment. Acknowledging that it is a 'romantic' image, they argue that Welsh miners and trade union activists in the early days of workers' self-education illustrate social motives for learning as a desire for 'universal transformation'. Group loyalties, such as commitment to a public service, allegiance to a craft, or subject discipline, a sense of professionalism, loyalty to family, community or colleagues, produce another social motive, namely 'vocational transformation'. Here the desire to do a job better is not synonymous with trying to get a better job. An indicator of changing attitudes to formal learning would therefore be if people no longer thought they should be compensated for enduring education.

There are undoubtedly important positive and progressive dimensions to ideas about social capital and social motivation (see Baron *et al.*, 2000). Nevertheless, there may also be signs that interest in how to motivate people for lifelong learning could become influenced increasingly by a view that those who do not participate in formal education or purposeful learning are 'at risk'. This trend has parallels in other countries: for example, Kelly (1999) argues that in Australia, vocational education policy is infected by moral panics about young people. This results both in new characterisations of 'risk' and in applications of new mechanisms for regulating risk to a growing range of groups and behaviours. In the UK, a discourse of 'being at risk' characterises some liberal and Leftist concerns about young people and adults who remain outside purposeful learning (see Colley, 2000; Bullen *et al.*, 2000).

Although these concerns emphasise empathy rather than the 'survival of the fittest' ethos of neo-liberal perspectives, they lead some educators and policy-makers to advocate stronger encouragement for non-participants to take up learning opportunities. In part, this stems from a view that not learning, for example at work, not only puts oneself at risk but also one's colleagues (see Tuckett, 1998). For those who believe that education is a force for social justice, the problem of giving people 'permission to have agency' (Tuckett, quoted in Ecclestone, 1999b) is acute when hope for the future is bleak without skills and where useful learning continues to benefit those who have already had it. Following this argument, if education really *does* empower people, stronger direction might overcome a prevailing belief amongst many adults that education is 'not for the likes of us'. From a perspective of empathy, then, marginalised adults or young people 'at risk' of exclusion need propelling into its liberating possibilities. At the same time, if political and professional consensus comes increasingly to view education as the main route to social and economic well-being for individuals and society as a whole, non-participants undermine a wider interest. Arguably, this view underpins new mentoring and careers guidance schemes for young people (see DfEE, 2000; Colley, 2001) and proposals to withdraw welfare benefits in order to make adults with literacy and numeracy problems take part in basic skills programmes.[1]

The idea that we have to 'be cruel to be kind' fits well with New Labour's much-vaunted moral purpose in all aspects of policy. It also reflects wider debate about compulsion and social obligation in welfare policy, evident in initiatives such as the New Deal initiative for unemployed people. Such responses may, as Alan Tuckett argues, signify a need to 'think differently' about the boundaries between choice and compulsion (see Ecclestone and Tuckett, 2000). For example, financial incentives to take up learning opportunties may precede stronger encouragement to provide through savings for strategic, purposeful learning rather than 'frittering it' on short-term courses without progression (see, for example, FEFC, 1998a). It is noticeable, too, that there is increasingly less dissent amongst educators for such proposals. And, as John Field argues, there is, in any case, no simple bi-polar distinction between compulsion and voluntarism in social democracies (Ecclestone and Field, 2001) nor in learners' reasons for taking part in formal education (Field, 2001). Yet such arguments do not obviate a need to counter and challenge authoritarian and moralistic tones in current policy.

For some critics of trends towards compulsion and moral judgements about 'an underclass' in welfare and social policy, current government policy merely continues neo-liberal Conservative policy (for example, 'Marxism Today', 1998; Ainley, 1999; Hill *et al.*, 1999). However, discussion here suggests a new dimension to these trends by relating them to growing 'risk consciousness' and to attempts in politics, scientific research, and increasingly, in social science, to 'make the incalculable calculable' (Beck quoted by Kelly, 1999: 196).

Although it has become commonplace to cite a 'risk society' as forming part of the context for lifelong learning, this is rarely deconstructed in detail for its possible effects on attitudes amongst educators. Yet is important to engage critically with the implications of the 'sociology of risk' arising from the work of Ulrich Beck (for example, Beck, 1992) and from Anthony Giddens' work on 'reflexive modernisation'. Beck argues that proliferating definitions of 'risk', new ways to regulate risk and the individualisation of people's responses to risk, are all logical outcomes of technological and scientific advance. Risk consciousness reflects a 'crisis of modernity' where society must become reflexive about the impact of advances in knowledge and science, particularly in relation to the risks they create. Fear of risk opens up new social and political dilemmas about who should define and regulate it and creates public scepticism about the authority of hitherto powerful agencies and bodies. Both Giddens and Beck therefore see new opportunities for democratic involvement in debating, defining and regulating risk and for new forms of trust to be fostered between people as ways of overcoming social 'difference'. This view is echoed by Alan Tuckett in his optimism that having to rethink boundaries between compulsion and choice in education is not something imposed by 'the state' but something 'we can all do' (Ecclestone and Tuckett, 2000). From the perspective of risk consciousness, moves towards stronger incentives to make people participate in lifelong learning reflect new definitions or risk caused by non-participation, and the need for new responses to the dangers of this risk, both on the part of the government and by educators and social communities.

In contrast to these benign interpretations, and acknowledging that we cannot avoid responding to new social and economic risks, it is nevertheless possible to see such responses as signalling a broader tendency towards moral authoritarianism, arising from a pessimistic, conservative view of human agency amongst liberals and the Left. Sociologist Frank Furedi evaluates the implications of risk consciousness for social and political perceptions of human agency. In doing so, he addresses research by Beck and Giddens, drawing upon extensive analysis of cultural studies, economics and the proliferation of 'risk' literature in medical and social policy research. He then applies this analysis to political and media campaigns in the UK and America over the last ten years around natural and manufactured disasters, health panics and a growing preoccupation with personal and emotional problems, culminating in 'defensive parenting' (Furedi, 1997; 1999a,b; 2001).

Liberal concerns to protect people from globalisation are, for Furedi, informed by 'risk consciousness' that both creates and arises from a cautious, anxious outlook on the future. While Beck focuses primarily on risk associated with scientific and technological problems, Furedi connects risk consciousness to state intervention in everyday life and to pessimistic views about human agency and scientific progress. He highlights themes of fear, risk aversion and increased state regulation in apparently disparate examples: myriad health panics; campaigns for 'safe' sex and healthy living; obsession with emotional and personal life in media reporting (such as correct parenting and children's safety, sexual abuse, family violence, work-place harassment and bullying); fear of environmental hazards and scientific initiatives such as genetically modified food; and a morbid, often voyeuristic obsession with the fate of victims and survivors from disasters and the minutiae of people's emotional responses to such events rather than analysis of what causes these phenomena. This soft approach to news has been criticised by John Pilger (1998) and reflects a move from the journalism of detachment and explanation to calls by some journalists in England for more 'morally sound' (i.e. attached) news coverage. A hopeless, almost hand-wringing account of human plight focuses predominantly on people's desperation and grief rather than analysing broader causes or highlighting strategies or discussing strategies for remediation. This is now commonplace in media coverage of natural and manufactured disasters.

The growing fragmentation of social communities and allegiances, and feelings that individual circumstances are created by conditions outside social and individuals' control, are, for Beck (1992) logical outcomes of a 'risk society'. Although Furedi does not underestimate fragmentation and alienation in communities, he emphasises, instead, a new dimension in media and political coverage of events. This portrays individuals as 'victims' of a growing range of events and life experiences, giving them a moral claim, not because of what they have done but because of what has been done to them. Yet an underlying pitying or judgemental tone depicts damaged people scarred irrevocably by events, unable to work out their own rational responses to problems.

One effect is to encourage dependence on 'experts' such as counsellors, psychologists, advice workers, the social services and, increasingly, adult and community educators. This dependence now goes far beyond support for deep-seated social or personal problems to help for everyday experiences and events once dealt with by family, friends and local communities. State agencies are therefore adopting a more interventionist role in private life, not as 'nanny' but, more subtly, as 'therapist'. For Beck, growing mistrust of politicians, scientists, companies and other agencies has progressive possibilities for democratic involvement in countering power and mystique in professional and political practices (Beck, 1992). In contrast, Furedi argues that fear of risk, combined with an emphasis on human helplessness and emotion rather than reason, fuels excessive dependency on professionals. This fosters individuation and mistrust amongst strangers, peers, neighbours, local communities, and within families, undermining both communal and human agency.

At the same time, political and media attempts to create public solidarity around tragedies, such as sexual abuse or the murders of children, also define new forms of risk and encourage mistrust. More subtly, this fosters the idea that such events have a broader 'moral significance'. For Furedi, moralisation accompanies risk consciousness, judging those in authority and public life for mundane and serious transgressions alike, and presenting a growing range of behaviours as 'putting others at risk'. Combined with dependency on experts and the fragmentation of communities, these trends create a tendency to question the scope available for human action and initiative. At the heart of risk consciousness is 'the diminished subject' where:

> increasingly we feel comfortable with seeing people as victims of their own circumstances rather than as authors of their own lives. The outcome of these developments is a world which equates the good life with self-limitation and risk aversion.
>
> (Furedi, 1997: 147)

The premise of a diminished subject is a misanthropic view of the world and of humanity's ability to solve problems. Instead, popular culture and the media emphasises and celebrates vulnerability, uncertainty and humility in the face of risks: even in stories purporting to show bravery or creative risks, cameras and interviews often linger on individuals' vulnerability and doubt. In a risk society, victimhood and vulnerability legitimise state intervention in personal life and behaviour by encouraging, then regulating, self-limitation and risk aversion. Intervention through guidelines, advice and legislation. comes from government and a growing number of organisations, covering parenting, education, health and social life. An important dimension is that such interventions also come increasingly from self-help groups or organisations that once campaigned for rights or equal opportunities. For example, the National Union of Students now spends much time moralising about the dangers of sex, drinking, drugs and potential violence from residents of university towns than campaign for education. Similarly, many trade unions devote more energy to codes of conduct about harassment and stress at work than they do to fundamental employment rights.

Of course, guidelines are not moralistic *per se* and are often common-sense attempts to alert people to risks or to clarify protocols and expectations. Yet they respond increasingly to mistrust and then reinforce it by anticipating and formalising expectations of transgression (Furedi, op. cit.). Guidelines can therefore transmogrify into rules or calls for legislation, thereby removing autonomy by codifying commonplace behaviour whilst appearing to solve problems. In this climate, 'risk' encompasses an increasing range of transgressional behaviours, including certain forms of autonomy. Those who transgress the guidelines threaten the community and become a source of mistrust.

Furedi contrasts his own thesis about the decline of 'subjectivity' (i.e. the potential for human action) with accounts by Beck and Giddens that attribute risk consciousness to the 'manufactured uncertainty' created by human intervention into social life, science and nature. From this perspective, advances in knowledge and technology themselves become risky but can be countered by 'reflexive modernisation', namely a social and political commitment to monitoring, defining and controlling risk. Yet, Furedi sees this view as ultimately conservative, citing Beck's observation that society increasingly unites to avert risks associated with the future instead of striving for unity based on progress (Beck, 1992). At the same time, low expectations of social and scientific progress and of human behaviour create uncertainty about personal and social issues. In the UK and USA, this is leading to the politicisation of moral values at all levels from government to individuals, accompanied by a rising tide of censure and prurience that erodes debate about deeper political and social issues.

Such uncertainty makes old conservative values in education and culture irrelevant. Instead, Furedi sees the moralisation of risk as the most insidious threat to beliefs in human agency, progress and creative risk. Low expectations of human behaviour, and belief in the power of fate over people's lives, undermine personal autonomy, trust and social responsibility whilst leading us to accept closer state regulation of both our public and private behaviour: everyday life itself becomes 'risky'.

A 'new etiquette for regulating the interactions between people' (Furedi, 1997: 150) offers a caring, seemingly non-judgemental morality which seeks to empower and protect the powerless. Indeed, in its attempts to 'protect us from ourselves', it explicitly rejects old-style conservative morality as irrelevant whilst lecturing those who take risks. Importantly, its inclusive language reaches out to the marginalised and critics of the system alike, appearing to confront social divisions whilst not attaching itself directly to any overt values. Yet, these new discourses are far from a cynical appropriation of liberal values to disguise more sinister motives or to reconcile us to a gloomy future. Instead, any drift towards moral authoritarianism is *disguised* or masked by liberal intentions but not deliberately. It is clearly much more subtle than this: as Ball (1997) points out, shifts of ideology and moral economy are never clear-cut, uncontested, or realised in standard ways.

Following arguments in this section, moralising about risk is deeply implicated in New Labour's 'new etiquette'. Some researchers have noted how empathy and concern for particular groups, such as 'disaffected young people', quickly become strongly moralistic and judgemental, signifying an underlying fear of deviance and portrayals of 'the other' (see Bullen *et al.*, 2000; Colley, 2000, 2001). Again, what is significant about this fear is that it seems, subtly, to becoming more commonplace amongst liberal educators. Depictions of 'the marginalised' and 'the excluded' at conferences, for example, now encompass long lists of the deficits and defects caused by non-participation and poor achievement in education. Crucially, these images are sympathetic and sometimes empathetic. But they conjure up all too easily images of an alien underclass in need of remediation through formal education.

In the light of arguments so far, concern about 'risk' for those excluded or marginalised from lifelong learning becomes tainted with an acceptance that there are no other solutions to social and economic problems. Instead, a relativist, apparently liberal morality helps people make sense of their individuation. Nevertheless, these low expectations sit uneasily with goals for autonomy, other than autonomy as synonymous with individual accountability for problems. This justifies what Giddens calls 'a fundamental impetus towards the re-moralising of everyday life' where morality demands commitment to a lifestyle rather than to a community (Giddens cited by Furedi, 1997: 163).

The new etiquette adds another dimension to blaming individuals for social problems or for their own fate through its demands for people to subject themselves to core values of safety and cautious, self-limiting behaviour. Once 'risk' encompasses any transgressional or controversial action, it cannot be seen as creative. A view that not learning at work risks colleagues' jobs, or that non-participation in education and training threatens economic prosperity, extends moral judgements about what constitutes risky behaviour, thereby encouraging mistrust. Such judgements are especially suspect when, as the first section of this chapter showed, all the social and human capital that individuals can accumulate will not stop high-tech employers leaving the UK.

A final implication of arguments in this section is that promotion of social capital as a counter to human capital could also become tainted by this underlying morality (see Ecclestone and Field, 2001). If so, the potential for compulsion, blame and low expectations of agency and community could erode faith amongst educators in trust, voluntarism and social commitments. Perhaps counter-intuitively, social commitment requires individual aspiration and a clearer distinction between *individuation* as a turning in on oneself and *individualism*. This implies that communal motivation and trust necessary to participate in learning that is genuinely meaningful to people, rather than deemed to be so by government agencies, require some individual aspiration. In fragmented communities, however, it may be tempting to manufacture communal feelings by inducing guilty obligation to others and to moralise about non-conforming types of social capital. As Tom Schuller points out, 'communitarian stances' on social capital raise problems about the 'complexity of norms' and how tightly they are enforced (Schuller, 1997: 121).

Summary

Macro factors of ideology examined so far contextualise the implicit and explicit types of motivation and autonomy that teachers and students might expect to develop through an assessment policy designed to foster such attributes. Concerns about non-participation in formal learning raise questions about the effects of a climate of risk aversion and low expectations of human agency on expectations amongst policy-makers, qualification designers, policy intermediaries, teachers and students of the types of motivation and autonomy that learners are 'realistically' capable of developing. This climate could make it difficult for teachers and learners to take risks, be innovative or creative or to negotiate their own curriculum, thereby encouraging a view in assessment and quality assurance systems that such activities are risky and undesirable. One effect may be to increase cynicism about the potential for learners to be intrinsically motivated and autonomous.

Although the book does not explore empirically constructs of 'risk' amongst policy-makers, teachers and students, notions about what qualities, attributes and skills comprise motivation and autonomy may be infected with the subtle constructs of risk explored in this chapter. In the light of arguments here, the next chapter analyses different meanings of motivation and autonomy as the basis for exploring how they are constructed through assessment policy and practice.

2 Theorising autonomy, motivation and formative assessment*

Introduction

If arguments in the previous chapter about links between structural conditions and a culture of fear and low expectations have any resonance, they have implications for discourses and meanings in relation to learners' autonomy and motivation. Yet ideological trends are not the only barrier in getting to grips with what it means to motivate learners and help them become autonomous. Examination of the conflicting epistemologies that underpin assessment systems highlights three specific problems.

First, views about autonomy and motivation amongst policy-makers, mediators of policy, teachers and students are often expressed in very general, comfortingly bland ways. These combine 'espoused theories' as genuine beliefs about what underpins practice, with implicit 'theories-in-use' where practices reveal other underlying but unrecognised theories (Argyris and Schon, 1974). Researchers therefore need a conceptual basis for gaining some empirical purchase on both types of theories. Second, the theories of learning that ideas about motivation and autonomy derive from, namely constructivism and behaviourism, are not widely understood, nor are their links to formative and summative assessment practices. This makes it important to connect theories about learning to promotion of understanding about what formative assessment is and what it is not. Last, if the numerous policy texts that comprise an assessment model have different notions of autonomy, motivation and formative assessment embedded in them, it is necessary to understand the technical nuances of assessment models and their interpretations by all the diverse constituencies involved in developing and implementing them.

It is therefore necessary to recognise such problems before we can appreciate the political complexity that characterises vocational assessment policy, and the different meanings of autonomy embedded within an assessment model such as the GNVQ. This recognition is also a necessary

* Parts of this chapter are reproduced with permission from Taylor and Francis Ltd, www.tandf.co.uk (see Ecclestone, 2000b).

precursor to analysis in subsequent chapters of the ways in which FE students and teachers conceptualised and then developed autonomy and motivation through the GNVQ assessment model. The first section proposes a theoretical framework that connects different types of motivation and autonomy to formative assessment practices. The second section relates different theories of formative assessment to the types of autonomy and motivation that FE students might develop.

A theoretical framework

Motivation

There are increased claims amongst policy-makers and growing numbers of educators that the UK has a cultural problem of poor motivation for learning (for example, Elliott, 1999; Fevre *et al.*, 1999). Recent research helps erode a long-running distinction in cognitive psychology where behaviourist perspectives emphasise extrinsic motives based on external goals, performance rewards and short-term goals while humanist perspectives prioritise a hierarchy of intrinsic motives. These include striving for self-regulation of personal attributes and subject expertise, followed by desire for higher levels of creativity and fulfilment and what Maslow termed 'self actualisation' (see, for example, Rogers, 1983; West, 1995).

In encouraging intrinsic motivation, cognitive psychologists explore the effects of learners' beliefs, values and emotions on attitudes to particular learning situations and advise teaching strategies that maximise intrinsic motivation and reduce extrinsic motivators. Intrinsic motivation is seen to derive from opportunities to develop the skills of metacognition, namely the ability to review and monitor the effectiveness of one's approaches to learning (Newton, 2000). There is particular research interest in whether learners attribute their achievement to ability, task difficulty or effort (Black and Wiliam, 1998a) and in the effects of self-concept (Dweck, 2000). This research promotes the idea that attributions of performance and achievement to effort are more productive than attributions to ability and more likely to foster intrinsic motivation. In addition, researchers emphasise how formal education can encourage unhelpful dispositions such as 'learned helplessness' (Dweck, op. cit.).

Criticism that 'behaviourist' outcome-based models atomise learning and encourage instrumental motivation (for example, Hyland, 1994) resonate with objections that National Curriculum assessment reinforces extrinsic motivation and encourages students to attribute achievement to intelligence or task difficulty rather than to effort and intrinsically worthwhile aspects of learning. Such features also undermine pupils' willingness to tolerate ambiguity (see Black and Wiliam, 1998; Broadfoot, 2000). Unless the power of intrinsic motivation to sustain deep, creative learning and to resist short-term rewards and surface engagement can be realised, the inspiring rhetoric of lifelong learning will have little effect (Coffield, 1997a; Broadfoot, 2000).

Despite recognition in this research of the importance of intrinsic motivation, there seems to be an enduring dichotomy between extrinsic and intrinsic motivation, creating two problems relevant to discussion here. First, there may be a tendency to contrast impoverished instrumentalism unfavourably with compelling but perhaps idealistic portrayals of intrinsic commitments. Desirable commitments might be to craft skills in specialised, small communities of practice (for example, Lave, 1997), the motivation generated by a 'love of learning' and the desire for mastery (for example, Bruner, 1966) or to feelings of civic and moral responsibility (for example, Barnett *et al.*, 1999). Second, there is a tendency to prioritise *individual* traits, dispositions and attributes and a diagnostic role for teachers in responding to them. In their review of theories of pedagogy in adult learning and higher education, Zukas and Malcolm (2000) argue that an overemphasis on individuals isolates them from social and personal histories and contexts. Similarly, interest in individual motivation through promotion of their self-interest overlooks the power of social motivation and commitment to groups and peers.

In response to these limitations, other research addresses the effects of social and cultural dispositions on teachers' strategies and children's attitudes and learning habits. A recent study compared attitudes and activities amongst school children and teachers in Russia, Kentucky and the northeast of England. It challenged the influential perspective on 'effects of attributional biases on goal-seeking behaviour' evident in current research on motivation (Elliott *et al.*, 1999: 77). Although researchers such as Carol Dweck have promoted the importance of individual self-concept and the effects of formal education on this, motivational theorists have only recently explored the importance of social goals in learners' goals for achievement. The study by Elliott *et al.* highlights the power of peer and family attitudes to both the intrinsic and extrinsic value of education and to the sustained effort necessary for high standards. Importantly, these researchers question whether current motivation research places too much emphasis on the importance of attributing achievement to effort since, in their study, pupils' attributions to effort did not necessarily improve workrates or performance. Further insights from sociological perspectives on motivation and social capital aim to capture social and cultural dimensions. By relating motivation to broader conditions such as changes to occupational structures and local job prospects, these perspectives illuminate how cultural change might transform instrumentalism and self-interest. Fevre *et al.* (1999) argue, for example, that divisions of labour within organisations and society as a whole, together with job opportunities, affect collective representations of motivation, as do community traditions of participation in non-formal and formal learning.

Motivation for particular goals and responses to assessment are also affected by students' attributions of achievement to factors outside their control such as the idea that ability is innate, difficulty with particular tasks, the effects of luck, or to intrinsic factors such as effort. These attributions are both individually and socially constructed and the idiosyncrasies of interactions between students, teachers, peers and families all affect how students view formative assessment (see Torrance and Pryor 1998; Reay and Wiliam, 1999). In particular, perceptions of job and social prospects, and of what counts as 'acceptable' behaviour, are simultaneously shaped and situated in specific cultural and peer contexts (see Elliott *et al.*, 1999; Fevre *et al.*, 2000). Similarly, dispositions amongst post-16 students towards learning and achievement are 'socially and culturally grounded' and profoundly affected by personal identities (Bloomer, 1997; Ball *et al.*, 2000). Approaches to learning cannot, therefore, be isolated from the unstable yet important contexts of learners' own interests, the strictures of externally imposed prescriptions for learning, and broader cultural attitudes within particular localities. In addition, Stephen Brookfield (2000) argues that theories of motivation rarely acknowledge the emotional and traumatic effects of learning on students' identities and sense of self. These socio-cultural dimensions lead Coffield (2000a) to argue that naive and very partial views of non-participation or low motivation for formal learning arise from any discussion that excludes the impact of social differentiation and cultural factors.

Recent research into post-16 learners' characteristic dispositions towards choices for career or study and for learning activities shows that 'pragmatic acceptance' of the need to gain a qualification is the most prevalent motive, where education is 'something to be got through'. Outside a core of pragmatic acceptors, are 'hangers on', reluctantly in education and vulnerable to sudden disruption of this choice (see Macrae *et al.*, 1997; Ball *et al.*, 2000). Their motives, ostensibly instrumental, relate to getting jobs and putting off life decisions by staying in education and are often interwoven with uncertainty, lack of real direction, lack of positive self-reinforcement or self-worth. Inside FE colleges, 'strategic compliance' dominates many students' attitudes, and for 'drifters', even extrinsic motivation is absent (Bloomer and Hodkinson, 1997; 1999). Under pressure of credentialism and individualistic self-interest, 'drifters' and 'hangers on' risk becoming marginalised (Ball *et al.*, 2000). In contrast, learners 'embedded' in the system see education as a natural development of previous experience and part of the process of 'becoming somebody'. They have a strong vested interest in the value of credentialism and are well-informed about available choices. These learners' sense of self and identification with peers is inextricably linked with gaining expertise in a subject, having good relationships with teachers and peers and intrinsic enjoyment of an identity built around being a student (Ball *et al.*, 2000).

The sociological accounts reviewed here therefore offer crucial insights for researchers hoping to construct an account of FE students' motivation and autonomy. It seems, then, that empirical evaluation of students' motivation has to differentiate between social and individual motivation, locate these forms in a socio-cultural and institutional context and account for progression between extrinsic and intrinsic motives. Nevertheless, there remains a need to guard against portraying fixed or static motivation during a course.

Acknowledging the powerful motivating influences of 'self-determination' and 'personal agency', Prenzel *et al.* (2000: 1) draw from different psychological traditions to offer 'a systematically ordered spectrum of constructs which are psychologically differentiated and at the same time, can be found within educational contexts'. Although Prenzel *et al.* aim to measure constructs of motivation through psychometric tests, the categories they offer are also extremely useful for sociological accounts of the types of motivation that learners might develop. They might also suggest reasons for fluctuations between these types:

1 Amotivated: lacking any direction for motivation, from indifference to apathy.
2 External: learning takes place only 'in association with reinforcement, reward, or to avoid threat or punishment'.
3 Introjected: learning happens when learners 'internalise' or 'incorporate' 'an external supportive structure'. Although it is internal, it is not a self-determined form of motivation.
4 Identified: learning occurs 'as a result of accepting content or activities which for its sake holds no incentive (it may even be a burden) but it is recognised as necessary and important in attaining a goal [the learner] has set'.
5 Intrinsic: learning 'results independently from external contingencies'. Learners perceive any incentives to be gained as being intrinsic to the content or activity.
6 Interested: learning does not merely recognise intrinsic value but takes place 'in accordance with subjective and meaningful attributes assigned to the object or object-specific skill'.   (Prenzel *et al.*, 1999: 1–2)

The spectrum mixes different psychological constructs, such as the psychodynamic notion of 'introjection', with behaviourist notions of stimulus and reward and a humanist view that identity, 'becoming somebody' and engagement with learning are integral to 'interested' motivation. This latter type therefore fuses motivation, learning activities and the positive enhancement or development of identity. For researchers wishing to explore motivation, Prenzel *et al.* argue that:

From an educational point of view, motivation theories take on relevance if they empirically predict how the different motivational states impact [on] learning and teaching processes. On this basis, it is possible to systematically differentiate between motivation states as being either (more or less) questionable or desirable with respect to educational objectives.

(ibid.)

The idea that motivational states might fluctuate across a spectrum of extrinsic and intrinsic types could help counter a tendency to portray distinctions between humanist and behaviourist, extrinsic and intrinsic, individual and social, as mutually exclusive. Humanist perspectives in particular seem to underplay the idea that extrinsic, individual motivation, represented as *external, introjected* and *identified,* may often be a springboard for *intrinsic, interested* and social motivation. In turn, the second section argues that motivation may link to different types of autonomy and then to different formative assessment practices and different purposes for using them.

Finally, two caveats remain in this discussion of motivation. First, post-16 students in FE fall between research that explores the motivation of children in compulsory settings and research which aims to account for 'distinctive' aspects of adult learning which is widely regarded as voluntarily chosen. Instead, the line between FE as a voluntary option and a natural but semi-compulsory progression for 16-year-olds is an increasingly blurred one.

Second, it is important to use more precise working definitions of learning, since, as Coffield (2000a) points out, a raft of policy injunctions for life-long learning remain devoid of any serious attempt to define 'learning'. In addition, as Chapter 1 showed, it is easy to conflate problems with motivation and participation in formal education and training with 'non-learning'. It is therefore helpful to adopt Michael Eraut's suggestion that we limit our meanings of learning to 'a significant change in capability or understanding and exclude the acquisition of further information when it does not contribute to such changes' (Eraut quoted by Coffield, 1997b: 5). Following this, we can differentiate further between:

- formal (organised and structured, as part of institutionally based programmes, one-off training events or development sessions, and written or computer-based guidance and learning packs);
- informal (*ad hoc,* incidental requests from friends or colleagues for help or joint problem-solving that are not usually recognised as 'learning activities' by those who take part);
- non-formal (events such as working groups, project teams, work shadowing and mentoring, structured amongst learners themselves or by middle managers, often in ad hoc ways, and which are often cited as important sources of learning).   (Eraut *et al.,* 2000)

Autonomy

Diverse terms, underlying constructs and goals slip confusingly, and often vaguely, through much academic and professional debate about autonomy. A review of research on autonomy in education shows that 'independent learning', 'taking responsibility for one's own learning', 'self-determination', 'self-regulation ', 'autonomy' are, as Boud (1988) points out, used generally and interchangeably. It can, for example, be seen as a general *goal* of education: an individual's ability to be independent from external authority and 'free from disabling conflicts' in one's personality, the freedom to act and work as s/he chooses (Gibbs quoted by Boud, 1988: 18–19). Autonomy might be the 'command of a repertoire of responses' for acting and thinking, the ability to transcend boundaries and social barriers, to challenge set ways of thinking or expectations about one's 'station in life' (Law, 1992). Rooted in Greek notions of political self-government, meritocracy and democratic citizenship based on 'free' but socially committed and fulfilled individuals, liberal humanist notions of 'self-determination' and 'self-actualisation' all underpin contemporary versions of these ideals. Although post-structuralist debates about structure, agency and identity have ruptured educational ideals of autonomy rooted in Western traditions of 'Enlightenment' and individual agency, liberal and humanist notions of autonomy exert a strong influence in the literature discussed here (see Bleakley, 2000 for discussion).

Whilst acknowledging that the term 'autonomy' is often used vaguely, Law applies some implicit meanings to careers guidance and to autonomy within a learning context:

> We have some idea of what we are talking about when we use it – when our students or clients are acting consciously (not without thought), independently (not compliantly), imaginatively (not routinely) and with commitment (not remotely).
>
> (Law, 1992: 152)

From this perspective, autonomy is not synonymous with critical thinking or independence but these skills and attributes are integral to an ability in acting autonomously to define what is morally acceptable, to choose alternatives between conflicting ideas, to have a 'mind of one's own' (Dearden, quoted by Boud, 1988: 19). In this light, autonomy becomes both a goal and a set of processes for realising it. Academic and mainstream uses of the term therefore tend to elide the qualities, skills and processes that comprise a goal of autonomy.

Some psychologists portray autonomy as a cognitive *process* that might be directed towards goals of critical thinking and acting but which might also address learning activities and their effectiveness. Autonomy from this perspective therefore derives from tacit and overt meta-cognitive planning and from monitoring and reviewing one's learning. Such processes are integral to intrinsic motivation and deep engagement with the content and processes of learning within subjects (Newton, 2000). Brookfield (2000) argues that adults develop a self-conscious capacity to 'know how they know what they know' and also to employ 'practical logic' to new situations, based on experience. These capabilities are, he argues, distinctive characteristics of adults' autonomy as learners. Carl Rogers links goals of democratic liberal humanism to these psychological processes to argue for a radical, naturalistic approach where learners are free to determine, set, carry out and assess their own goals (Rogers, 1983).

However, discussion in the relevant literature on autonomy slips quickly from democratic ideals, personal agency and cognitive processes to portray autonomy as a more instrumental *procedure* or *method*, such as action planning, flexible access to resources, independence for working outside formal structures and didactic teaching. Nevertheless, 'a person may be exposed to so-called autonomous methods of learning without internalising the values of autonomy or necessarily being enabled to think and act autonomously' (Candy, quoted by Boud, 1988: 21). It is therefore important to differentiate between 'independence' and 'autonomy'.

Slippage between terms and underlying purposes of autonomy and motivation suggests a need to gain some empirical purchase on them. Although no typology can capture the complexity and overlap between different types of autonomy, discussion below draws on debate about different goals for action research in pursuit of teachers' professional autonomy by Wilfred Carr and Stephen Kemmis (Carr and Kemmis, 1986; Carr 1995). It extends a theoretical framework that explored different goals for reflective practice in professional development programmes (Ecclestone, 1996b). The typology attempts to differentiate between autonomy as a broader educational and social goal and the processes and conditions that enable people to act autonomously. This raises broader questions about the extent to which formal education can and should aim to foster the different meanings of autonomy discussed below. It focuses on the autonomy that formal learning programmes and their assessment models may consciously and indirectly develop in learners or, conversely, the autonomy they claim to develop but might not.

Following Carr and Kemmis, the typology proposes that autonomy can be *procedural* (technical); *personal* (practical – as in one's own 'practice'); *critical* and, ultimately, *emancipatory*. It relates autonomy to three different models of teaching and learning: *transmission, transaction* or *transformation* (see Haywood, 1997). Each type of autonomy suggests a different underlying motive (or motives). The typology also suggests that there is overlap and fluctuation between different motives and forms of autonomy during a learning programme. In addition, different formative assessment practices may encourage one type of autonomy more than another. Of course, the distinctions and overlaps indicated by a model based on categories are imperfect and sometimes arbitrary. It needs further theoretical refining but offers a basis in this study for analysing and evaluating links between assessment, autonomy and motivation in post-compulsory education.[1] It is summarised in Appendix 3.

Procedural autonomy

The ability to determine some control over pace, timing and evaluation of work, to negotiate types of learning activities and 'appropriate' evidence of achievement, to become more proactive within specified rules, outcomes and assessment criteria is a form of autonomy. This might develop independence in using techniques or processes, as well as confidence with a body of technical or specialist language. Some qualification frameworks, for example, formulate procedural autonomy at different levels through competences such as 'undertake directed activities with limited autonomy within time constraints (level 2); select from considerable choice in familiar and unfamiliar contexts (level 3)' (NICATs, 1998). 'Proactivity', 'independence', 'self-reliance' and 'confidence with language' are integral to procedural autonomy.

The typology proposes that procedural autonomy relates to *transmission* of pre-defined outcomes, knowledge, processes and content by teachers, or through open-learning and computer-based materials. It might involve *transaction* over how tasks might be done, underpinned by Prenzel *et al.*'s categories of *external* and *introjected* motivation, although, at a push, teachers might be able to coax and cajole *amotivated* students through the assessment requirements! Teacher and self-assessment focuses on checking that criteria are met whilst rewarding short-term goals and the replication of information. Side-effects are likely to be 'surface' learning to 'get through' the criteria.

If procedural autonomy in an outcome-based model is the only goal and is underpinned solely by instrumental motivation, it becomes an imposed 'technical empowerment' where students are little more than 'hunters and gatherers' of information without deep engagement with either content or process (see Bates, 1998a; Helsby *et al.*, 1998; Bloomer, 1998). Procedural autonomy in outcome-based models prepares students for work and quality assurance practices where team-work, initiative and self-reliance from devolved responsibility within 'much stricter frameworks of accountability and performance appraisal' (Bates, 1998a: 13) combine with notions of enterprise and responsibility for one's own employability. Lack of any critical engagement with rules and their rationale can therefore turn autonomy in outcome-based assessment systems into what critics regard as a 'technology' of self-surveillance (see Edwards and Usher, 1994; Bates, 1991).

Nevertheless, dismissal of procedural autonomy as unprogressive may, however, overlook its initial importance at the beginning of learning programmes. Confidence with procedures, systems, and the technical language underpinning particular subjects, is integral to gaining confidence with more sophisticated forms of planning, new activities or engaging with concepts behind terminology and the contested nature of the rules themselves. There may also be a necessary progression from learners' ability to make decisions with the support of prescribed procedures and their subsequent ability to judge when it is and is not needed. Although there is an important but easily overlooked distinction between learners' *self-direction* and their *accountability* (Bates, 1998b), procedural autonomy may actually be a pre-requisite or a co-requisite for more sophisticated forms of personal and critical autonomy. This view is supported by Newton who argues for a deliberate progression:

> Paradoxically, facility in self-regulation (of learning) can develop from external regulation. Success is when external support is removed and self-regulation stands alone.
>
> (Newton, 2000: 166)

Personal (practical) autonomy

Humanist ideas about people's drive to become self-directing suggest another form of autonomy based on knowledge of one's strengths and weaknesses, learning habits and potential choices for action and progression. These insights are perhaps the beginning of a 'repertoire of responses' discussed earlier as a broad goal for autonomy as a basis for 'self actualisation'. For Carr and Kemmis (1986) and Carr (1995), personal autonomy within occupational or professional practice cannot be isolated from the ethical and moral dilemmas that this practice raises. Thus, engagement with these issues can enhance self-knowledge and the ability to make moral choices. Nevertheless, as John Vorhaus points out, it is possible for someone to be personally autonomous in a professional role, 'frequently making decisions which others are required to conform to, and who yet rarely engages in any sustained critical reflection' (Vorhaus, informal communication). Similarly, it would be possible, from Carr and Kemmis' interpretation, for someone to be personally autonomous in one context, but unable to be so in a learning programme if motivation and engagement are limited.

The typology proposes that personal autonomy is situated precisely within a particular learning context, underpinned by Prenzel *et al.*'s categories of *identified, intrinsic* and, ideally, *interested* motivation. Its development also requires learners and teachers to attribute achievement to effort and engagement, developed through good relationships and *transaction* between teachers and peers. Learning becomes more student-centred, based on negotiation of intended outcomes and how to achieve them. There is an emphasis on positive interdependence amongst learners, co-operative

approaches to problem-setting and problem-solving, and negotiated processes of evaluation, review and recording of achievement.

Personal autonomy therefore derives from social processes as well as
individual traits and activities and from constructivist ideas about learning,
discussed in the next section. Thus, people who draw on experiences outside
immediate family or schooling 'nourish a diversity of perspectives in
conceiving a future and alternative futures' (Law, 1992: 164). Learning,
non-formal and informal activities that encourage peer assessment and
mentoring while ipsative targets, individualised feedback and criteria for
assessing individual progress are also important.

Yet, unless personal autonomy is related to procedural and critical autonomy, it is prone to reductionist equations with procedural autonomy.
Ultimately, then, students' ability to 'see it all another way' (Law, 1992),
to go beyond awareness of their strengths and weaknesses within a set of
procedures or a preoccupation with personal attributes, is shaped by the
ability to appraise their position within a wider context. It is difficult, then,
to separate personal autonomy from learners' broader life chances and the
socio-economic and cultural conditions affecting these chances.

Critical autonomy

The last point is why, for many educators, critical autonomy is the ultimate
goal of education since notions of democratic citizenship based on critical
intelligence enable students 'to free themselves from the constraints under
which they are already thinking and acting' (Barnett, 1994: 191). In higher
education, critical autonomy is seen to emerge through subject expertise,
where engagement with established bodies of thought and participation in
associated conversations enables people to develop their understanding
beyond conventional insights and wisdom. From a more radical tradition,
learners 'participate in determining the content of learning . . . or what
counts as educational knowledge' (Young cited by Bates, 1998: 11, and see
also Ainley, 1999). Without the capacity to see the world another way,
Law asserts that 'there is no negotiation' between teachers and students
(1992: 164). For some students in higher education, critical autonomy is
inseparable from their social and cultural needs which demand intellectual
depth and the ability to make connections between ideas. Echoing the
social motivation of Fevre *et al.*'s 'universal transformers' cited earlier,
these adults want to contribute actively to their deprived communities
(Ross, 1995). The ability to think critically is therefore integral to critical
and personal autonomy but is not synonymous with either form of
autonomy.

We therefore need to show more precisely where critical autonomy is
integral to learning about a vocational subject, to coping with a job or life
or simply a desirable, important goal within formal education. It is possible,

for example, that calls for critical autonomy may be seen by designers of vocational qualifications as no more than 'academic drift' in education and training situations where learners might not want or need it. This implies a need for closer theoretical exploration of critical autonomy, together with empirical accounts of where and how it might be fostered, and what role formative assessment practices might play in this. Without more clarity and discussion about when critical autonomy might *not* be necessary, its promotion tends to attract worthy but vacuous proselytising, a problem that applies also to notions of 'empowerment' (Fielding, 1996).

But if critical autonomy is a legitimate goal, then analysing and evaluating issues critically within a subject or occupation is more than a 'core skill' designed to bridge the academic/vocational divide since its appropriation as a skill obscures different interpretations of 'critical' (Halliday, 2000). It can, for example, be equated with being a 'good thinker' and therefore a 'canny' worker or with challenging accepted ideas or thinking independently: 'in this sense a critical thinker might be something of a maverick, always challenging accepted norms even when it seems foolish to do so' (ibid: 7). Brookfield argues that such tensions can be particularly traumatic for adults 'becoming critical' through educational experiences, where peers or family may resent this new attribute (2000). In addition, if critical autonomy means a critique of one's own position, to challenge or even transform situations collectively, it is important to question how far educational institutions can realistically promote learners' ability to act autonomously in these ways, either inside or outside them (Fielding, op. cit.).

In addition, the particular cultures of academic or vocational subjects, professions or occupations affect whether certain forms of critical thinking and autonomy are accepted or valued. If critical thinking in university teaching, for example, is located very precisely within individual teachers' own engagement with their subject and teaching methods (see a special edition of *Teaching and Learning in Higher Education*, 1999), then critical autonomy is also likely to be context specific. Halliday argues that it is essential to connect critical thinking within a subject and a community of practice that can debate actively what it implies and what it is for. It is also important to recognise that critical autonomy may take many years and specialist expertise to develop and that it disappears, temporarily, when learners confront a new subject domain (Candy, 1998). In many cases, as Halliday observes, people have to balance a critical approach with acquiscence. Progress is therefore difficult without reconciling a tension between conforming to norms and values within communities and the need, sometimes, to challenge them (Halliday, 2000).

In a context of risk aversion, critical autonomy may be seen as risky or as putting others at risk. It is therefore important not to elide the types of *critical thinking* that students might engage in, and the aims behind them, with *critical autonomy*. Imprecise, ambiguous notions around autonomy

have important implications for how qualification designers, policy intermediaries, teachers, students and end 'users' of qualifications, such as
employers and further and higher education institutions, variously construct
autonomy. Confusion also makes critique that programmes do not develop
critical autonomy ultimately unconvincing.

The typology proposes that critical autonomy is developed through *transaction* and *transformation* which, in turn, build upon problem-solving and
collaboration within a particular subject or occupational context and a
belief that knowledge is dynamic, uncertain and contestable. Diverse
activities, formal and informal discourses, openness and creativity build a
community of practice where constructive, self-regulating processes enable
learners to climb to a 'high ground' for surveying their own knowledge
and processes of learning (Bruner cited by Torrance and Pryor, 1998: 39)
(see also Brookfield, 2000).

Formative assessment has to encourage critical reflection and engagement
with dilemmas in subject disciplines, social and occupationally related
issues. Oral and written 'critical conversations' should encourage learners
to assess their own work and relate its quality to that of peers and immediate superiors. They need confidence to transform feedback into a more
sophisticated critical understanding and know how to use teachers' often
idiosyncratic comments about their work. Teachers and students therefore
have to extend their understanding of formative assessment as feedback
and review to include questions for understanding (or to diagnose barriers
to understanding), climates where people feel able to challenge or to ask
curriculum-related questions of each other and teachers, and strategic
debriefing of learning processes.

Behaviourist and constructivist theories of formative assessment

A growing body of research aims to theorise the goals and processes
involved in realising the potential of formative assessment to motivate and
engage learners. The previous section suggested how formative assessment
practices might relate to three types of autonomy. Some activities are cate-
gorised easily as 'assessment', such as giving students feedback about their
progress and setting targets for improvement. Others are associated with
classroom questioning, debriefing and feedback, and tutorials. As a result,
theoretical and practical understanding of links between formative assessment, autonomy and motivation depend on formative assessment being
seen as:

> a moment of learning, and students have to be active in their own
> assessment and to picture their own learning in light of an understand-
> ing of what it means to get better.
>
> (Black and Wiliam, 1998a: 29)

Yet, Black and Wiliam's work also suggests that few teachers, whether in schools or FE, are likely to be confident about the differences between formative, diagnostic and summative assessment. Further problems arise because the term 'formative assessment' 'does not have a tightly defined and widely accepted meaning' (ibid: 7). In addition, a major difficulty in conceptualising and operationalising it is that claims for its benefits have been both over-stated and over-simplified (ibid; see also Torrance and Pryor, 1998).

From a constructivist perspective, formative assessment is inseparable from classroom activities identified above. It requires a belief in learners' potential and active discouragement of ideas about fixed or 'innate' ability. Instead, teachers need to help learners attribute achievement to effort and to encourage collaboration within a community of practice, committed, ideally, to developing everyone's potential for learning. Constructivist models of learning encourage teachers and more expert peers amongst students and the wider community to work collaboratively with less expert learners. 'Scaffolding' tasks and questions focuses on the gap between where learners are, the work they can produce with help from a teacher or a more expert peer, and achievement of the desired standard. The aim is to help learners 'internalise' the standard of work implied in the criteria and to appreciate what it means to 'close the gap'. Feedback moves from detailed support to more general advice or questions as learners gain confidence and expertise in translating feedback into improvements and new goals (see, for example, Gipps, 1994; Black and Wiliam, op. cit.). It is therefore necessary to use diagnostic assessment, followed by differentiated activities and feedback and remedial support. As part of their response to political injunctions to raise achievement, many colleges now use strategies such as diagnostic tests on entry to learning programmes, reviews and tutor feedback.

Commitment both to the idea of a community of practice and the assessment strategies themselves is affected, however, by socio-cultural expectations of achievement and 'the broader context of assumptions about the motivations and self-perceptions of learners' which shape learners' dispositions towards learning and assessment activities (Black and Wiliam, 1998a: 16). Unless diagnostic and formative assessment, such as the college strategies mentioned above, are incorporated into techniques for encouraging motivation and forms of autonomy, then into pedagogy linked to subject content, feedback and support, such strategies are unlikely to engage learners on a deep level.

Fostering commitment and addressing deeply held, often implicit, expectations also requires attention to the enduring influence of a behaviourist tradition that begins in primary schools (see Torrance and Pryor, 1998). One effect is that extrinsic motivation based on 'rewards', 'performance goals' and 'punishments' is deeply entrenched in teachers' assessment practices and in their feedback to students (see also Gipps and Tunstall, 1995).

This tradition is exacerbated by pressures on teachers to get as many pupils as possible through external tests whilst minimising the demotivation of those who do not succeed. Yet, once this pressure percolates through the compulsory system into post-compulsory education and training, this may confirm low expectations of achievement and a narrow view of what constitutes 'purposeful' learning. Torrance and Pryor show, for example, that teachers 'protect' children they see as vulnerable from having to engage with robust feedback and its implications about their achievement. In addition, children vary considerably in their understanding of their own role in the social rituals that surround assessment and their expected responses (Torrance and Pryor, 1998; see also Pollard and Filer, 1999).

Similar pressures are likely to be evident in post-compulsory education where teachers often want to maximise students' achievement in order to give them the best chance possible in difficult socio-economic circumstances. Yet, this cultural disposition can, inadvertently, reinforce low expectations of achievement (Elliott *et al.*, 1999) and lead to unchallenging forms of assessment. This reduces expectations of the rigour and commitment necessary for critical autonomy, especially if students need to see themselves as 'embedded' learners willing to exploit assessment feedback to improve learning, not merely to get better grades. Previous 'learning careers' and identities shaped in response to increasingly rigid assessment in the National Curriculum are therefore essential variables (see Bloomer, 1997; Reay and Wiliam, 1999). So too are the particular dynamics of informal and formal learning within a community of practice which also produce feelings and responses to assessment demands. The effects in activities outside formal learning may not necessarily be progressive since groups can create their own norms about what counts as desirable learning and marginalise peers who do not conform (for example, Ecclestone and Field, 2001).

Given that internalising the standard of assessment implies much more than merely knowing what it is and aiming for it, there is therefore a need to examine the social dynamics, and emotional effects, of assessment relationships. As Black and Wiliam argue:

> beliefs about the goals of learning, about one's capacity to respond, about the risks involved in responding in various ways and about what learning should be like [all] affect the motivation to take action, the ability to choose action and commitment to it.
>
> (1998a: 20–1)

Social and conditioned dispositions influence students' views about whether questions and feedback are opportunities to learn, a potential threat to self-esteem, or merely an unfair hurdle. Groups and sub-cultures will also be important, perhaps affecting individuals' willingness and ability to develop different types of motivation and autonomy within a peer group. An important factor in these social dimensions is the distinction made by

Eraut and colleagues between informal learning and non-formal learning, identified earlier in the chapter. Courses in FE colleges have many more opportunities for informal and non-formal learning than for formal learning. These create their own norms, 'maps of meanings' and dispositions, making them a significant part of students' experiences and attitudes to assessment requirements.

These considerations all imply that the quality and use of feedback, and of relationships between teachers and students are subtle and have unpredictable effects (see, for example, Tunstall and Gipps, 1996; Torrance and Pryor, 1998). To add further complexity, the idea of internalising a standard also has both behaviourist and constructivist dimensions. From a behaviourist perspective, for example, an early aim in GNVQs was that precise specifications of outcomes could create shared understandings of the required standard amongst teachers and between teachers and students (see discussion in the next chapter). Yet, an assessment community requires induction and socialisation, where reinterpretations of 'standards' occur through moderation processes, and regular discussion between colleagues about the quality of grading and comments to students (see Wolf, 1995; Winter and Maisch, 1996; Ecclestone, 2001). This has direct parallels with strategies to develop self and peer assessment amongst students in order to encourage this shared standard. 'Checking compliance' or 'encouraging critical conversations' therefore seems to summarise the main tension in creating an assessment community. A heartfelt perspective is offered by Graham (1998) who argues that the pressures of summative assessment destroy the type of authentic relationships between teachers and students that can allow learning to be real and genuinely empathetic (see also Rogers, 1983).

The fusion of constructivist and behaviourist epistemologies also creates a misleading rhetoric that formative assessment can 'lead naturally' into the requirements of summative assessment (see Torrance, 1993 for discussion). In addition, merging purposes and processes alters relationships between teachers and students while prioritising teacher (internal) assessment, also alters the relationship between government, awarding bodies and teachers (see Harlen, 1995; Wilmut, 1999). Black and Wiliam (1998a) argue, for example, that formative assessment requires 'radical change' in classroom pedagogy since it is integral to the learning and teaching process. This implies that if teachers see formative assessment as 'just part of what I do anyway', they will not appreciate the need to understand theories about assessment and then to relate them to changes in practice. Without this, formative assessment is little more than continuous summative assessment.

More broadly, it is possible to connect behaviourist and constructivist notions of assessment with theories of human and social capital. Specification of outcomes and criteria lend themselves, for example, to conditions where there are less resources and demand for group contact: in theory, individuals can pursue their own goals with minimal recourse to peers or teachers and without any social commitment to or from them. This may be particularly tempting in areas where a shortage of good jobs, low expectations of progression, or of the value of education, creates growing numbers of 'hangers on', 'pragmatic acceptors', 'drifters' and 'strategic compliers'. Behaviourist approaches to assessment therefore respond pragmatically to low expectations amongst teachers and students of shared social goals and commitments, thereby encouraging teachers and institutions to overlook their importance in assessment communities. They also underpin the ideology of risk aversion, discussed in Chapter 1, where the seemingly neutral authority of guidance and specifications codifies and then regulates human behaviour and reduces an inclination to depart from the specifications.

In contrast, theories of constructivism require communal motivation, together with creation of, and commitment to, the networks and mutual development that underpins social capital. Ideally, this requires teachers to focus on relationships and networks, both in the particular community of practice that a learning programme fosters within an institution, and in a wider community of employers, parents and peers in the institution itself. Yet, constructivist assessment is less predictable, less amenable to regulation than behaviourist assessment and therefore more risky. Seen in this light, when behaviourist models incorporate constructivist techniques and a liberal humanist discourse, they offer a comforting, low risk approach to learning. This feature might confirm fears that humanist beliefs can become a mere technology in the pursuit of more instrumental goals (Rogers, 1983).

Summary

The typology has raised difficult philosophical and political questions about what we mean by autonomy. Nevertheless, it offers a basis for conceptualising and categorising different types of autonomy and motivation. It is probably self-evident that the diverse constituencies involved in policy development and implementation will have different views about goals and processes relating to each attribute. The typology offers a basis for exploring constructions of autonomy, motivation and formative assessment within the 'black boxes' of policy processes, college classrooms and relationships between teachers and students and amongst students. It also enables curriculum designers, awarding bodies and teachers a way of beginning to think strategically about how teachers within particular subject disciplines and occupational areas might encourage different forms of autonomy and motivation.

Yet, developing the potential of formative assessment techniques in order to motivate learners and make them more autonomous requires attention to the lack of understanding amongst teachers and designers of assessment models about how formative assessment translates into classroom interaction. This is compounded by a dominant summative mindset about the goals of assessment. Such problems suggest that research and professional development have to help teachers see formative assessment as a conscious strategy for changing learning in the everyday constraints of FE colleges rather than merely part of 'good' tutoring or teaching. This requires them to re-conceptualise, then practise, formative assessment in the context of everyday activities and constraints (Black and Wiliam, 1998; Ecclestone and Swann, 1999).

The complexities of motivation also highlight a need to differentiate between the effects of an assessment model, institutional and structural factors, students' dispositions to learning and their expectations of progression and achievement. Lastly, it is important to reiterate that, while the motivational labels or 'ideal types' used in the first part of this chapter are useful as initial organising and analytical categories, they should not become essentialising characterisations of students' traits and dispositions.

3   Constructing GNVQ assessment policy*

Introduction

As the latest of a series of initiatives to motivate more 16-year-olds to stay on in full-time education and to raise the status of vocational education GNVQs were announced in the Conservative 1992 election manifesto, introduced in 1992 after nine months of development and funded until 1995 by the Employment Department (ED). GNVQs were introduced initially at Advanced and Intermediate (Key Stage 4) levels as a parallel to job-specific NVQs and to provide a route into higher education. They were developed between 1992 and 1999 in a rolling programme of fourteen vocational areas at three levels (Foundation and Intermediate (post-14 and post-16) and Advanced (post-16) and re-launched as 'vocational GCSEs' (Intermediate GNVQ) and 'vocational A-levels (Advanced) in 2000. The new qualifications are therefore a major route at Key Stage 3 and KS4.

The government's intention in 1993 was that 25 per cent of all 16-year-olds would take Advanced GNVQ and that they should have a strong profile in further education, sixth form colleges and schools. By 1997, figures from the Further Education Funding Council (FEFC) show that 75 per cent of Advanced GNVQ registrations were in the further education sector: of these, 85 per cent were in FE colleges, 15 per cent in sixth form colleges, and 70 per cent of FE college registrations were with the EdExcel awarding body (formerly BTEC) (FEFC, 1997). Yet, of the total number of full-time 16–19-year-olds in FE and sixth form colleges, 24 per cent took Advanced GNVQ, 46 per cent took GCE A-levels, and across the post-16 sector as a whole, including schools, recruitment to general A-levels outnumbered that in GNVQs by eight to one (Spours, 1997). There were also problems with retention and completion. More tellingly in terms of status and location, GNVQs made little impact in schools where few subjects were offered in small cohorts (Wolf, 1997a). Finally, 75 per cent of those completing Advanced GNVQ in 1996 applied to university for degrees or

*Parts of this chapter are reproduced with permission from Taylor and Francis Ltd, www.tandf.co.uk (see Ecclestone, 2000a).

Higher National Diplomas (HNDs) and of these, almost two-thirds had offers for HNDs. Of those completing Intermediate GNVQ, 75 per cent progressed to Advanced GNVQ. It is also important to note that, despite fourteen subjects offered at Advanced level, four of the original five (Business, Health and Social Care, Leisure and Tourism, Art and Design) dominated recruitment, taking over 75 per cent of all students (Wolf, 1997a) while Engineering, IT and Manufacturing never attracted large numbers.

A case study of Advanced GNVQs illuminates political debates surrounding the aims and claims made for autonomy and motivation in outcome-based assessment models. It also reveals the broader influences, processes and debates in policy-making for the vocational curriculum (see also Raggatt and Williams, 1999). In addition, policy analysis enables researchers to 'people policy' with personalities, beliefs, values and dilemmas, gain data unavailable elsewhere, confirm or adjust publicly available accounts of policy and identify networks of individuals and agencies (Walford, 1994). 'Elite-based' research into education policy can illuminate the nature of power and how policy-makers realise their aims and familiarise researchers (and practitioners) with the assumptive worlds of policy-makers and key actors who set policies in motion (Fitz and Halpin, 1994). The values and missions of policy-makers, their personal and professional experiences and the particular institutional context they operate in, are essential factors in understanding the debates which surround policy (Bates, 1989b).

The twenty-five policy-makers and representatives from other constituencies involved in designing and developing GNVQ assessment policy between 1991 and 2000 formed a 'purposive' sample and relied heavily on 'snow-balling' where participants indicated other important or expert actors to interview.[1] In order to be as immersed as possible in policy-based issues, each broad constituency of interviewees was represented at similar times over an intensive period between March and June 1998. Twelve of the twenty-five interviewees were from the National Council Vocational Qualifications (NCVQ) and although there was no uniform 'NCVQ view' about GNVQ assessment, this set up an organisational bias. I aimed to offset this through concerted efforts to take account of participants' comments on two draft accounts of the emerging analysis, with particular reference to the views of external constituencies.

Analysis of data used multiple perspectives offered by Malen and Knapp (1997), outlined in the introduction to this book. Combining these perspectives addresses the central themes of policy and 'encourages a comparative analysis of prominent perspectives in terms of their capacity to account for patterns of policy activity within and across settings; they suggest 'avenues for influence', notably targets and strategies actors might consider should they seek to affect policy developments' (ibid.: 421).

The first section summarises official claims that an outcome-based assessment model can promote autonomy and motivation, using the typology developed in Chapter 2 to examine implicit constructions in the Advanced GNVQ assessment specifications. The second section focuses on the ways in which different constituencies viewed the aims of the model's designers. The third section evaluates how the assessment model was affected by broader political debates about 'standards' in assessment systems. The fourth section draws out some implications of the case study for avenues of influence in post-16 assessment policy.

This sets the scene for discussion in Chapter 4 about the effects of vocational initiatives on ideas about autonomy in FE colleges and on current forms of political intervention in FE colleges.

Autonomy and motivation in GNVQs

The official claims for autonomy and motivation in outcome-based assessment models can be summarised as follows:

- teachers and students can design assignments that generate evidence to meet the required outcomes;
- assignments and learning activities respond to individual interests and needs;
- students can determine their pace of work and receive interim feedback on progress;
- students can assess their own effectiveness in planning, executing and evaluating their work;
- processes of reviewing and recording achievement and setting targets encourage students to take more control over their learning;
- teachers have to share the basis of their assessment decisions with students and negotiate appropriate evidence of achievement;
- knowledge of outcomes enables students to plan progression both within a programme and to the next stage of education or employment;
- an upbeat public focus on achievement and opportunities to succeed erodes traditional associations of assessment with selection and norm-referencing.

Supporters of these features claim that they encourage independence from formal time-served courses run in groups and teachers. They also promote a dichotomy between 'traditional' teacher-centred pedagogy and 'active learning' suggested by projects and other investigative activities. Individuality, personal development and independence are all integral to outcome-based assessment:

> The outcomes model is based on the assumption that learning is a personal and individual experience and that to standardise it by adopting specific modes and time periods is not an effective means for a group to achieve a set of learning outcomes. Individuals need to manage their

own learning experiences in a manner which recognises where they tart from, their preferred styles and modes of learning and the time and opportunities they have for learning.

(Jessup, 1995: 34)

Specifications of learning outcomes shift attention from traditional course structures and teaching inputs, to 'what is actually learned' (UDACE, 1994: 4), contrasting ways for individuals to achieve the outcomes with time-serving and formal attendance in groups and open access to the criteria with 'a tutor-led system with fuzzy objectives and undisclosed criteria' (Otter, 1995). An important aim in NVQs and GNVQs was, then, to reduce the influence of teachers with assumptions that learning is not a social but an individual process:

> There seems to be an assumption that educators exert proprietary con-trol over the process of learning . . . Yet if anyone can exercise control over the process of learning, it is the individual. It is only the learner who can make sense of the diverse inputs he or she receives.
>
> (Jessup, 1991: 4)

Claims for outcome-based assessment therefore offer ambiguous, confus-ing and largely implicit perspectives on autonomy and motivation, inter-twined with notions of self-reliance, flexibility and responsibility (see Bates, 1998a). Interest in outcome-based assessment resonates with two wider political and social trends. One is for more individuality and informality in everyday life. At the same time, increased routinisation in education and other parts of the public sector respond to calls for people to have equal treatment and for public services to be accountable. The two shifts are frequently incompatible.

Although the model and its claims for autonomy were widely supported amongst many teachers in vocational education, it was both politically and educationally contentious. Deriving from principles in the TVEI and CPVE, such as unit assessment, negotiation of assignments around learning out-comes and portfolios of achievement, GNVQs were influenced heavily by the competence-based model of NVQs. This challenged powerful traditions of norm-referenced, examination-based assessment, on one hand, and learn-ing programmes or activities that did not lead to formal recognition of achievement, on the other. They also raised questions about the balance between teacher (internal) and external assessment similar to those which have dogged the National Curriculum (see Wilmut, 1999).

In addition, the assessment model is a telling example of the way in which two contradictory psychological traditions underpin many assessment systems, where behaviourist objectives rooted in positivist epistemology sit alongside constructivist ideas about negotiation through formative assess-ment over both course content and assessment evidence. By examining official guidance in GNVQs, and specifications from the three models between 1992 and 2000, discussed below, that boundaries between generating and assessing knowledge, and processes for planning, managing and evaluating learning were, to some extent, negotiable and transactionary. They were also fixed and prescriptive! Assessment criteria, course outlines, learning outcomes, assessment criteria, official guidance to teachers and awarding bodies, inspection and awarding body reports, commercial texts and official exemplars of students' work all illuminate explicit and implicit expectations of autonomy and motivation.

Official advice to students emphasised general activities:

Ways of working

- GNVQs give you an opportunity to try out all sorts of ways of working, for example: *working on your own* and as part of a team;
- doing short projects and longer assignments;
- looking into processes and products, planning and organising events, designing products and services;
- getting work experience.

Generally, you are expected to take responsibility for your own learning, for example, deciding what to do and how to go about it. (Mandatory Unit Guidance Booklet, QCA, 1997, my emphasis.)

The assessment model was overhauled three times between 1993 and 2000, culminating in Vocational A-levels. Reasons for perceived problems inside policy processes are discussed below. As a precursor, a brief review here of each model reveals different notions of autonomy.

The 1993–1995 model reveals very general notions of autonomy such as the freedom of teachers and students to design their own courses around outcomes and the potential for all students to achieve Distinctions, provided they met the criteria. As guidance from Gilbert Jessup, the model's architect, shows below, there are implicit resonances with ideas about internalising the criteria discussed in the assessment chapter above.

Summative criteria rewarded generic skills of self-reliance, procedural autonomy and a form of personal autonomy based on knowing one's strengths and weaknesses in planning assignments, assessing strengths and weaknesses in managing work and evaluating improvements. Students accumulated evidence of achievement across the programme in individual portfolios. Distinction criteria encouraged students to meet criteria without direct guidance while criteria such as 'complex sources' and 'range of sources' indicated a deeper interpretation of independence, with fleeting and erratic general images of critical autonomy in relation to specific topics.

Official advice to teachers about formative assessment placed 'information for students to plan their learning at the next stage' at the top of a list of functions for summative evidence (Jessup, 1994: 12). Advice emphasised regular, consistent feedback to students about their progress as essential for their motivation and the ability to plan their programme. In response to widespread anecdotal evidence amongst GNVQ teachers that they 'were not allowed' to help, advice pointed out:

> But this [independence] does not mean they never ask for help – independent students will often ask questions based on their own initiative and information. A dependent student does not take initiatives, needs ideas and options given to them and needs advice about what to choose and why.
>
> (ibid.: 1994)

The 1995 model reduced the 1993 grading criteria and the proportion of the portfolio required for summative assessment. However, there was significantly more detail in the actual specifications as 'amplification' and 'evidence indicators', accompanied by advice to teachers that students should experience 'active learning' and 'have to make informed judgements about their learning'.

The 1996 model was introduced as a pilot of new specifications after an official review of the assessment model was commissioned in 1995 by the NCVQ and chaired by John Capey, principal of Exeter college and a member of the NCVQ Council. The review and subsequent pilot of a new model in ninety centres between 1996 and 2000 responded to widespread criticisms of an overburdened, confusing model and criticisms from OFSTED about Advanced level students' lack of 'cognitive depth' within a subject, discussed below.

This model was the basis for Vocational A-levels, introduced in September 2000. Instead of generic grading themes, criteria of planning, review and evaluation are embedded within subject (unit) specifications with grading at five levels to correspond to general A-levels. There is strong emphasis on externally-set and moderated assignments and external tests require more engagement than the simple multiple choice tests of the 1993 and 1995 models. Pass criteria emphasise procedures such as selecting material and deciding on a focus for the study, with verbs of 'explain', 'identify' and 'describe'. To progress from Pass to Distinction, there is a pattern of adding criteria of 'synthesis' and 'comprehension', then 'analysis', 'critical analysis' and 'evaluation', indicating that Bloom's *Taxonomy of Cognitive Objectives* (1956) is alive and influential!

To gain a Merit in the 1996 model, students had to meet all Pass criteria, and then the Merit ones. For Distinction, students had to meet all Pass and Merit criteria and then 'critically evaluate' or 'critically analyse' either the learning processes used in an assignment or issues raised by the subject content, such as the application of a particular theory or procedure to a context or practice:

Higher grades build on achievement at lower grades. This does not mean that the students have to do additional tasks to get a merit or distinction grade. It means that they show increased sophistication and independence in their work, for example in the planning and organisation of their work, and their production of better-quality work which shows a deeper understanding of what they have learnt. Independence is therefore subject related rather than seen as a generic skill across the course.

(QCA, 1997: 19)

A major change in the 1996 model and Vocational A-levels was to locate implicit notions of procedural, personal and critical autonomy within specific subject criteria instead of presenting them as generic, 'transferable' skills across the course as earlier models had done. An overview of specifications in each of the two courses in the fieldwork show that implicit notions of autonomy for Distinction grades were, potentially, sophisticated but confusing and switched erratically between assignments, with no sense of a progression over the two years that students were on the course. Variation appears, for example, in whether units emphasised cognitive skills, application of theory to practice, self-reliance and independence in planning, managing and evaluating one's own work. 'Evaluation' criteria sometimes prioritised personal strengths and weaknesses in an assignment, or the applicability of particular theories or approaches to research. For example, the Social Policy unit in Advanced Health and Social Care (HSC) required students to explore ideology in social issues. In contrast, the college-based fieldwork discussed later in the book showed that the externally set assignment for 'Planning a Health Campaign' encouraged the 'hunting and gathering of information' that school students in Bates' study showed (Bates, 1998a) and fairly superficial evaluations of these processes gained a Distinction.

In spite of aims in the earlier models that formative and summative assessment were iterative, official guidance to GNVQ teachers after 1996 was vague about the role of feedback. Guidance focused on boundaries of 'acceptable' help, summative evidence and how to reduce the administrative burden of recording (QCA, 1998). The QCA's Code of Practice governing assessment procedures for teachers and awarding body verifiers also discussed 'internal assessment' (coursework) entirely in summative terms. Similarly, advice to students in unit specifications concentrated on what summative evidence would be required, how it could be recorded and where it could derive from.

The model in Vocational A-levels that emerged over eight years of policy development, discussed next, therefore reflects a major shift from principles underpinning ideas about autonomy and motivation in the models of 1993 and 1995:

- from content-free specifications based on outcomes to a syllabus;
- from 100 per cent mastery of outcomes to sampling parts of the syllabus and isolated grade criteria rather than cumulative achievement;
- from continuous assessment, plus knowledge-based tests to more robust external testing and assignments designed and moderated by QCA and awarding bodies;
- from creative activities and 'real life' assignments to a more hypothetical application of theory to pre-defined contexts and scenarios;
- from generic skills of independence to subject-focused autonomy.

The technical minutiae of each model, and the political debates that have accompanied them, are complicated. Yet, some understanding of them is important if researchers are to evaluate the impact of a particular assessment system on learners' motivation and autonomy and to compare apparently different assessment systems such as general and vocational A-levels (see Table 3.1 for examples of changes to assessment specifications in the three models).

Constructions of autonomy and motivation inside policy

The political origins of GNVQs have been analysed by Raggatt and Williams (1999) and Sharp (1998) and the debates and controversies that surrounded the development of the assessment model are discussed at length in Ecclestone (2000b). Some themes in my earlier analysis help to illuminate discussion here about the ways in which generic goals for autonomy and motivation in an outcome-based assessment model were finally overcome. This section uses some of this earlier analysis as the basis for drawing out issues in relation to constructs of autonomy and motivation inside policy processes.

An inference of a 'passionate' vision emerged strongly from the interview data and detailed fieldnotes. The GNVQ initiative generated strong personal and professional commitments, particularly inside NCVQ, but from other constituencies too. Interviews revealed aspirations heavily permeated by liberal humanism and vocational progressivism, albeit from different interests. Inside NCVQ, strong normative themes amongst interviewees in Gilbert Jessup's small enthusiastic team encompassed general themes of autonomy and motivation arising through more student choice:

> I thought [GNVQs] presented real opportunities for transference . . .
> that I've never encountered in my educational experience, either as
> a teacher or as a student learner before. It also related to the concept
> of the adult learner, the learning contract etc which philosophically I
> felt was really appropriate for the population that we were talking
> about, which was mostly . . . young adults, which is to do with their

Table 3.1 Changes to advanced level GNVQ assessment models 1992–2000

The charts show examples of changes to assessment characteristics in Business and Health and Social Care (HSC) specifications.

Changes to Advanced GNVQs in Business 1993–2000

Model	Key features	Manageability	Cognitive depth	Student autonomy	Creativity and motivation
1993 Model	• portfolios of achievement • grading themes emphasised process • external multiple choice tests 'bolted on'	• 8 mandatory units • 25 outcomes all of which are assessed	• lower end of Bloom's taxonomy predominates: 'describe', 'identify', 'explain'	• language of specifications aimed at teachers • heavy demands on students' procedural autonomy • scope for personal autonomy at merit and distinction level	• design elements in units 3B8 and 3B2 • role-play and peer assessment in unit 3B4 • emphasis on local design of 'real life' assignments • flexible approaches to meeting the criteria
1995 Model	• introduction of amplification, guidance and evidence indicators • summative feedback from teachers used formatively • reduction in portfolio evidence • 100 per cent mastery of outcomes	• 8 mandatory units • 29 outcomes of which only one-third are assessed	• lower end of Bloom's taxonomy predominates: 'describe', 'identify', 'explain'	• increased detail and technical language make specifications less clear • procedural, personal and critical autonomy as 1993	• proposals required for unit 2 • proposals, role-play and assessment elements in unit 4

1996 Model	• reduction of assessment burden, evidence indicators become 'bullets' • introduction of more 'cognitively challenging' criteria • externally set and moderated assignments • feedback becomes summative confirmation of achievement	• 8 mandatory units • 8 outcomes to be assessed • grades are cumulative: Distinction must encompass Merit and pass	• introduction of a progression from pass: 'explain' and 'describe' to merit: 'compare' and 'detailed explanation' to distinction: 'analyse' and 'appraise critically'	• redesigned for students, clarity of language and presentation improved • extension of pass criteria not clear • procedural autonomy embedded at Pass level • critical autonomy at Distinction level for evaluating processes and subject-related issues	• proposals required for distinction in unit 1 • creative elements embedded in unit 5 at all levels with emphasis on role-play and peer/self-assessment • possibility that teachers can merely give students specifications rather than design assignments
2000 Model	• grades a, c and e replace distinction, merit and pass • external testing for one-third total mark • requirement for 100 per cent mastery removed	• 6 mandatory units • 4 outcomes to be assessed and 2 externally set and moderated exams • grades are no longer cumulative	• progression not as evident: 'analyse' used at e/pass level • comparative elements removed from outcomes, requiring only one business case study	• commitment to student understanding continues	• creative elements mainly replaced by descriptive or analytic tasks • requirements for role-play and peer assessment removed • hypothetical application of theory and less emphasis on 'real life'

Table 3.1 continued on next page

Table 3.1 (continued)
Changes to Advanced GNVQs in Health and Social Care 1993–2000

Model	Key features	Manageability	Cognitive depth	Student autonomy	Creativity and motivation
1993 Model	• portfolios of achievement • grading themes emphasised process • external multiple choice tests 'bolted on'	• 8 mandatory units • 24 outcomes all of which are assessed	• lower end of Bloom's taxonomy predominates: 'describe', 'identify', 'explain' but 'analyse' appears in unit 3HSC	• language of specifications aimed at teachers • heavy demands on students' procedural autonomy • scope for personal autonomy at merit and distinction level	• opportunity for rehearsal and peer assessment in unit 3HSC2 • emphasis on local design of assignments • flexible approaches to meeting the criteria
1995 Model	• introduction of amplification, guidance and evidence indicators • summative feedback from teachers used formatively • reduction in portfolio evidence • 100 per cent mastery of outcomes	• 8 mandatory units • 24 outcomes of which only one-third are assessed	• lower end of Bloom's taxonomy predominates in unit 1 • unit 2 requires higher order skills	• increased detail and technical language make specifications less clear • procedural, personal and critical autonomy as 1993	• recommendations required in unit 3HSC • opportunity for rehearsal and peer assessment in unit 3HSC

1996 (Capey) Model	• reduction of assessment burden, evidence indicators become 'bullets' • introduction of more 'cognitively challenging' criteria • externally set and moderated assignments • feedback becomes summative confirmation of achievement	• 8 mandatory units • 10 outcomes to be assessed • grades are cumulative: Distinction must encompass Merit and Pass	• introduction of a progression pass to merit to distinction • process elements a significant feature in merit criteria	• redesigned for students, clarity of language and presentation improved • extension of pass criteria not as clear in some units as others • procedural autonomy embedded at Pass level • critical autonomy at Distinction level in relation to evaluation of learning processes and/or subject related issues	• explicit ownership and management of research in unit 1 • opportunity for rehearsal and peer assessment in unit 2 • possibility that teachers can merely give students specifications rather than design assignments
2000 Model	• grades a, c and e replace distinction, merit and pass • external testing for one-third total mark	• 6 mandatory units • 4 outcomes to be assessed and 2 externally moderated assessments. • grades are no longer cumulative	• influence of Bloom's taxonomy continues • process elements removed	• clarity and transparency affected by the reduction of evidence indicators	• explicit ownership and management of research in unit 1 removed • opportunity for peer assessment in unit 2 • hypothetical application of theory and less emphasis on 'real life' contexts

intellectual development and the way they feel about themselves and their autonomy and their right to decide.

(NCVQ official 6)

Designers brought into NCVQ for their assessment expertise also had an absorbing technical interest in applying principles of outcome-based assessment in order to achieve such goals in a mainstream qualification:

> I've done enough teaching and enough educational psychology to know that for a lot of kids, it's not fit to have an exclusive diet of examinations so this looked like an interesting way forward and the whole issue around what could loosely be called criterion-referencing and whether that would work or not work, having also been part of the National Curriculum.
>
> (NCVQ official 7)

Frustration with didactic, uninspiring forms of education and what were seen as inappropriate notions of 'standards' in assessment were not only prevalent inside NCVQ. There were strongly held views, and therefore strong normative themes, about what counts as a 'good' education:

> Having been to a secondary modern school, I identified strongly with the sort of kids that might do [GNVQ], and also from my background in occupational psychology and learning . . . if you could make the qualification about something that was real to these kids then they wouldn't give up. That's very idealistic but . . .
>
> (civil servant 1)

There were initial hopes that such goals would resonate with existing traditions in FE colleges:

> There was great potential for a tremendous alliance between the NCVQ and the best of its idealism, and the FE sector, at least that part of the sector which shared ideas about access and flexibility and also, like NCVQ, felt beleaguered . . . because FE people did not feel part of the education system, you know, and I think they would have welcomed an alliance.
>
> (External body official 2/General Policy Committee (GPC))[2]

Yet, in keeping with the general injunctions for autonomy, empowerment and choice, noted above, these aims had numerous themes running through them:

> The whole idea of the student accumulating evidence towards a portfolio and being able to say 'I've got it together and I'm now ready to

be assessed'. So that they take the time they need and they determine when they think they've got the right quality and . . . have the option also to go back and say 'I want to improve, can I do this again?'. . . We didn't say it was a free-for-all and the students are in charge . . . it wasn't a case of autonomy or independence running mad but it was saying . . . for young adults, they may have very valid reasons for saying 'I can't do it this week, can I do it next week' . . .

(NCVQ official 6)

Outcome-based assessment might also offer teachers more autonomy in designing locally appropriate assignments to motivate students:

I remember making lots of speeches about how we were liberating teachers from the tyranny of curriculum and syllabus by saying we specify the outcome and you decide what it is people need to do in order to get there. You decide how much you need to teach them, how much they can learn for themselves and you decide on the route they are going to take. You've got to decide on the basis of each individual in each group of students and you are constrained by the economics and all the other things that constrain you but that's your job, that's what being a professional teacher is. They used to cheer 'that's wonderful stuff'. Whether anybody could actually do that I don't know, but that's the theory.

(NCVQ official 5)

Some designers saw autonomy as an entitlement of equal access to worthwhile certification, built both through political recognition of parity of esteem but also through assessment processes that inspire confidence, and thereby, motivation. This is a meritocratic view of autonomy:

If you judge people on how well they meet a series of outcomes regardless of how they got there, that is really important for enabling open access and things . . . I've thought a lot about outcomes and I thought about them in terms of people internalising, seeing what they needed for an outcome, and then trying to match that to their own feelings of how they were doing. . . . But when you get working with the outcome in one hand and the learner's own perception on the other, with no intermediary, it can be a big problem.

(NCVQ official 1)

The last part of this quote indicates more caution than Gilbert Jessup's radical view that access to assessment outcomes and criteria empower students to be the lever for pedagogic change, bypassing the mediocre, uninspiring teachers he saw as barriers to learning:

> One can't have this great faith in teachers. They aren't going to change overnight to become inspirational. Improve teachers by all means but there must be other means.
>
> (interview, March 1998)

Autonomy is therefore associated with independence from institutional timetables and from teachers' idiosyncratic and often lacklustre approaches. From these perspectives, self-regulation of procedures precedes engagement with subject content. Initial motivation through choice over relevant, authentic learning activities and by not being subjected to artificial, invalid external testing offered a naturalistic view of learning as a basis for progressing to intrinsic motivation and engagement with subject content. The grading criteria in the first two models would therefore encourage the 'student's ability to use his or her own resources to solve a problem' (NCVQ official 4) and 'to go away and do projects and think things through for themselves a lot more' (NCVQ official 8).

However, it was the contention that students' access to clear specifications of learning outcomes and assessment criteria played a key role in their autonomy that offered the strongest contrast with traditional models of assessment:

> It was always this tension that we didn't want to finish up with just another A-level . . . at each step of that, there's been some soul searching about whether this is the right way and what are the implications . . . the Gilbert Jessup perspective, that once you start moving this, you're putting control back to the teacher and not to the student because assessment is no longer clear . . . somebody has to interpret it and that kind of educational control and those issues . . .
>
> (NCVQ official 7)

Despite such aims and enthusiasm, these were not closely articulated either inside the NCVQ, nor externally through early publicity conferences for GNVQ and the guidance to teachers discussed above. When asked directly whether the aim of using assessment to develop autonomy and motivation was discussed or communicated, both inside policy and to external constituencies, every interviewee believed that it was left implicit. As GNVQs moved out from the policy margins of vocational assessment, the *ad hoc*, rushed, even chaotic, development of the assessment specifications combined with fraught internecine turf wars between awarding bodies and other constituencies, reminiscent of previous initiatives (see Ecclestone, 2000b for discussion; also Radnor *et al.*, 1989; Raggatt and Williams, 1999). Each awarding body took overall responsibility for a particular subject area (e.g. RSA and Science, BTEC and Business) and for developing the assessment specifications. Individual subject development was overseen by a GNVQ Development Group led by an NCVQ official.

Specifications were written at enormous haste, first by the small team of NCVQ designers which developed the model and then, after the first pilot, by small subject committees. These comprised development officers from Further Education Unit, school and college inspectors, the awarding bodies, employers' and professional organisations, subject associations, representatives from colleges, schools and universities. Groups determined the content of units which writers then turned into assessment specifications against a 'template' written by the NCVQ design team. The first units drew on expertise from commercial consultants and NCVQ officials who had developed occupational specifications in NVQs. Everyone brought their own normative perspectives about assessment, and through this, about autonomy and motivation in associated activities:

> It was iterative, you brought in someone who had knowledge of, say, health and social care – what we were desperate for was subject knowledge – and then they'd write a few units and we had a look at them . . . it was a very difficult process . . . there are very few people who are able to write units [according to the assessment model's principles] . . . what they were essentially doing was just replicating what they thought was important which was OK because they were experts in their field . . . we did use writers who were more familiar with vocationally-oriented programmes [and] with adult learning and obviously the people who were involved in the NVQ standards' programme . . . understood what state of the art vocational provision should look like . . . but it was very led by their own perceptions of what was required and we didn't have time to consult very widely at that stage.
>
> (NCVQ official 2)

There were, therefore, clashes between supporters of different assessment traditions, even inside the NCVQ itself:

> I think one of the things that may have happened is that we . . . turned to the same fairly limited [number of] people often drawn on because they were familiar with NVQ and we then asked them to go through a kind of cultural conversion and come out with a new style of stuff . . .
>
> (NCVQ official 7)

Leaders of subject groups had to write specifications around the epistemological principles determined by the NCVQ whilst trying to impose common interpretations and mediate interests between competing constituencies. The pressures were extreme:

> We didn't have a master plan. We never did. I think the most you could say is we had an idea about what it would look like and we could recognise when it wasn't there. But I don't think that at any stage you

> could say we knew all the time what [specification writers] should be
> doing and it was just a terrible job to get them to do it.
>
> (NCVQ official 5)

> It was very intense work . . . it was very much learning and developing
> from what you learned. It didn't seem there were lots of things you
> could borrow from . . . and we did produce lots of information [about
> the conventions of writing GNVQ units], lots of drafts and masses of
> paper about how to do this.
>
> (NCVQ official 1)

As this chapter's first section showed, these processes produced assessment specifications with erratic notions of autonomy embedded in them
across a subject area and over two years of a course. Given the tensions
between the awarding bodies and the NCVQ, it is not surprising that there
was criticism outside the NCVQ of a model 'out of control':

> There was no template produced, lots of little groups all over the
> country were just allowed to go off and just invent something with
> virtually no guidance as to what was the purpose and what this was
> supposed to look like.
>
> (awarding body official 2)

Initially, the original team edited unit specifications against the model they
had designed and there was an organisational culture of intense personal
commitment to the model and its aims. But keeping a tight rein on it rapidly
became impossible. The subject committees reconciling competing interests
in the specifications were often, as one official points out, made up of the
very lobbyists who wanted 'their bits' in the GNVQ. A recurring image in
interviews is the phrase 'a camel designed by a committee' ('and pastured
on a water meadow', according to awarding body official 2). Any potential
for discussing and developing clear goals around autonomy was lost in the
messy processes which led to what Eraut calls 'Parkinson's Law of curriculum development', where approaches to designing the National Curriculum,
NVQs and GNVQs allow disparate constituencies to add their requirements
to an overloaded, compromised curriculum (Eraut, 1997):

> The subject committees [were] saying 'we ought to have this' but they
> always overloaded the qualification so the job comes down to the
> subject adviser, the problem being that they were at the mercy of the
> various constituencies and often were not subject specialists, which I
> suspect was an NCVQ weakness, that you hadn't got people with the
> knowledge themselves to say 'I'm cutting out a third of this unit' . . .
> the SCAA officers . . . have got enough kind of clout to say 'this has

just got too much or this hasn't got enough in and you've missed out something that is important'. [In NCVQ] there wasn't that culture sufficiently, you've got people doing subjects . . . but doing it as kind of administrators almost.

(NCVQ official 7)

Things got added in and there are . . . very simple things about revising any qualification: you use the subect committee and you have consultations. Everyone will say 'it's too big but there is nothing you can take out'.

(NCVQ official 1)

As a result, there was no overt discussion, even in the subject groups, about the link between autonomy seen as generic research skills and subject content:

I don't think people ever discussed it, I didn't come across that type of debate at all . . . we were thinking of people's research skills . . . an emphasis on autonomy through depth of subject matter was never an issue in any of the meetings I was at.

(NCVQ official 8)

Inside NCVQ itself, there was not unanimous support for GNVQ and NCVQ officials describe a 'two buildings culture' at the head office of NCVQ in London, with little interaction between mainstream NVQ developments and the GNVQ initiative. Internal dissension began to emerge over the extent to which specifications of outcomes in isolation could empower learners and whether having to account for one's autonomy through the grading criteria became merely bolted-on and 'false' (NCVQ official 5).

Instead of a mainstream initiative with coherent underpinning principles, a piecemeal process of bidding to the Employment Department to fund each stage led to a model constructed by an unprecedented array of constituencies from diverse subjects, educational and assessment cultures. Between 1992 and the new model for 2000, the assessment model was overhauled three times, with many accompanying attempts to improve guidance and explication of specifications and expected standards for students' work (see Table 3.2). As new political imperatives arose, or new problems were seen, the NCVQ had to bolt-on additional features of assessment or change parts of the model frequently and at great speed. One civil servant pointed out that no other qualification has had so many people 'dabbling in it'.

Problems of communication were exacerbated by the ways that awarding body verifiers, inspectors, ministers and civil servants, staff running the

Table 3.2 An outline of developments in GNVQs (1990–2000)

Year	Development	Focus	Organisations or individuals involved
1990	Internal meetings in NCVQ	Discussion of 'ideal' assessment principles, in a new qualification	Gilbert Jessup and NCVQ officials
1991	Tim Eggar's briefing letter to NCVQ	Internal, formal launch of GNVQ developments	NCVQ officials and a newly formed General Policy Committee (GPC)
(May)	White Paper 'Education and Training for the 21st Century'	Public launch of initiative by DES, limited funding from ED	GNVQ team in NCVQ, awarding bodies
1992	Consultation amongst diverse constituencies about principles for the assessment model	Assessment principles and characteristics of the qualification	Colleges, awarding bodied, inspectorates, FEU, subject and professional associations
1992		First model of assessment specifications	GPC, subject groups convened by NCVQ
	DES instruction to include grading and external tests	Design of grading themes, delegation of the design of external tests to awarding bodies	NVQ, awarding bodies, subject groups
1993	Launch of first GNVQ	5 subjects, Advanced and Intermediate level	
1994	Smithers' report for 'Dispatches', Channel 4	Public criticism of quality of GNVQs. Notion of 'standards' and 'rigour' gain ground as a result of the publicity	Smithers, via Channel 4 Television, wide press coverage.
1994	First Further Education Funding Council (FEFC) inspection report	Informal feedback to NCVQ about burden of assessment	GPC, and on Radio 4's 'Today' programme FEFC chief inspector defends quality of GNVQs
1994	Report for the Employment Department by Alison Wolf	Internal criticism about quality of grading and burden of bureaucracy on teachers and students	Civil servants, NCVQ Officials

May 1995	Following FEFC and Wolf's reports, preparation for revised assessment specifications in Sept 1995 had started before the '6-point plan' to improve GNVQs, announced by Tim Boswell at CBI Conference in May	Public emphasis in Boswell's speech was on burden and manageability of assessment rather than on 'reliability' and 'standards'	Gilbert Jessup sets up Capey committee in response to Boswell's speech
Sept 1995	Revision to model. Much more detailed assessment guidance issued to teachers	• requirement for total coverage removed • clear rules for allocation of final grades • introduce external element to portfolio assessment • review to balance and relationship of internal and external verifiers	Gilbert Jessup, NCVQ and awarding bodies
May–Nov 1995	Review of assessment by John Capey's committee Report published November	Shift in emphasis from early principles of valid 'standards' • manageability of assessment: specifications reduced • grading themes integrated into units • attention to cognitive/intellectual skills in Distinction criteria • external tests (short answer) • externally set and moderated assignments	Representatives from UCAS, FEDA, OFSTED, FEFC inspectorate, teachers, awarding body verifiers, universities
Nov 1995	First OFSTED report on Advanced GNVQs in schools	Criticisms of: • poor quality work compared to A-levels • poor reliability of grading	Informal meetings OFSTED and civil ministers, discussion in GPC
1995	DfEE sets up Dearing Review of 16–19 qualifications	Review of assessment issues across 16–19 curriculum.	Ron Dearing liased closely with John Capey

Table 3.2 continued on next page

Table 3.2 (continued)

Year	Development	Focus	Organisations or individuals involved
Autumn 1995– May 1996	NCVQ design the pilot of new model in light of Capey's report	Rapid growth of NCVQ officials working on GNVQs, first large injection of public funding	NCVQ and awarding body subject groups
Sep 1996	Pilot of new 'Capey' model in 90 centres	New forms of moderation and shift in emphasis within the assessment regime (see above)	Institutions, NCVQ officials, awarding body verifiers
1996	Publication of second FEFC inspection report on GNVQs in colleges	FEFC concerns with 'standards of achievement' and 'reliability' move from burden/ manageability closer to OFSTED's interpretation of problems with reliability.	Informal OFSTED meetings with civil servants, GPC before publication of 1996 report
1996	Second OFSTED report (on Part 1 GNVQs in schools)	OFSTED voice concerns about GNVQ at key stage 4	
1997	GNVQ Scrutiny Report published by NCVQ	Following a review of consistency in teachers' grading decisions (Goff, 1996), NCVQ develop a monitoring programme to improve teachers' reliability in grading	NCVQ officials
October 1997	SCAA and NCVQ merge to form QCA		Gilbert Jessup leaves NCVQ; many GNVQ designers from NCVQ take on new roles in QCA

Date	Event	Details	Involved
October 1997	FEDA GNVQ Survey report	GNVQs confirmed as route to HE and to employment, with reservations Parity of esteem with A levels questioned	FEDA, Nuffield Foundation, Institute of Education
1997	Publication of third OFSTED report	Continued criticism of 'standards' and concerns about Part 1 GNVQs in school	
1999	DfEE/FEDA report on retention	Reducing demands of portfolio could improve retention	
Sept 1999	FEFC/OFSTED report on assessment pilot	4 areas of recommendation: • specifications: fewer units and more global summative assessment • assessment: reducing the burden, increasing 'rigour' in testing to achieve parity with A levels • standards moderation in a national moderation system • staff development, training and guidance	QCA officials, awarding bodies
2000	'Vocational A-levels' replace GNVQs, based on revisions to the 'Capey' model	• reduced assessment burden • external assessment now forms one third of summative requirement • new grade criteria • key skills as separate qualification	QCA officials, awarding bodies

GNVQ support programme in the Further Education Development Agency and textbook writers all contributed their own interpretations of the goals and characteristics of the model to teachers and other audiences. It is therefore helpful to see GNVQ specifications as the cannibalised 'policy texts' in Ball's analysis of policy-making (Ball, 1994), discussed in the introduction to this book. In this light, their production seems particularly chaotic and contentious in GNVQs.

Outside the NCVQ's team, further political confusion arose over whether the NCVQ's role was to design a whole new qualification, or merely the principles and features around which awarding bodies could submit their qualifications for accreditation (see Ecclestone, 2000b and also Raggatt and Williams, 1999). Confusion over the ambitious remit adopted by NCVQ placed unfamiliar pressures on relationships and responsibilities between government departments, NCVQ as a regulatory or accrediting body and commercial awarding bodies:

> [by 1992] the whole bandwagon was rolling. So the whole thing had shifted and . . . I don't know why it happened or if DfEE officials knew about it, but we were no longer working to [Eggar's] briefing letter . . . NCVQ chose not to accept the role of regulatory body but instead chose to design a whole new qualification.
>
> (GPC member/external body official 2)

In this turmoil, disagreements began to surface about whether the notion of autonomy through flexibility was realistic, or even desirable in the everyday reality of education institutions:

> You need to promote as much flexibility as you can, or as near as you can get to it, yet people nevertheless do adopt certain kinds of pathways, there are certain standard kind of packages . . . in terms of allocating resources . . . I always felt . . . that total autonomy, learning autonomy, was an unrealisable goal . . . because you are trading off things that are of great value like coherence, programme or peer group support. The kind of nightmare scenario of each individual pursuing a slightly different programme and having to access support in a slightly different way, just didn't seem to ring true.
>
> (civil servant 2)

In this quote, autonomy is synonymous with individual freedom of choice over options and pathways. However, it was fierce disagreement about what counts as 'standards' in assessment that made generic and vague views of autonomy vulnerable to political imperatives. This finally overcame educational images of autonomy, as the next section shows.

Slipping over 'standards'

Two contradictory notions of 'standards' slid past each other in GNVQ policy debates, sometimes disingenuously, sometimes unwittingly. One notion measures achievement as 'reliability' in performance between candidates and institutions and consistency of demands made on candidates in different years and in different subjects. Until the 1980s, defining and maintaining standards in public examinations relied on strong norm-referenced assessment, where the proportion of permitted grades at each level is set in relation to cohort performance and then regulated by examination boards. Both A-levels and GCSEs have moved away from this 'strong norm-referencing' towards 'weak criterion-referencing' (see Baird *et al.*, 2000). Despite this shift, and despite the complexity and mystique surrounding grades in public examinations and university degrees, the enduring public image of A-levels as a 'gold standard' draws on implicit psychometric notions of a limited 'pool' of innate ability where only a minority can attain the highest grades.

But analysis here of debates and changes to the model suggest that it is a populist portrayal of norm-referenced reliability that now underpins comparisons in league tables of qualification results between schools, FE and sixth form colleges. Similarly, the claim that overall achievement in Advanced GNVQ became 'the same' as in A-levels (DfEE, 2000) and that Vocational A-levels have 'parity' with general A-levels relies on this populist image of standards. OFSTED's criticism of students accumulating evidence mechanistically, without gaining autonomy within a cognitive base of a subject resonated with civil servants and Ministers who were becoming concerned about modular A-levels (Tim Boswell, interview May 1998). The idea that a foundation of knowledge and skills is needed as the basis for generic research skills therefore became influential:

> When you say 'fostering autonomy', that in itself is no good at all. What does autonomy mean in isolation? It is also about applying it, it's to do with styles of learning and giving a young person greater responsibility, if you like, but it also has to achieve something, and our concern in the early days of GNVQs was that actually achieving some kind of knowledge, as well as vague ideas of competence.
>
> (OFSTED inspector 2)

> We were concerned [about] what is the subject matter? What is the knowledge element in this, because we always felt that there was something missing in GNVQs.
>
> (civil servant 2)

This subject-based notion of autonomy became a source of profound disagreement over what was meant by 'standards': OFSTED saw standards as differentiated levels of knowledge and skills, drawing from clear foundations and hierarchies of subject knowledge. For them, parity of esteem would only arise if GNVQs showed the public that they had this foundation: otherwise, the quality of students' work would always be seen as inferior to A-levels. This view was powerfully illustrated by the way that critics used questions from external tests in GNVQs to raise concerns with ministers and through the media about rigour (see Ecclestone, 2000b). In the light of the typology in Chapter 2, these critics saw procedural and personal autonomy as poor substitutes for autonomy derived from command of subject knowledge.

This view, based on a particular view of 'standards' was proselytised through OFSTED's statutory role which gives them a direct line to Ministers. Such influence was resented by the vocational side of the standards' argument since the FEFC inspectorate had no similar lever or avenue of influence. The following parody of OFSTED's influence illuminates the political and populist sway that the traditional view holds:

> When NCVQ talked about 'standards', they meant standards that had been validated by the awarding body and the concerns are whether they are being validly assessed. . . . OFSTED used ordinary language; (interviewee adopts a conspirational whisper) 'it's inconsistent Minister, we could show you two pieces of work, both of which have been passed at very different standards' – they switched the meaning of it.
>
> (external official 2/GPC member)

Once GNVQs moved into the post-14 curriculum through Part One provision, this populist political perspective on assessment had become an imperative:

> There are strong public perceptions of what rigorous assessment looks like . . . if we were not seen to be taking clear and firm action in the response to concerns that had been passed to the public domain through OFSTED . . . that would damage the qualification.
>
> (civil servant 3)

And, as Tim Boswell believed: 'You need to be seen as addresssing the problems' (interview, May 1999).

In contrast to familiarity with notions of reliability seen to be embedded in A-levels over fifty years, designers of GNVQs had to counter low status associations of older initiatives such as the CPVE, TVEI and BTEC First and Diploma with erratic and unrigorous 'standards'. Designers portrayed standards achievable in an outcome-based model as high expectations of coverage and attainment of pre-specified, precise outcomes, assessed against public criteria that claimed to measure authentic performance. This definition allowed all candidates to achieve the highest grade if they met all the criteria. More contentiously, Gilbert Jessup argued that rigorously defined criteria, supported by the right quality assurance procedures to ensure teachers' compliance with the assessment criteria, would promote valid, consistent assessment decisions. This aim places a premium on the ability of assessment to discriminate validly between satisfactory and unsatisfactory performance. In theory, by achieving high levels of validity, Jessup hoped the model would deliver reliability (see Jessup, 1991; Wolf, 1995; West, 2000 for discussion).

The FEFC inspectorate had more affinity with this notion of standards, focusing their early criticism on 'burdensome' assessment and mechanistic approaches to covering the criteria which demotivated students. Inspectors were also conscious that, in contrast to schools, FE colleges had experienced a series of vocational initiatives and were also experiencing major restructuring. These factors are discussed in the next chapter. This coincided with the introduction of GNVQs and FEFC inspectors believed that GNVQ had to be given the chance to 'bed down' and become established. In addition, NCVQ officials saw the FEFC inspectorate as having a more realistic view of what 'parity of esteem' meant:

> FEFC were much more in sympathy with the objectives because they recognised the type of student we were talking about . . . my view is that OFSTED weren't anti but they were rather like some of the hardliners in SCAA . . . I think what underlay their views was 'we don't mind you doing what you are doing – it meets the needs of a group – but please shut up and recognise that they aren't as good as the ones doing [A-level]. So don't make waves about what you are doing for parity or equivalence'. Nobody ever said that, it's not written down anywhere, but it's my impression that that's what the sticking point came to.
>
> (NCVQ official 6)

In the midst of technical confusion and organisational rivalries over the assessment specifications, the Department of Education (DfE) began to see the political significance of GNVQs. A much cooler, more rational tone appears in interview data:

> We increasingly felt it would be an acid test of the viability of this thing that we had to provide a progression route into higher education.
>
> (civil servant 2)

The phrase 'this thing' symbolises a distance, rather than the more intense vision of NCVQ. It also symbolises something which had grown unexpectedly and problematically, important. Referring to GNVQs as 'this thing' or 'the thing' and GNVQ students as 'this type of student' emerged in interviews with civil servants from the education wing of the DfEE, OFSTED, and inspectors. It symbolised concern about Advanced GNVQs' credibility in universities and, through the Part One GNVQ, in the post-14 curriculum. Despite the fact that school-based GNVQs formed only 25 per cent of provision at Advanced level, all interviewees saw OFSTED as pivotal in moving debates about desirable forms of assessment firmly to the 'traditional reliability' side of the standards' faultline outlined earlier. Officials in NCVQ and external bodies resented the way that credibility in schools dominated political concerns.

OFSTED's statutory access to Ministers had an important political impact. Nevertheless, other less dramaticinfluences were also attributed to:

> a whole range of interactions [which] were going on, correspondence going from Ministers and [NCVQ] officials, separate meetings . . . with the inspectorates . . . so there were lots of levers operating.
>
> (civil servant 3)

It is therefore important to recognise that political concerns about standards in GSCEs, raised by Prime Minister Major in an influential speech about returning to 'simple paper and pencil' tests, together with lobbying by academics and groups wanting a return to 'traditional' forms of testing, were also happening in parallel to developments in GNVQs.

Within Advanced GNVQs, slippage over different meanings of 'standards' intensified as concerns about the effects of over-loaded assessment on students' motivation began to slide into issues of public credibility and rigour of 'standards' in comparison to A-levels. Press coverage of 'mickey mouse' tests, and criticism inside policy of test questions, were paralleled in Alan Smithers' high profile television report (1994). At the same time, OFSTED reports (1995, 1997) and Dearing's review of 16–19 qualifications pushed initially strong support amongst FEFC inspectorate, NCVQ, the awarding bodies and the FEU for 'distinctive yet manageable assessment' into more traditional concerns about 'credibility', 'reliability' and 'rigour'. This division was very apparent in interviews with inspectors, as well as in official inspection reports, but the last report, jointly written by OFSTED and FEFC, shows how far the shift went over seven years (OFSTED/FEFC, 1999). Symbolically, this report was published by the FEFC but OFSTED was the first author. This suggests that the demise of the FEFC inspectorate in the Learning and Skills Act of 2001, and its replacement for inspection in the vocational curriculum in colleges by OFSTED, reflected, in part at least, these divisions over credible standards.

Initial political concerns about assessment focused on manageability and concerns over 'rigour, consistency and reliability' were not raised at the CBI conference in 1995 where Tim Boswell outlined a six-point plan for simplifying GNVQ assessment. Changes to simplify the grading themes and portfolio had already been introduced in 1995 but NCVQ asked a high-profile committee, chaired by John Capey, principal of Exeter College and an NCVQ Council member, to carry out a more radical overhaul. The final outcomes of the review were that, in addition to the many levers of influence mentioned above, political imperatives elsewhere in the system came to affect those in a particular initiative. The DfE's review of 16–19 qualifications chaired by Ron Dearing soon dominated Capey's task of resolving the burden of assessment. By the time that Capey reported in 1995, slippage from manageability to rigour and credibility was clear, as the NCVQ official serving the Capey Committee pointed out:

> Whenever you ask for a review, it doesn't matter what the terms of reference are, you get other agendas coming in. So the thing to simplify the assessment . . . also got pretty mired with 'make it more reliable and rigorous' and these didn't sit particularly comfortably . . . there was a whole sub-plot there about increasing the rigour and reliability of the qualification.
>
> (NCVQ official 7)

The higher political status of the Dearing Review was therefore influential:

> If you look at the recommendations of Capey . . . it was a much more tentative recommendation you know . . . but by the time Capey got to Dearing and summarised in his study, it was set in stone, 'it will be this and you will do this and you will do that'.
>
> (NCVQ official 7)

Following a three-year pilot of changes from Capey's 1996, external assessment now forms one-third of the model for Vocational A-levels, together with changes to grading criteria, levels of grades and to the format and content of the unit specifications. Key skills have been displaced to a discrete qualification and systems of quality assurance emphasise national moderation of grading. These changes overturn many fundamental principles of the first model discussed in the first section.

Change was therefore politically expedient for creating an image of reliable standards. Yet the new model, designed between the autumn of 1995 and spring 1996 and piloted in ninety centres from September 1996, induced great tensions inside NCVQ as subject officials struggled to reconcile Capey's recommendations in new assessment specifications whilst countering teachers' 'initiative fatigue' (NCVQ official 8). New symbolism appears over competing notions of standards embedded in the new model. Instead of missionary zeal and crusades, NCVQ officials in the fieldwork used the political symbols of 'betrayal', 'revisionism', 'political pragmatism', 'being under seige', 'hawks and doves'. In contrast, the cool neutrality of 'reporting without fear or favour', ' evidence-based interventions' appear in OFSTED inspectors' and civil servants' version of events. Presenting resistance from NCVQ officials as 'zealotry' or 'purism' only serves to reinforce the rationality of the side which sees itself as having the political upper hand.

Nevertheless, analysis here suggests that it was an *image* of reliability, rather than any robust measure of it, which eventually dominated assessment policy for GNVQs. Difficulties in realising Jessup's claim that reliability would come through robust validity were, in part, epistemological as well as technical. On the ground, in colleges and schools, problems were financial and professional: despite lobbying by the FEFC for the model to be allowed to bed down, almost continual change meant that assessors could not develop a sense over time about what the standards meant. Instead, political panic over reliability led to formal Standards' Moderation procedures in the 1996 pilot mode accompanied by detailed and extensive Standards' Moderation 'kits' for teachers to use. Underpinned by quality assurance protocols, these new forms of regulation were extremely influential on the activities of teachers in the fieldwork for this book, examined in Chapter 6.

Drawing on moderation processes associated with A-levels, regional grading exercises and postal moderation were designed to standardise teachers' grading decisions in line with the criteria. They were accompanied by analysis in the NCVQ of statistical discrepancies in grades between centres and subjects. Such processes produced an impression of norm-referencing by bringing the proportion of Distinction grades awarded in line across the country: by 1998, after only two years of intensive moderation activities, QCA figures showed that the national proportion of Distinctions was about 28 per cent (Ecclestone and Hall, 2000). This interpretation of 'national standards' appears to increase reliability without the demotivating effects of belief in innate ability, overt comparisons between students' work or producing normal curves of distribution of grades, once associated with A-levels. Symbolically, it enabled an NCVQ official in the fieldwork to claim that GNVQs would have 'parity from Penzance to Penrith'.

Assessment policy in GNVQs therefore illustrates that different meanings of 'standards' reflect disagreement about values and goals in different qualifications and learning processes. This produces dissent and confusion over whether assessment should be a norm-referenced measure of consistent but selective achievement in order to promote reliable assessment decisions or a criterion-referenced measure of attainment to produce valid, authentic decisions. Each interpretation offers a different meaning of what constitutes 'fair' assessment. As John West, a senior official working on vocational qualifications in the ED argues, policy-makers and qualification designers must always balance these two notions as well as reconciling the technical mechanisms that promote them (West, 2000).[3] The technical tension reflects different purposes for qualifications, where reliability meets a need for fair treatment of candidates in high stakes or selective assessment and validity fulfils a requirement to confirm publicly that someone is competent or is licensed to practise. As a result, technical issues are extremely complex even before political considerations are added to them.

Yet, debate around standards in GNVQs also illustrates a deep-rooted ideological disagreement about which type of assessment should have higher social status (see Young, 1998). The resulting 'fault line' 'bedevils our qualifications' (Stanton, 1998: 50), producing assessment policy which panders to, and fuels, the annual media hysteria around A-level and GCSE results whilst simultaneously setting 'tougher' targets to motivate more people to achieve formal qualifications. When these tensions became embroiled in GNVQs through the 'messy realities of influence, pressure, dogma, expediency, conflict, compromise, intransigence, resistance, error, opposition and pragmatism' that characterise education policy in the UK (Ball, 1990: 9), they created passionate political and organisational commitments and competing normative perspectives about what counts as 'good' assessment.

The case study therefore highlights the extent to which meanings of 'standards' in education policy are perhaps more prone to both deliberate and unwitting misuse than ever. As Raymond Williams argues, certain words embody practices and institutions embedded within culture and society at any given time. Problems over meanings are therefore 'inextricably bound up' with the problem the word is being used to discuss (Williams, 1983: 15) in a particular historical and political context. This is strikingly evident in his detailed analysis of the word 'standards' as 'an exceptional kind of plural . . . a plural singular' (p. 296), where disagreeing with one meaning implies, in the case of 'standards', disagreeing with the idea of quality itself. Analysis here shows that diverse normative values underpin 'standards' in assessment policy and it is not insignificant that 'morals' and 'values' are the other two examples Williams gives of plural singulars.

The historical evolution of 'a standard' shows its symbolic status as a flag or banner behind which warring sides would rally. This image is particularly apposite in the case of political and organisational feuds over standards in GNVQs! The elision of 'standard' as a rallying call, into a moral appeal to 'standards' image is evident in accusations from SCAA and OFSTED officials that the NCVQ 'did not care about standards'. It confirms the populist image discussed above and explains the damage done to Advanced GNVQs by parodies of external test questions by the media and individuals criticising GNVQs inside policy processes. A banner or 'standard' therefore aligns with the moral status of 'standards' as a quality of performance or behaviour that must both be defended and maintained and this moral dimension was a powerful theme in different perspectives discussed in the second section. Yet, heated defences of what was meant by 'standards' were finally overcome by the political imperative to present an image of norm-referenced assessment. The banner behind which all sides in the GNVQ battle finally rallied was a populist political one.

Other meanings of 'standards' were also powerful and created further confusion. The notion of standardising a product to a particular level of quality is represented, as Williams argues, in the British Standard or the 'standard rose'. This image underpinned both the exhaustive specifications of occupational standards in NVQs and the approach taken to making sure that GNVQ teachers interpreted criteria consistently in Standards' Moderation exercises. A quality assurance vision of standards, based on strict protocols for examination and moderation processes, is exemplified in the bureaucratic approach adopted in the QCA's Code of Practice for awarding bodies (see also Baird *et al.*, 2000).

It is clear that each of the three meanings discussed above was used implicitly or overtly to attack or defend a particular stance in assessment policy. At the same time, each notion also underpins a sophisticated technological armoury of testing, monitoring and moderation methods that are enormously complicated to the uninitiated. The overall effect is to create an ideological, political and epistemological quagmire around the notion of standards, compounded by its technical complexity in an outcome-based model. When qualifications are required to fulfil competing purposes, as GNVQs were, any bid for parity of esteem seems to drift inexorably towards the problems of reliability discussed here. Yet, a standardising approach to reliability seems to dominate thinking inside the DfEE, winning out over validity and strict criterion-referenced grading in GNVQs promoted by the ex-Employment department or old-style forms of cohort referencing (see also Raggatt and Williams, 1999; West, 2000).

Avenues of influence

In divisions over 'standards', normative themes of autonomy and motivation in learning coalesced in GNVQs around three discernible ideological standpoints (see Ball, 1990 and Hickox and Moore, 1995):

- *'cultural restorationism'* (or what Ball calls 'old humanism') implicit in traditional notions of standards, heirarchical achievement within discernible subjects and policy processes associated with 'the way we do things' (OFSTED inspector);
- *'liberal humanism'* associated with progressive, student-centred approaches, access for disadvantaged learners;
- *'vocational modernism'*, associated with a meritocratic rather than norm-referenced view of standards, and frustration with established 'ways of doing things', whether in college (and school) procedures and cultures or policy processes.

In the data, the second and third standpoints, evident amongst the 'vocational side of the divide' (including the civil servant from the ED) show more intense normative themes and more personal investment of individual visions or a championing of 'an FE ethos' (see also next chapter). In contrast, OFSTED inspectors, DfE civil servants, those still with incumbent senior roles in QCA and the development of GNVQs, or who were more distant from the original vision, were much cooler and more politically adept at being 'neutral'.

Interview data showed the extent to which organisational frustration, rivalry and political dissent started to dominate attributions of blame for problems, displacing the early visionary aspirations. Strong views about disputes which had to be mediated, won or conceded showed the extent to which the standards debate became a battle: NCVQ would hold 'war cabinets' to reconcile new problems and there were internal 'battle royals' over tensions in the assessment model (NCVQ officals 5, 2). OFSTED were 'the hawks' over directions in assessment (NCVQ official 7), while Tim Boswell invoked historical battle imagery to describe OFSTED's political role:

> Certainly I think the OFSTED side of it was very, very important in terms of putting a warning shot across the bows of NCVQ . . . we may even have used them at some point as a sort of third party endorsement for some change. To put it vulgarly and slightly unfairly, as a sort of battering ram on NCVQ.
>
> (Tim Boswell)

The case study has a powerful, disconcerting sense of people and organisations 'talking past each other' technically, epistemologically, and politically. There was fierce, sometimes acrimonious debates about 'standards', particularly in the GPC, with fierce accusations that NCVQ officials 'did not care about standards' (external official 2, NCVQ officials 2, 1, 5, 6). The ensuing 'turf wars' produced what one civil servant called a 'not invented here syndrome' amongst critics of GNVQs. This became increasingly difficult for the DfE to manage and one interpretation of the decision to merge the NCVQ with SCAA is that 'we got fed up with the "not invented here" going on all the time . . .' (civil servant 2).

Further problems of organisational culture and ethos arose from the need for NCVQ to operate politically in unfamiliar territory dominated by 'the movers and the shakers in the education policy world' (NCVQ official 6), namely SCAA, the DES/DfE and OFSTED. NCVQ officials found it hard to influence assessment policy and lobby for their case in these different cultures (NCVQ official 3), especially manoeuvring between the 'constant back-door stuff that went on' (NCVQ official 5). An alien policy culture, with its own subtle, informal channels of communication, made it difficult to resist pressures for more traditional notions of reliability and to portray, instead, how NCVQ saw it being achieved:

> Perhaps what we didn't recognise was that the move from validity and the solid groundwork on content, to reliability[4] had to be made fast, very fast.
>
> (NCVQ official 6)

Yet it was difficult to influence policy discussions. The FEFC inspectorate believed that criticising a new vocational qualification would undermine its precarious public status and wanted to play down what it saw as 'teething problems' (FEFC inspector). In contrast, OFSTED had 'the ear of Ministers' and access to the 'cocktail parties and networks' that some NCVQ officials saw as the real arenas of decision-making (NCVQ official 6). Representatives from vocational assessment traditions therefore moved into processes and cultures that were familiar with assessment principles and formats for academic qualifications. A sense of cultural and political alienation is reflected by a view from one senior NCVQ official who pointed out that: 'the DES would never have hired someone like me. Never in a million years'. In addition, GNVQ assessment required individuals in government departments, the inspectorates, external constituencies such as FEU/FEDA and awarding bodies to develop new levels of conceptual, technical and political understanding of assessment principles. One effect was that individuals were expected to represent an official policy position for their organisation in fraught, unfamiliar debates inside or on the periphery of an alien policy culture.

In this context, political debates about what constitutes a desirable equilibrium between validity and reliability in qualifications at different levels remain fraught if not impossible. Indeed, the notion of political debates is somewhat of a misnomer since any debate is confined largely to academic discussion, such as the one here! As I argued above, apart from some acrimonious arguments in the General Policy Committee over standards, no concerted discussion took place outside the NCVQ's GNVQ team over either the technical issues or the political ones. This absence is paralleled in political discussion about National Curriculum assessment, confirmed by Nick Tate, ex-head of the QCA (see West, 2000). Instead, interviews for this study revealed the extent to which debate operated largely at the level of populist traditional images of 'reliable' standards of assessment and NCVQ officials acknowledged that they never succeeded in explaining their notion of reliability, let alone convincing sceptics that it might work.

Throughout its tortuous political development, the GNVQ assessment model was dogged with the image that its technical complexity was only understandable by specialists in competence and outcome-based assessment (see also Raggatt and Williams, 1999). This added further defensiveness, confusion and political disingenuity to the debate, especially for external constituencies lacking in-depth technical and political expertise in assessment. For one civil servant, the 'assessment technology' and NCVQ's organisational *esprit de corps*, were:

a serious impediment to moving the policy on . . . debates were difficult because the language was awfully difficult . . . it was actually very difficult to get a consensus because the two sides of the argument were using completly different terms and language . . . there was a sense in which you were not qualified to take part in the discussion unless you were steeped in that.

(civil servant 2)

Tensions over 'standards' create difficulties for constituencies wishing to influence assessment policy, including the awarding bodies who, in theory are best placed to have most expertise and influence. Discussion here, together with research by Baird *et al.* (2000) and West (2000), confirm that assumptions about the nature of standards in public examinations remain largely implicit as do expectations about how to maintain them. This suggests that awarding bodies and other constituencies involved in assessment policy need to be more open about these problems, rather than colluding with the political populism that obscures fundamental contradictions in defining standards and establishing technical processes to maintain them.

The cumulative effect of problems and dissent is that GNVQ developments set precedents for high levels of political intervention and new powers for QCA as a regulatory body. One civil servant believes that stronger control by the DfEE is now based on more robust specialist knowledge and understanding about assessment amongst civil servants and Ministers:

I think it was the DfE that really made the difference because people like [name of civil servant 3] were instrumental in this and developed a lot of internal expertise . . . when I first started on qualifications stuff way back in the 80s, civil servants were simply not expected to understand anything. We just got expertise from outside. We realised that you couldn't deal with the issues [in GNVQs] unless we had a lot of internal expertise . . . Tim Boswell developed a lot of knowledge and understanding and was able to challenge . . . he was very assiduous and asked very penetrating questions.[5]

(civil servant 2)

New expertise allowed the DfE to effect changes in GNVQs by transferring actors to other parts of the policy process, such as the appointment in 1995 of a civil servant from GNVQ policy to run the FEU. This coincided with a £5 million government grant to FEDA to set up a curriculum and staff development programme for GNVQs. His experience in both roles led him to argue that what appeared to be mere technical issues were, in fact, 'policy-laden', enabling him to 'work behind the scenes' by placing certain individuals in GNVQ development groups (civil servant 2). This again implies the need for external constituencies, including researchers in assessment policy and practice, to understand something of these technical processes and groups. Another interpretation of the DfE's role was that 'inappropriate' attention by DfE civil servants to the minutiae of assessment in GNVQs meant that they did not control how NCVQ changed the remit it had been given (external official 1). This interpretation of the changing role of civil servants resonates with a more general shift from being impartial advisers to more 'hands-on' promoters of government policy (see Whitty and Edwards, 1994).[6]

Although external constituencies became embroiled in a political maelstrom over assessment and its unfamiliar policy processes and debates, it seems that many policy-makers take a fairly sanguine view of any ensuing chaos and compromise. As one OFSTED inspector pointed out, 'that, sadly, is the British way of doing things'. The apparent irrationality and messiness of 'policy on the hoof' becomes neutral and rational:

> I think if I'm honest, [the problems] could have been predicted . . . people worry about the classification of the upper secondary and tertiary education system and to some extent, the assessment model is only a proxy for that debate.
>
> (Tim Boswell)

> We were working to a pretty tight timescale, for perfectly reasonable policy reasons . . . everyone learned as we went along . . . the outcome of Capey was entirely predictable, I think the themes of Capey you could map all the way back, more or less, to the beginning, just a culmination of all that.
>
> (civil servant 2)

Analysis of how competing visions for GNVQs transmogrified into a politically acceptable model shows that normative themes in the data dissolve rapidly into organisational ones under the pressure of devising the assessment 'technology' of the specifications, then into political conflict over reliability and 'rigour'. In coding and analysing data, a focus on the period after the formation of the QCA shows how different constituencies rationalised, retrospectively, the sequence of events, their consequences and the personal performances of individuals. An apparent chronology of events, pivotal decisions and influential individuals symbolised a rational reconciliation of political and organisational conflict. Yet, the use of organisational, normative and symbolic perspectives in policy analysis reveals the mayhem underneath.

Summary

It is important to remember that, in addition to confused images of autonomy, GNVQs also had to address diverse, conflicting visions about the qualification's place in the post-16 sector. These multiple aims set up huge, if not impossible, demands for the assessment model which had to, simultaneously:

- motivate learners who would otherwise not stay on in post-16 education or who were disaffected in Key Stage 4 by responding to, and rewarding, learners' expressed interests and notions of relevance;
- expand routes into higher education whilst also making sure that expansion did not lead to over-subscription for limited places;
- prepare for progression into work and job-related NVQs;
- keep students labelled by defenders of A-levels and GCSEs as 'less-able' from 'undermining' standards in these qualifications;
- convince learners, teachers, admissions tutors that GNVQs had parity of esteem with A-levels and GCSEs;
- ameliorate poor levels of achievement in numeracy and literacy;
- unify disparate and confusing post-16 qualification pathways;
- satisfy demands from different constituencies to include 'essential' content and skills.

Although some of these diverse purposes had been addressed in previous attempts to provide a meaningful vocational curriculum, the profound political and pedagogical challenge was to combine them all in a mainstream qualification intended to have parity of esteem with traditional forms of assessment in A-levels. The next chapter explores how political intervention in the vocational curriculum over a period of fifteen years changed FE colleges and images of autonomy and paved the way for GNVQs.

4 Changing FE colleges

Introduction

The preparedness of FE colleges to implement the radical aims of a new assessment model in any qualification cannot be isolated from contextual and political factors discussed so far. Colleges are under extreme pressures to motivate and retain more learners and now deal with more young people and adults whose motivation for being in further education is complex and often fragile. A series of vocational initiatives came to set great store by outcome-based assessment as a key feature to address these challenges, culminating in GNVQs. Over a period of twenty-five years, political and professional interpretations of vocational education have changed ideas about formative assessment and pedagogy in FE colleges. Nevertheless, the controversies and disagreements about the purposes of assessment, reflected in the previous chapter, offer extremely confused messages for teachers.

In addition, and despite some good opportunities through TVEI and CPVE for staff development, theoretical analysis and academic critiques have rarely informed FE teachers' insights about assessment over the past twenty years. Most FE teachers derive their ideas about assessment from the particular specifications they use for different qualifications and do not make explicit connections between them. This fragmentation is reinforced by lack of general understanding about the principles and purposes of assessment throughout schools (Black and Wiliam, 1998a) and the further and adult education sectors (Ecclestone, 1994a, 1996a). As Chapter 2 suggested, changing teachers' ideas and practices at a deep level, as opposed to securing their conformity to policy injunctions, is really only possible by working intensively with teachers facing problems that are meaningful to them in their everyday teaching contexts (see, for example, Black *et al.*, 2001; Swann and Ecclestone, 1999). A barrier to this possibility is that since incorporation of colleges in 1993, professional development in all aspects of pedagogy and assessment has been poor and under-funded (FEFC, 1999d). At the same time, political intervention in vocational education has grown, alongside upheaval in funding, quality assurance and institutional restructuring in colleges since incorporation in 1993. Restructuring and an intensification of workloads have altered both the nature of FE colleges as work-places and lecturing as a labour process. Evaluating the effects of these influences on occupational cultures and ideology amongst FE teachers is made more difficult by a lack of research in this area. Last, and more specifically, understanding the impact of an assessment model on values and practice requires insight into the specific local contexts of colleges.

As a prelude to discussion of students' and teachers' experience of the Advanced GNVQ assessment model, this chapter explores the changing landscape in FE colleges. The first section relates theoretical and political perspectives on autonomy discussed in the book so far to traditions amongst vocational education teachers in FE. The second section evaluates how political intervention through vocational initiatives began to reshape professional perspectives about change in curricula, institutional structures and quality assurance. The third section examines conflicting discourses and practices emerging from the rise of 'performativity' in FE colleges. The fourth section describes the college sites and samples in the college-based fieldwork.

New kids on the YOP: themes of autonomy in vocational education

At the beginning of the twenty-first century, mass youth unemployment is obscured by the fact that 69 per cent of 16 year olds now stay on in full-time post-16 education. In 1999, this was split 34 per cent in school sixth forms, 35 per cent between FE and sixth form colleges and a further 7 per cent in employment training schemes and 8 per cent in part-time education. This leaves about 15 per cent unemployed and without social security benefit. The total participation rate in education and training of 85 per cent at 16 drops to 77 per cent at 17 (FEFC, 1999a). In the north-east, where research for this book was carried out, participation in post-16 education and training is about 71 per cent, with 62 per cent in full-time education while participation in training dropped from 12.7 per cent in 1997 to 9.8 per cent in 1999 (OFSTED, 2000). Participation in education and attainment of qualifications is therefore significantly lower than the national average while participation in training is higher.

A series of initiatives to respond to mass youth unemployment began in 1979. It heralded major changes in thinking about pedagogy and assessment in post-compulsory education and an influx into FE colleges of new students and trainees from government schemes for the unemployed. In schools, the raising of the school leaving age in 1975 led to an alternative curriculum for those not entered for examinations at 16 and to GCSEs in 1988. By 1979, mass youth unemployment initiated the extension of this new curriculum in FE colleges, through uncertificated work and community experience and Social and Life Skills (SLS) programmes taught by a new type of pedagogue, namely the 'supervisors' working on government schemes for unemployed 16–19-year-olds. Many of these scheme workers moved into mainstream FE in the mid-1980s and a significant number of them went on to middle management and principals' roles in the 1990s. Funded by the Employment Department (ED), through the Manpower Services Commission (MSC), the Youth Opportunities Programme (YOP) was introduced in 1978. It began an *ad hoc* series of attempts to engage growing numbers of young people who would not otherwise choose FE (see Table 4.1 for a summary of initiatives leading up to the introduction of Vocational A-levels in 2000).

The emerging new curriculum gave teachers and supervisors scope to negotiate a programme covering diverse social, political, personal, leisure pursuits and work-related issues. Yet, meaningful summative assessment was not part of initial responses to mass youth unemployment. Nor was diagnosis of needs, action planning or recording of achievement. And while such curricula were often relevant, interesting and genuinely experiential, they rarely prepared young people formally for progression to employment or FE or saw their work experience as a serious focus for learning. By the mid-1980s, 'govvy schemes', with their breadline training allowance and a curriculum criticised for merely 'warehousing' participants, were the much-derided but often only alternative in many areas to the dole (see Coffield *et al.*, 1986). Accreditation for off-the job training gradually improved as YOP became the Youth Training Scheme, then Youth Training and Modern Apprenticeships and used National Vocational Qualifications (Raggatt and Williams, 1999).

In parallel to SLS for unemployed young people and Unified Vocational Preparation for work-based trainees, apprentices on day-release education in colleges took part in liberal and general studies. Promoted by the City & Guilds awarding body, and emanating from interpretations of its founding charter of 1900 which aimed to promote democracy and contribute to the well-being of society in general, liberal studies tried to immerse working class young people in 'arts, music, culture and political education'. Satirised realistically in novels by Tom Sharpe and his accounts of teaching 'Meat V', it suffered from being treated, and seen as, separate from work-related issues. Teachers had high levels of professional autonomy to appropriate liberal studies for diverse purposes, from film studies, elective studies, life and social skills to political education. The demise of liberal studies began with new ideas about careers education during the 1970s and early 1980s (see also Bates, 1984), SLS and vocational preparation promoted by the Further Education Unit (FEU, 1992) encouraged many colleges to adopt 'Communication Studies', alongside the 'Personal, Health and Social Education' component of the TVEI initiative. Since incorporation in 1993, few colleges have offered any extra-curricular provision although there are new calls for a 'citizenship' curriculum to accredit community work and address health and election-related political issues.

Absence of summative assessment and scope for teachers' own interpretations of SLS and general studies were challenged by a large-scale incursion of general vocational preparation into schools and colleges that began through the Technical and Vocational Education Initiative (TVEI). Overseen by the MSC from 1982 until 1989 and run through the LEAs, it was tellingly described by David Young, then chair of the MSC, as a 'dawn raid on education' (Young, 1990). The origins of centralised assessment policy, including the National Curriculum, were evident in the TVEI (see Helsby, 1999). Also evident is the reshaping of general education both in goals, content and organisational structures. TVEI offered vocational and technical education for 14–18-year-olds, both within mainstream subjects and as separate options. In many areas, LEAs connected it with the Certificate of Pre-Vocational Education (CPVE), introduced by the Department of Education and Science (DES) in 1985 as a belated competitor to the TVEI (Radnor *et al.*, 1989).[1] CPVE provided general vocational preparation as a basis for further study or employment, became the Diploma of Vocational Education in 1987 and was withdrawn in 1991 to pave the way for GNVQs. Both TVEI and CPVE offered new possibilities for school/college co-operation and promoted vocational relevance and formative assessment as a progressive way to motivate students who would otherwise not stay on in education.

Alongside interest in the progressive potential of new forms of assessment that emerged through TVEI and CPVE, there was also great optimism amongst adult educators about developments in National Vocational Qualifications (NVQs) and in outcome and credit-based assessment. Organisations such as the Unit for the Development of Adult and Continuing Education (UDACE, part of the National Institute of Adult and Continuing Education (NIACE) and the Further Education Unit (FEU)[2] saw these developments as both a political and educational key to widening participation in formal learning for adults (UDACE, 1989, 1994; Jessup, 1991). In the early 1990s, the notion of Assessment and Accreditation of Prior Learning emerged from the margins of access and adult education programmes into NVQs and some university credit systems. There was much technical and ideological promise in the air that these forms of assessment could motivate adults and widen access by accrediting diverse achievements and giving them status in credit frameworks (see Jessup, 1991; McNair, 1995). There were also moves in the early 1990s to extend assessment to non-accredited provision and this debate is re-emerging as organisations like the Workers' Educational Association and LEAs providing adult education consider their curriculum under the new Learning and Skills Councils (LSCs).

It is important for understanding how GNVQ teachers in this book responded to goals of autonomy embedded within the assessment model to review themes of autonomy in vocational education during the 1980s and 1990s. The typology in Chapter 2 and the ideological positions of policy-makers and their intermediaries in GNVQs in the previous chapter,

Table 4.1 Vocational initiatives 1979–2000

Date	Initiatives/Support	Key features	Problems	Implications/Precedents
1978	Unified Vocational Preparation Scheme for young workers : MSC and the ED	General vocational preparation, life and social skills and some job-related training	No accreditation; marginalised in FE colleges	New genre of education, incorporating youth work traditions, personal and social education and bringing in a new 'style' of teacher and student into FE colleges
	Youth Opportunities Programme : MSc and ED	As above	As above; diverse and patchy provision; poor quality control	
1980	DES Consultation Paper 'Examinations 16–18'	Proposals to rationalise courses for non A-level students	Friction between vocational awarding bodies and school bodies (e.g. Schools' Council)	Turf wars to come later in CPVE and GNVQs
1982	DES Consultation Paper '17+ : A New Qualification'	Proposals for new pre-vocational courses with nationally-recognised certification		
1982	FEU report 'A Basis for Choice'	An influential report promoting new forms of assessment (e.g. portfolios) in pre-vocational programmes in FE colleges		Regarded as an important report from FEU, raising its profile in colleges
1982	DES merges the Business and Technician Councils to form the Business and Technology Education Council (BTEC)	A quango accrediting vocational programmes in colleges	Not an independent awarding body like City and Guilds of London Institute: independent in 1992	Confusion over boundaries and roles in relation to awarding bodies in CPVE and later in GNVQs

1984	MSc and the ED introduce the Technical Vocational Education Initiative (TVEI) in post-14 curricula in schools and colleges	ED/MSc sponsored and funded; LEA-organised; separate vocational and technical options in schools and colleges; integrated options; opportunities for collaboration and curriculum development; personal and social education	No formal accreditation often marginalised in schools and colleges	New forms of intervention in schools and FE colleges; 'vocationalising' of post-14 curriculum for particular learners: government saw it as for 'low achieving' students not as a mechanism for 'parity of esteem' with O-levels and A-levels (Young, 1990)
1984	DES announces the Certificate of Pre-Vocational Education (CPVE) in post-16 curriculum in schools and colleges	A new nationally-recognised qualification to replace BTEC General Certificate and the City and Guilds '365' general vocational preparation qualification; new forms of assessment (portfolios, unit-based, competence-based specifications); jointly-awarded by BTEC and CGLI	Marginalisation in many schools and colleges; extreme turf wars between awarding bodies; lack of national recognition of certificate	Introduction of outcome-based assessment (OBA); turf wars to come later; public, political and professional association of 'pre-vocational' with 'low ability' students, despite attempts to characterise them as 'low achieving' rather than 'less able' First indications of bureaucracy in an OBA system
1986	BTEC introduces the First Diploma in most subjects covered by CPVE, as pre-cursor for their National Diplomas	Similar assessment features to CPVE; offered in colleges	Direct 'rival' to the CPVE which begins to become seen as a 'special needs' provision	Continuing proliferation of qualification systems and rivalry between awarding bodies and BTEC

Table 4.1 continued on next page

Table 4.1 (continued)

Date	Initiatives/Support	Key features	Problems	Implications/Precedents
1986	Review of vocational qualifications by ED and ED and MSc set up National Council for Vocational Qualifications (NCVQ)	Recommendations for a rationalised, national system of vocational qualifications Remit to NCVQ of rationalising a confining system of vocational qualifications and work-based training at diverse levels; Jessop's idea of a national framework; competence-based assessment	Growing interest in the MSC for competence-based assessment system for vocational qualifications	Separation of NCVQ from education 'establishment'; OBA becomes a profound challenge to traditional assessment
1988	Social security benefits withdrawn for 16–18 year olds	Young people could no longer 'choose' unemployment and must go into employment, youth training or further education	Rise in unmotivated young people in FE; masks unemployment rate amongst young people	FE and/or training become the 'natural' alternative to aspirations for work
	Closing of MSC and merging of ED and new Department of Education from the DES			
1988	DES report 'Advancing A-levels' (Higginson Report)	Report criticises narrowness of A-level curriculum	DES decides not to act on the report; political maintenance of notion of A-level as 'gold standard'	A-level seen as different, better, higher than vocational alternatives

Year			
1991	NCVQ begin to design a new general NVQ DfE announces end of Diploma of Vocational Education (CGLI's alternative to CPVE) and asks NCVQ to rationalise general vocational qualifications; awarding bodies (BTEC, RSA and CGLI told to work with NCVQ)	Confusion over precise nature of remit given to NCVQ (see Chapter 6); extension of OBA into the mainstream education system	Friction and turf wars; speed of development; scale of GNVQ initiative	See Chapter 3 for discussion of implications
1992	First five GNVQs introduced at Advanced, Intermediate and Foundation levels	OBA based upon portfolios of achievement, 100 per cent mastery of specified outcomes; external tests of 'underpinning knowledge'; unit-based structure; locally-designed assignments	Diverse issues discussed in Chapters 5, 6 and 7	Discussed in Chapters 5, 6 and 7
1993	Further and Higher Education Act	FE colleges incorporated and overseen by FEFC	Major changes to funding, quality assurance and staffing structures and conditions in colleges First independent FE inspectorate set up, run by the FEFC	See Chapters 5, 6 and 7
	Pilot of a Part One GNVQs for KS4 in schools	Units from foundation and Intermediate level GNVQ could be taken at Key Stage 4	See Chapters 3 and 4	See Chapters 5, 6 and 7

Table 4.1 continued on next page

Table 4.1 (continued)

Date	Initiatives/Support	Key features	Problems	Implications/Precedents
	Changes to model introduced following criticism by FEFC of confusion over evidence for grading themes	GNVQ model is amplified by specifications of guidance; new grading themes	Specifications more detailed	See Chapters 3, 6, 7 and 8
1995	Review of problems with GNVQ assessment model by the NCVQ	John Capey, principal of Exeter College, chairs a review aimed to rationalise and simplify the assessment model	See Chapter 3	See Chapter 3
1995	DfE and ED merge to form Department for Education and Employment (DfEE)	Announces review of 16–19 qualifications to be chaired by Ron Dearing	See Chapter 3	See Chapter 3 for implications for post-compulsory education policy
1996	Pilot of a new model taken up by 90 GNVQ centres	Stronger external aspect to model; unit-based rather than generic grading; moderation of teachers' grades by Awarding bodies	See Chapters 3, 5, 6 and 7	See Chapters 3, 5, 6 and 7
1996	DfE Review of 16–19 Qualifications published	Ron Dearing proposes more convergence between A-levels and GNVQs	Emphasis on 'reliability' and 'rigour' as a basis for 'parity of esteem' between GNVQs and A-levels	See Chapters 3 and 8

1997	Schools Assessment and Curriculum Authority merged with NCVQ to form the Qualifications and Curriculum Authority (QCA)	Administrative systems, offices and executive positions from SCAA.	See Chapters 3 and 8
		GNVQs no longer the responsibility of a cohesive, designated team	
1998	The introduction of a revised model for GNVQs, based on pilot, is delayed until 2000		
1999	DfEE announces new structure for A-levels and GNVQs; GNVQs launched as Vocational A-levels and Vocational GCSEs as part of reforms under 'Qualifying for Success' White Paper	Voluntary structure that schools, sixth form colleges and FE colleges can adopt to make units (modules) from GNVQs and A-levels easier to combine; stronger external testing in GNVQs; grading in GNVQs aligned to 5 grades in A-levels	See Chapter 9
			See Chapter 3

illuminate different meanings of autonomy within academic and vocational qualifications. The history of the FE curriculum therefore reveals tensions between notions of autonomy promoted through work-related competence, liberal humanist ideas about helping people deal with work and life changes and roles (Hodkinson, 1989) and the type of critical thinking that enables people to engage rationally with choices, conflict, information and propaganda, and to relate their personal circumstances to a broader context (see Hodkinson op. cit.; Bates *et al.*, 1998). The academic curriculum promotes the beginning of subject-based critical autonomy supported by 'cultural restorationists' and proselytised in the policy case study in Chapter 3 by OFSTED and the civil servants from the education 'side' of the DfEE (see also Ball, 1990).

This history also suggests that many general education teachers working on vocational programmes, together with their SLS colleagues, were influenced strongly by belief in 'the intrinsic, non-instrumental value of education, a distrust of vocational studies and a technical education' (Helsby, 1999: 16; see also Hodkinson op. cit.; Bates *et al.*, op. cit.). Mistrust of manipulative forms of vocationalism that merely prepare people for degrading or limiting jobs whilst masking this with rhetoric about 'empowerment' (see Bates, 1984) has undoubtedly been a powerful strand in 'progressive pedagogy' in FE colleges. Progressivism has also been associated with antipathy to summative assessment amongst many youth workers and the new pedagogues on unemployment schemes in FE during the 1980s, seen as the cause of failure, stigmatisation and demotivation for young people on schemes and vocational preparation courses. However, it is also apparent that there are conflicting ideas within 'progressive' curricula and assessment fragments further over generic and interpersonal skills, active teaching, learning and assessment methods, student choices about processes and procedures and critical engagement with the political and socio-economic context that affects their lives (see Bates *et al.*, 1998). It is not therefore surprising that notions of autonomy embedded within GNVQ were bland and vague: they had to address competing commitments without being seen to promote one over others.

Access to extra-curricular provision is another factor in considering to what extent any qualification can encompass all three forms of autonomy in the typology. Emphasis on formative assessment in Records of Achievement and portfolios accompanied the demise of commitment to liberal studies and general education in vocational courses (see Pring, 1994; Yeomans, 1998). BTEC abandoned a separate general studies curriculum in its National Diplomas in 1986, merging notions of personal development and general education with vocational preparation and work-related personal skills. Enthusiasm for 'student-centred' pedagogy, active learning and vocational relevance accompanied interest in affective dimensions to learning, seen in SLS programmes. This reinforced a polarisation between progressive vocational teachers supporting personal development and those committed to a critical curriculum. It also consolidated existing divisions between vocational curricula and 'conservative' academic pedagogy with its commitment, ostensibly at least, to critical thinking embedded within subject disciplines and progressive approaches (see Hargreaves, 1989; Bates *et al.*, 1998). And, although some academics saw potential for a more coherent notion of personal and critical autonomy to bridge the post-16 academic/vocational divide (Hodkinson, 1989), this has not happened. Indeed, the history of the post-16 curriculum as a whole is characterised by absence of any serious professional and political debate about what it should comprise and why (Bloomer, 1997). Criticism that new forms of vocational assessment celebrate individual experience and 'self-realisation and personal awareness' at the expense of interest in 'deeper structures' of personal development in a social context (Ball, 1990: 83; also Hargreaves, 1989; Avis, 1995) therefore has little professional resonance. Nor is there much overt professional support for criticism that vocationalism in GNVQs is instrumental and narrow (Hyland, 1994) or that they offer mere 'technical' empowerment and accountability masquerading as autonomy (see Bates, 1998a,b; Bloomer, 1998; Helsby *et al.*, 1998).

Initiatives such as TVEI, CPVE and GNVQs both reflected and created instability in the vocational curriculum. They also reinforced divisions between general, academic and vocational traditions that have characterised the English education system from the nineteenth century (see for example, Edwards *et al.*, 1997; Raggatt and Williams, 1999). Further barriers to debating the goals and purposes of vocational education within FE colleges arise from divisions over the many purposes of the FE sector as a whole. Broadly, these include: access, equity and entitlement for 'non-traditional' learners; vocational, craft and professional training as licences to practise; accreditation for professional development; progression routes into higher education; local community education; provision for learners with learning difficulties and disabilities. Less obviously, allegiances also coalesce within subject areas around the particular awarding body that teachers deal with, since procedures for assessment and quality assurance embody certain professional traditions and values (Ecclestone, 1993; Ecclestone and Hall, 1999).

In a context of fragmentation, poorly funded professional development and lack of a coherent vision for the post-16 curriculum, vocational relevance as a goal for general education has had a powerful resonance. As Hickox and Moore (1995: 283) explain:

> Vocationalism's anti-academic, anti-elitist rhetoric recalls progressivism's earlier criticisms of traditionalism. It derives much of its recent success from the ability to appeal to a range of distinct political constituencies and to a diverse range of arguments tough-minded, 'right wing' arguments concerning economic modernisation and, also, appeals to social justice, consumer choice and expanded opportunities.

The co-existence of different progressive perspectives in FE colleges there-fore forms an important context for discussion of different types of motiva-tion and autonomy valued by students and teachers in the following chapters. As the next section shows, different initiatives in the vocational curriculum have also enabled policy-makers to attempt to shape pedagogy and underlying aims for autonomy through assessment models and different styles of political intervention.

Political intervention in the vocational curriculum

The vocational initiatives discussed so far set important precedents for both the origins and styles of political intervention in GNVQs and for management of change within FE colleges. Indeed, the origins of centralised assessment policy, including the National Curriculum, were evident in the TVEI (see Helsby, 1999). Also evident is the reshaping of general education in goals, content and organisational structures. As the previous chapter showed, GNVQs also set new precedents for regulation and quality assur-ance from the QCA as a regulatory body and the awarding bodies adminis-tering GNVQs. Teachers in the FE sector, able to remember initiatives before GNVQ, have therefore experienced important contrasts between the cultural ethos of the Department for Education and Science (DES) over-seeing the CPVE and the MSC which set up the TVEI. A brief summary of key features is relevant here as a precursor to evaluating the effects of GNVQ developments on forms and styles of political intervention.

The DES was a rule-bound bureaucracy unable to compel compliance, while, in contrast, the MSC was set up deliberately as an arm of govern-ment. The MSC was a corporate body of different interests which could act quickly and saw education as a means of bringing about radical, system-wide changes while the DES worked to persuade and cajole within strongly set policy boundaries (Dale *et al.*, 1989; see also Ainley, 1999 and Raggatt and Williams, 1999). Thus, the MSC saw TVEI as a means of 'exploring and testing ways of organising and managing the education of 14–19-year-old young people' (MSC cited by Dale *et al.*, 1989: 85) and pushed for system-wide reform and centralised control. In contrast, the DES emphasised local innovations via the LEAs. The culture of the NCVQ, and the pace and authority with which it introduced GNVQs, emanated from its roots in MSC's interventionary style (Raggatt and Williams, 1999).

TVEI and CPVE also set precedents for swift timescales in new initiatives, the rapid movement of resources to priority areas and for regular external monitoring at national and local levels. TVEI, in particular, paved the way for more structure and control of the curriculum, alongside overt commit-ments to student involvement in managing their own learning processes (Dale *et al.*, 1989). Both initiatives began to erode the professional auton-omy of designing curricula, often in conjunction with students, that teachers of SLS, liberal and general studies had hitherto experienced. Indeed, TVEI raised suspicions about professional autonomy in ways that CPVE, despite more hegemony in its prescriptive curriculum and assessment model, did not: the 'perceived monolithic facelessness of the MSC' generated 'professional paranoia'. At the same time, the new mandate reflected in the TVEI meant that:

> the degree of autonomy of the education system, schools and teachers, and the ways that autonomy was alleged to have been used, made the system as much part of the problem the new mandate addressed . . . The mandate implied not only changes in the orientation of education policy but changes in the way these changes were devised and introduced into the system.
>
> (Dale *et al.*, 1989: 86)

Antipathy towards the power of non-educational state agencies, voiced by some critics about TVEI, have had parallels in hostile responses to the NCVQ's apparently hegemonic role in developing GNVQs (for example, Hyland, 1994). Nevertheless, the MSC was able in TVEI to insinuate what has turned out to be an enduring 'vocational ethos into the conventional rhetorics of education policy-making and implementation' (Dale *et al.*, 1989: 87) whilst maintaining a general language of specification which allowed a diversity of local responses. Importantly, despite David Young's resistance as Secretary of State to the influence of the LEAs (Young, 1990), TVEI was mediated by LEAs and their advisers whose 'delicate task of incursive diplomacy' did not threaten the identities and autonomy of educationalists. Instead, it provided 'a basis for transformation which appear[ed] to articulate with conventionally established perspectives at all levels' (Dale *et al.*, 1989: 87) and, like CPVE, offered some teachers scope for innovation and career prospects. Combined with powerful rhetorics of access for 'non-traditional' students, progressive pedagogy and autonomy, TVEI and CPVE together had strong support amongst FE teachers in vocational and pre-vocational education.

Equally important was the way in which TVEI challenged the rhythm and pace of educational development so that change became a requirement rather than a response to exhortation by the DES. This requirement was much less apparent in CPVE and obligatory in GNVQ. In TVEI, evocations of 'participation' appeared in guidance from LEAs to schools and colleges and were used in communicative processes from MSC, to the DES, through every level of implementation and the teacher/pupil relationship itself (Dale *et al.*, 1989: 88). New discourses of intervention, regulation and pedagogy for new groups of students paved the way for outcome-based assessment to be communicated to teachers via what Bates calls a 'textually mediated discourse' (1998b: 45) and a prescriptive GNVQ assessment system.

In addition to changing discourses, political imperatives led to more overt control over 'standards' of assessment in GNVQs. As Chapter 3 argued, this created a new hegemony of design, guidance and advice to teachers and new styles of regulation in post-compulsory qualification systems, overseen by the QCA. The bid for parity of esteem was partly achieved by standardising content, design and forms of regulation in GNVQs and by diluting the previously distinctive 'brands' of awarding bodies.[3] This has eroded the power of awarding bodies such as RSA, BTEC and City & Guilds in determining the design and scope of vocational qualifications. Although other European countries have state-run vocational systems, they also have the active involvement of other partners, such as trade unions, professional associations, employers and academic researchers (see, for example, Johansson *et al.*, 2002 forthcoming; Brown and Keep, 2001). It is also rare for them to have major overhauls of qualifications: this stability and social partnership prevent qualifications systems being used for political purposes as they are in the UK. In contrast, the combination of reduced power for awarding bodies and the marginal influence of educational interests in designing and evaluating GNVQs has given government unprecedented control over general vocational qualifications. And, as Brown and Keep observe, vocational education research is extremely fragmented in the UK, unlike, for example, Germany (op. cit., 2001).

Yet, political hegemony belies the extent to which extreme degrees of intervention, dissension, organisational turf wars and political *ad hocery* dogged the GNVQ assessment model and undermined the opportunity to create a coherent vision for vocational education. Chaotic development led to different perceptions of problems in the assessment model and different attributions of blame. Nevertheless, even those in fieldwork for this book who held the NCVQ responsible for problems believed that a unique opportunity offered by GNVQs for dramatic change in vocational education has passed and is unlikely to appear again. In the absence of a clear vision or public debate about vocational education, the merging of academic and vocational assessment models in order to create a populist image of 'parity' merely reinforces the current lack of distinctiveness for assessment in the vocational curriculum. In the policy-based fieldwork, all interviewees outside OFSTED, SCAA and the education 'side' of the DfEE believed that no one now champions vocational education with the political and professional conviction it needs to survive as something distinctive and worthwhile. Ironically, given the hostility that the NCVQ attracted from some academic and professional critics committed to vocational education, and whatever one's view of its role and impact in GNVQs, the NCVQ may turn out to be the last high-profile champion of vocational education.

In addition, although the Department for Education and Skills (DfES) now proclaims its commitment to 'evidence-based policy', analysis highlights a pragmatic, almost world-weary, acceptance of what might be characterised outside policy processes as confusion, even chaos. This would never be tolerated in reforming A-levels (Stanton, 1998) and it is in relation to this dimension of GNVQ assessment policy that most criticism might be levelled. Just as policy slipped in the government's remit to the NCVQ for NVQs, it slid unnoticed from Minister Tim Eggar's original remit into a large-scale initiative with minimal initial funding and no development strategy or political oversight (see Raggatt ánd Williams, 1999 for similar developments in NVQs). It then ran into what Gilbert Jessup argues is the UK's 'unique obsession' with particular notions of reliability and parity of esteem (interview, March 1998). The ensuing mess, and a long-running failure to learn from past mistakes in NVQs and National Curriculum assessment policy (Stanton, 1998), imply profound problems in creating a coherent post-16 curriculum. Far from open debate and the contribution of evidence from well-informed external constituencies to policy, the previous chapter shows that interviewees seemed to portray, and accept that fraught policy design and regression to traditional notions of 'standards' are inevitable features of the assessment policy landscape in the UK.

Political, organisational and technical conflicts mean that institutional managers and teachers had to implement complex technical changes in GNVQs without any coherent underlying rationale. This confusion also obscured contradictory theories of learning embedded in GNVQs. In spite of the importance that GNVQ designers attached to the radical implications of their assessment principles, discussion of motivation, autonomy and formative assessment was erratic and cursory. Nor were these attributes defended either publicly or inside the difficult policy processes depicted in the previous chapter. Unsurprisingly, then, such discussion did not appear in official guidance and other texts, the research and development pro- gramme run inside the NCVQ and QCA, the FEDA support programme or in FEFC and OFSTED reports. And, apart from an official attempt to articulate the fusion that Jessup envisaged between formative and sum- mative assessment (Jessup, 1994) advice about the summative purposes of collecting evidence dominated official guidance while autonomy and moti- vation were elided as self-reliance and independence from teachers, class- rooms and groups.

Turmoil also reflects low expectations amongst policy-makers about the nature of change in institutions. NCVQ officials were not optimistic that teachers could be 'student-centred' or foster autonomy, or that awarding bodies would relinquish their market interest while OFSTED did not appear to expect vocational teachers to understand traditional interpreta- tions of 'standards'. None of the constituencies represented in the study seemed to expect government to resource the professional training and development necessary to secure both the desired learning approaches and effective assessment. At the same time, these constituencies expected policy-making to be chaotic, as part of 'the way we do things in Britain'. As a result, securing and regulating teachers' compliance was attempted through prescriptive guidance added into the 1995 model and then replaced with stronger regulation by the QCA using the awarding bodies, FEDA and inspectors as mediators.

GNVQ developments therefore mean that FE teachers now deal with new intermediaries of policy and regulation, such as inspectors, awarding body officials and curriculum support agencies such as the Further Education Development Agency, now the Learning and Skills Development Agency. These agencies are no longer at a distance from government policy. Instead, they are crucial in proselytising it and for making practice reflect policy. They also legitimate new communicative styles in assessment and quality assurance systems, thereby contributing to the rise in FE colleges (and schools) of 'performativity' (see, for example, Broadfoot, 2000; Ball, 2000). This proposal is discussed next.

Upheaval and the rise of 'performativity'

The period of incorporation from 1993 to 2001 saw financial crises for 50 per cent of the 450 colleges funded by the Further Education Funding Council (FEFC), acrimonious disputes over contracts and conditions, repeated restructuring in colleges and growing political concerns about mis-management. One effect has been the loss of 150,000 full-time staff between 1993 and 1999 through retirement, voluntary and compulsory redundancy. These have been replaced by growing numbers of part-time and temporary staff and an intensification of full-time teaching contracts. As a result, and second only to the catering industry, colleges have one of the most casualised workforces in Britain with over 50 per cent employed on some form of temporary, fractional or part-time contract. This reflects a rise in such contracts of 28 per cent between 1996 and 1998 (FEFC, 2000a), with accompanying divisions within teaching teams and departments over appro-priate responses to change (see, for example, Ainley and Bailey, 1997). In addition, there is a growing recruitment problem, an ageing workforce and serious under-funding of professional development (FEFC, 1999d).

During the same period, FE colleges expanded their student base in response to political injunctions to 'widen participation' whilst meeting tighter targets for retaining students and helping them achieve formal quali-fications. Political concerns about teaching quality, and disputes about inspection and quality assurance, began to affect FE in May 1999 with moves by government towards a more overt tone in inspection of 'naming and shaming' failing colleges. At the time of writing in 2001, FE is still reeling from clashing discourses during its incorporated era of 'sleaze', 'mis-management', 'failing colleges', 'inclusiveness', 'widening participation' and 'community responsiveness'. New pressures arise from exhortations by the Learning and Skills Council (LSC) for FE colleges to become world-class organisations and specialist centres of vocational excellence. Competing dis-courses therefore accompany the current round of far-reaching change in

2001 as FE colleges prepare to both compete and collaborate with other post-16 providers under the LSC.

It is tempting to portray political intervention as the most potent element in connecting policy injunctions and rationale with the organisational and personal realities of college managers, teachers and students (see Avis *et al.*, 1996; Gleeson and Shain, 1998a; Gleeson, 2001). Yet, it is also important to relate a climate of risk aversion, mistrust and low expectations, discussed in Chapter 1, to trends in 'managerialism' and new forms of external regulation through audit, inspection and quality assurance and, in GNVQs, through official processes to regulate vocational teachers' assessment decisions. Regulation of assessment in general vocational education such as BTEC National Diplomas, CPVE and the Diploma of Vocational Education was, until GNVQs, a more supportive form of moderation of students' work and advice about the course, based on personal links with awarding body officials (see Ecclestone and Hall, 1999).

In understanding responses amongst teachers to new forms of regulation introduced for GNVQs, it is important to recognise how assessment models and quality assurance systems are based increasingly on what Habermas calls 'technical rationality' (see, for example, Hodkinson, 1998a). The inexorable advance of 'performativity' both causes and reinforces technical rationality so that the 'simulcra' of targets become a self-fulfilling rationale and response, whether or not the targets have any real meaning (Ball, 2000; Broadfoot, 2000; Torrance, 2000). 'Performativity' has been a central feature of changes in FE colleges, leading Adrian Perry, principal of Lambeth College, to argue that obsession with targets has had 'ludicrous' effects, including high expenditure on creative accounting and divisive attributions of blame and 'cover up' when targets are not met (Perry, 1999). In this context, performativity is transforming professional and personal subjectivities and values at all levels of the education system. Professionals might rail against the lunacy of targets and even admit their cynical manipulation of targets or their creative compliance with them. Nevertheless, managers and teachers alike become deeply implicated in legitimating them, even at the cost of undermining genuine collegiality and trust (see Ball, 2000 for discussion). From this perspective, educators and managers internalise and then promote self-interest and self-regulation through a series of 'micro disciplinary' practices (Ball, 1997). It is difficult to see how this ethos does not transmit itself to students.

Performativity is also secured, or attempted, through managers and policy-makers emphasising 'empowerment' and the need to:

> give more responsibility to employers to determine how tasks can best be done and reducing the extent to which they are closely supervised through hierarchical and bureaucratically structured tiers of management.
>
> (Bates, 1998a: 11)

Despite rhetoric about empowerment, rituals of verification and audit in all areas of government lead to what Power calls the 'pathologicality of excessive checking'. This reflects the cessation of trust, but with little idea of what must be checked and what can be taken on trust against economic criteria (Power, 1997). This has a number of subtle effects. It substitutes democratic political accountability with managerialist accountability and creates new definitions of risk and reliance on guidelines and auditing. Following arguments in Chapter 1, notions of risk and transgression erode expectations of trust between colleagues and managers within organisations, and between institutions and external agencies.

At both the meso level of college organisational structures, and at the micro level of day-to-day staff rooms, classrooms and visits by awarding body officials and inspectors, interactions seem to rely increasingly on codes of conduct, guidelines, assessment and quality specifications. At one level, these make clear what is required of the diverse groups and individuals who use them: outcome-based assessment systems in particular codify attributes and learning activities hitherto at the discretion of teachers and awarding bodies to disclose. As earlier discussion showed, this makes them potentially empowering. Yet such systems belie a deeper tension where the well-known phenomenon of 'spiralling specifications' in an assessment model (see Wolf, 1995) combines with political pressures to secure common, standardised interpretations. Thus, 'guidelines', whether in assessment or quality assurance systems, soon become 'exemplars of good practice' and then rules, whilst criteria become checklists for self and external regulation. In announcing an inspection handbook, for example, the chief inspector for the inspection regime run by Further Education Funding Council from 1993 to 2001 pointed out that 'we have tried hard to get the balance right between producing rules and offering guidelines' (FEFC, 1998b).

In assessment and quality assurance models, specifications perform two functions. On the one hand, as the next chapter shows, they can codify progressive practice in providing students with a basis to take part in discussions about what counts as 'quality' for a particular grade in GNVQ. They might also make teachers adopt progressive forms of pedagogy (see Oates and Harkin, 1995) and offer feedback on progress. Yet, in a climate of risk aversion where remote checking happens alongside fewer resources for learning programmes and greater pressure on teachers' working conditions, specifications encourage defensiveness by becoming checklists to cover gaps in understanding, to pre-empt transgression from prescribed procedures or to justify compliance. In a context where assessment has increasingly high stakes, both for students progressing with good qualifications and for institutions justifying their funding, these tensions present teachers with conflicting assessment roles. They are, increasingly, as facilitators of learning, gatekeepers for access to the next stage of progression and accountable for quality and 'national standards' of achievement.

Similar tensions appear over inspection protocols and guidelines that simultaneously clarify processes, protect inspectors from institutional appeals against grading decisions and can be used by institutional managers to blame staff for poor inspection grades! In the light of arguments about risk aversion and mistrust discussed in Chapter 1, a cumulative but unintended effect is to reinforce calls for formal regulation. This can fuel a reluctance to interpret independently what guidelines mean or to collaborate in order to define and solve problems. Such tendencies can, in turn, feed demand for more external clarification and regulation, followed by fear of transgression, and then resentful challenges to regulation. As the previous chapter showed, awarding body moderation and quality assurance procedures, regulated by the QCA, are likely to show these tendencies.

A context of upheaval, increasing regulation and under-funding of professional development in FE colleges makes it hardly surprising that theoretical requirements for dealing with educational change, such as personal vision building, inquiry, mastery and collaboration will be evident (see Fullan, 1991, 1993; Helsby, 1999). Another important but often overlooked factor in evaluating teachers' responses to interventions designed to change practice is their own and researchers' images of these responses. Portrayals of teachers as, variously, 'heroic resisters', 'realistic subverters', 'career opportunists' or 'managerial compliers', emerge in analyses of the National Curriculum (Helsby, 1999), developments in FE (Ainley and Bailey, 1997; Avis, 1999) and in studies of change in Australian technical colleges (Seddon, 1998). These studies show polarisation between those who object to change and their colleagues and managers who might actively support both change and its underlying values or go along with it strategically but without commitment.

However, it is important not to overplay divisions since, despite discernible effects of 'new managerialism' in FE, colleges as workplaces are not as controlled as some accounts suggest (see Gleeson and Shain, 1998; Gleeson, 2001). And, despite upheaval and resistance from teaching unions in FE, there has been little public demonstration. Scenes of teachers at union conferences protesting about huge piles of government guidelines have not been replicated in FE. Nor, in contrast with opposition to National Curriculum assessment and inspection in schools and to intensified quality assurance in universities, particularly through satirical columns in the *Times Educational Supplements*, has there has been much media coverage. Absence of protest about conditions in colleges partly reflects preoccupation with union disputes between 1993 and 2000 over conditions of service, but it also reflects how FE teachers are divided into diverse assessment cultures and traditions, each with different pedagogies and assessment models. It may also reflect the effectiveness of 'performativity' in securing compliance.

The two fieldwork colleges and samples

Fieldwork data which form the basis for analysis in the next two chapters came from a series of activities in two Advanced GNVQ subjects, namely Business (BS) and Health and Social Care (HSC), over two years in two urban colleges with reasonably sound inspection grades in the two subjects. The college-based fieldwork aimed to explore 'what is, what may be and what could be' (Schofield, 1990), focusing on 'what is' by trying to maximise typical, ordinary features of a site. Being open to 'what could be' might reveal examples of good practice in fostering motivation and autonomy. Yet choosing a 'typical' site was problematic because of variation in student cohorts, different socio-economic contexts, urban and rural settings, college league table positions and inspection grades. Identifying what is typical in sites and samples is complicated further by the micro-politics of colleges so that features thought to be 'typical' might turn out to be atypical. This can be countered by highlighting any atypical features (Schofield, 1990) and aiming to portray something of the complexity in both culture and ethos in post-16 institutions since, as Hodkinson and Bloomer (2000) show, these dimensions are crucial variables in developing students' dispositions to learning.

College A is the largest urban college in the north-east in a city of 260,000. (In order to maintain anonymity, I use pseudonyms here and different names later.) Despite some success in attracting new industries, unemployment in the city is high, with the fourth highest male unemployment rate of metropolitan districts in the UK. The college recruits an increasing proportion of students from local disadvantaged areas, although over half come from outside the city, including some of the prosperous small towns to the west of the city. Just over 31 per cent of the city's 16-year-olds gain grades A–C at GCSE, compared to a national average of 46 per cent. The college attracts very few students from the city's nine independent schools. Courses at Advanced level (which includes A-levels and GNVQs) account for 41 per cent of the intake and 11 per cent of the full-time intake are 16–19-year-olds (FEFC 1996b, 1999b). Higher education forms 7 per cent of the college's provision. The proportion of 16 year-olds continuing in full-time post-16 education (schools, sixth form colleges and FE) in the city is 60 per cent, compared to a national average of 69 per cent.

The site in which the study took place is in one of the most deprived areas of the city, currently undergoing a regeneration programme. The college on this site comprises a collection of three large and fairly characterless 1960s buildings around an attractive large piazza built in 1999 to replace a dingy Victorian school building. The piazza forms a windswept but dramatic focus and fine weather social area for the college. Like the buildings, the piazza has open access from the surrounding roads yet vandalism, graffiti and intrusions into buildings and classrooms are infrequent. The two courses in the study are housed in the same seven-storey building in plain classrooms without student work or decoration but with large cupboards for storing GNVQ students' assessment portfolios. Each course is located on its own corridor, with busy shared staffrooms on each floor and there is a strong sense of separation with few opportunities for staff, or students, to meet colleagues in other Advanced GNVQs. Small teams of core, full-time teachers share space with a flow of part-time staff who 'hot desk' whatever table and shelf space is available on a particular day. There is no communal space for staff and breaks are taken in shared staff rooms but often at different times in a staggered system of breaks in teaching.

An unattractive student refectory, mainly used by 16–19-year-old students, is on the ground floor whilst adult students and staff tend to use a smaller coffee bar. In the building where the courses are housed, there is no reception area and, instead, a bare entrance hall with lifts. In contrast to this anonymity and to the youth club feel of the refectory, the Learning Centre is in another building across the piazza and is a busy and welcoming place with a library and IT resources. A steady stream of adult and younger students moves around the college and piazza at most times of the day and year. Interestingly, and in spite of the upheavals noted earlier, both colleges retain a very traditional flow during the academic year of both staff and students: after the spring bank holiday and until the middle of September, both colleges are quiet places.

Although both colleges went through a major restructuring with new principals in 1998, another, more acrimonious intensive restructuring and redundancy programme took place in College A in 2000, with the second new principal in three years.

College B is a merger of two former tertiary colleges in a city of 300,000. The loss of heavy industry has been only partly compensated by an influx of call centres and a large car manufacturer, making the university, health service and local authority the main employers: 52 per cent of 16-year-olds continue in education, an increase of 60 per cent since 1989, whilst 30 per cent participate in training schemes (twice the national average). Unlike College A, there is less competition with schools for 16-year-olds and much less higher education in the college's remit. However, it faces strong competition with four other FE colleges (FEFC 1995, 1999c).

GNVQ courses are run in three city sites, each one attracting its own very local intake. One of the two centres where the study took place is an ex-grammar school with attractive redbrick 1930s buildings around a somewhat dilapidated grassed square. A welcoming reception area and a busy and modern Learning Centre give the building a more cohesive feel. Like College A, classrooms are bare and functional and staff rooms crowded and busy. There is no communal staff area and, like College A, subject teams meet and teach in discrete subject and course-related areas with little cross-curricular or cross-college contact. In this building, Business staff in the study created a social area within a small crowded staff room and a strong team ethos. In year two of the study, they were moved to a cramped basement and the team'ssmall social space disappeared. The other centre, where the Health and Social Care course was run, is modern, located between two housing estates in a deprived part of the city and some way from the city centre. It has a busy and well-equipped Learning Centre, an efficient, pleasant reception and waiting area but also a dingy refectory, plain classrooms and 'hot-desking' in busy staff rooms. There is a remarkably homogeneous intake of 16–19-year-old students in terms of their appearance and dress and this is the only centre where an outsider, such as a researcher, feels out of place rather than merely anonymous. Unlike College A, both centres in College B feel much more like schools than FE colleges and have a parochial atmosphere.

The teachers' sample was partly 'purposive', comprising course leaders who would understand the complexities of GNVQ assessment and have to implement a new model for Vocational A-levels in September 2000, and 'opportunistic' since course leaders selected colleagues who might be interested to take part in the research. The eventual sample comprised three men and six women, reflecting, in part, the growing feminisation of FE teaching staff and a gender bias on Health and Social Care courses. It covered subject units with academic roots (for example, Pyschology, Sociology, Behaviour and Motivation at Work) and vocational roots (for example, Human Resources, Planning a Health Campaign, Social Policy, Health Services, Planning a Business Activity). As Chapter 2 suggested, notions of autonomy are rooted in subjects and this range in the fieldwork enabled me to explore how subject discipline might affect teachers' values, beliefs and approaches to assessment. An alternative to random selection would have been to construct a sample to cover specific subject traditions. Some triangulation of attitudes and beliefs from the in-depth study occurred through a questionnaire to a wider regional sample of sixth form college and FE staff teaching on the same courses.

All nine teachers had been involved with GNVQs for over three years. As a precursor to analysing their educational goals and responses to the competing demands they had to reconcile in GNVQs, I summarise here teachers' general views of the GNVQ assessment system. It is crucial to acknowledge, though, that this summary, and the in-depth account in the next three chapters, is a snapshot of students' and teachers' views and beliefs articulated within a very specific context at a particular moment in time. This makes it essential for qualitative researchers to highlight the effects of timing, both of fieldwork itself and of other factors affecting respondents.

Broadly, two (Neil, unit tutor, and Jim, course leader) were negative, even hostile, about the effects of GNVQ assessment on their own goals for education and on the quality of students' engagement with their subject. After twenty years in College B, Neil was reluctantly moved in the college's restructuring in 1998 from teaching A-level sociology and humanities to Advanced GNVQ. Refusal to change would have meant compulsory redundancy. He now teaches Social Policy and Sociology units in GNVQ, together with Access to Higher Education courses and a BTEC National Diploma in Nursery Nursing. After fifteen years' experience in FE, five of those in College A, Jim had been similarly displaced in a college restructuring from a senior management role on higher level management and accountancy courses to be course leader for Advanced GNVQ Business and to teach BTEC National Diploma. In the second year of the study, all middle and senior managers in College A were applying for their jobs in the second major restructuring in three years. In College B, another round of early retirement in 2000 took out another layer of experienced staff at very short notice.

Five of the sample had been involved with general vocational education for a number of years and were generally supportive of the aims of GNVQ but critical of their complex assessment model. As a unit tutor for 'Planning a Health Campaign' and 'Health Services', and with a background in nursing, Madeline has worked in College A for twenty years on health and social care courses. At the time of the study, her colleague Caroline had been in FE for three years, two of them in College A: Caroline left FE in 2000 to work for an awarding body. Both Madeline and Caroline were broadly supportive of the aims of GNVQ but were feeling increasingly pressured by the demands of the 1996 pilot model. As a unit and personal tutor, Barbara worked for fifteen years in College B on pre-vocational courses such as CPVE, TVEI and also in BTEC National Diploma. Her close colleague, Gill, worked for twenty-five years in similar courses and was course leader for Advanced GNVQ until she retired from teaching in 2000. Danny also worked on BTEC National for seven years and moved to GNVQs in 1993. This close-knit team were, until becoming involved with the 1996 pilot model, generally positive about the emphasis in GNVQ on 'real life' relevance of assignments and the overt promotion of students' independence. They also believed, initially at least, that GNVQ would offer better national standards of progression and status for students than BTEC National Diploma had.

The two younger teachers who saw themselves at the beginning of careers in FE, Mary, course leader for Health and Social Care in College B, and Jo, year one tutor for Business in College A, were both enthusiastic about GNVQs with minor reservations about some features of the assessment system. At the start of the fieldwork, three of the four GNVQ teams had been piloting the 1996 specifications for one year. One team was therefore continuing to work with the 1995 model and this enabled some contrast between the two models. It also enables me to relate implications from the 1996 model to Vocational A-levels since, as the previous chapter showed, these are based on the 1996 specifications.

Given earlier arguments about the need to identify non-GNVQ and GNVQ-related effects on autonomy, motivation and formative assessment practices, I focused on the 'best' students' experiences and responses. This, in theory, would enable the claims of GNVQ designers for benefits of autonomy and motivation to have an optimum chance of being realised. I asked teachers to select five students in each year group whom they saw as 'autonomous' and 'motivated'. This gave me an initial insight into teachers' constructs of autonomy and motivation, followed by early discussion with students about why they had been selected as autonomous and motivated.

In terms of qualifications and expectations of GNVQs, the sample conformed to data about GNVQ students in other studies in terms of lower entry GSCEs, confidence and their image of themselves as 'non-academic' students (see Wolf, 1997a; Edwards *et al.*, 1997). Over the two years, the total sample reduced to the eighteen with whom I maintained contact through interviews and then to nine after a group activity in the second year of the course to explore constructs of autonomy and motivation. Interview data, observation and fieldwork notes and analytical memos were coded in relation to teachers and students from each college, course and year, then by individual students, and last by six students (Michael, Britney, Louise, Darren, Annette and Jacqui) who showed deeper forms of autonomy than the others. Some triangulation of emerging constructs of autonomy, motivation and formative assessment also occurred through a questionnaire given to seventy students from the four courses in my study and completed by 80 per cent (62) students from the four groups covered by this study. Fifty-seven per cent of the respondents were at Bridgeview College and 43 per cent at Riverside College, whilst 60 per cent were taking the Business GNVQ and 39 per cent taking HSC. Forty-four per cent were in Year 1 and 45 per cent in Year 2.

Summary

This chapter has outlined traditions of autonomy in vocational education and shown how political intervention in vocational initiatives combined with performativity to create new 'micro disciplinary' practices and responses in FE colleges. At the same time, FE teachers have been dealing with these changes while responding to upheaval caused by incorporation of colleges in 1993. The chapter also aimed to relate some of the micro-disciplinary practices associated with performativity in assessment, inspection and quality assurance systems to tensions between openness and empowerment and risk aversion and mistrust, discussed in Chapter 1.

5 Getting through: motivation in GNVQs

Introduction

Policy and practices in post-16 pedagogy and assessment have been transformed in FE colleges by the need to engage the 69 per cent of 16-year-olds who now stay on in full-time education in England. Reflecting broader cultural dispositions in the UK, discussed in Chapter 2, increasing numbers of FE students are likely to be 'pragmatically compliant' at best and 'hanging on' or 'drifting' at worst. Indeed, it might be argued that political and professional concerns about motivation, retention and achievement in formal learning have acquired something of the status of a moral panic, with a growing tone of blame for colleges who fail on these counts. Teachers therefore have to motivate students, many of whom face precarious job and social prospects and have fragile learning identities from past experiences in formal education. They must also achieve 'national standards' in vocational qualifications. The tension that these two pressures create has to be located in organisational settings where teachers themselves have experienced repeated restructuring, resource constraints and pressures on conditions of service since 1993.

Activities within the college fieldwork were influenced by evidence that implementing policy depends largely on how teachers think about their everyday practices, how far they agree with an initiative and how far they can reconcile it with their assumptions about learning and aims for students. It is not difficult to envisage 'situations where various centralised initiatives may be met in terms of paperwork, while teachers continue with their traditional practices and approaches in the classroom' (Swann and Brown, 1997: 97). The effects of policy on practice is obscured further because teachers become proficient in using the 'official patterns of discourse and terminology' (ibid.: 97), a trait reinforced through official evaluations, such as inspections and awarding body procedures for quality assurance, which base their questions around this terminology. A rounded picture of teachers' interpretations of policy imperatives in relation to their own goals for education, the actions they take to realise them and the conditions that they see as affecting goals and actions is therefore important. Nevertheless, although it is important to explore gaps between policy rhetoric and the reality of implementation, it also necessary to present any congruence between the two that might be evident.

These dimensions implied as deep an immersion in the life of a GNVQ programme as possible, together with a relationship with participants that could encourage discussion of authentic constructs. Focused interviews carried out immediately after observing a lesson or assessment activity asked teachers to consider what went well in the session, their values and goals for students and factors affecting achievement of these. Avoiding a hypothetical focus on the effects of policy, and exploring real activities instead is more likely to avoid 'espoused theories' and get closer to 'theories-in-use' (Argyris and Schon, 1974). An intensive sequence of activities might therefore produce a richer account and the chance to explore meanings with participants and to develop shared understandings. Activities are summarised in Appendix 2.

This chapter uses the typology of motivation, autonomy and formative assessment developed earlier in the book to analyse the implications of students' and teachers' experiences in sustaining students' motivation throughout two years of the Advanced GNVQ course. The first section analyses the goals and aims that motivated students and teachers during the GNVQ. The second section examines the various actions they took to sustain goals for motivation, and the third section explores limitations to their goals and actions and therefore to the forms of motivation they developed. The fouth section considers the particular motivational characteristics of the six students in the sample who consistently achieved Distinction grades.

Aims and goals

A good qualification

Students were asked in the questionnaire to pick the 'two most important reasons for doing GNVQ': 77.4 per cent chose *gaining the qualification*, 72.6 per cent added *subject content* and 24.2 per cent added '*college atmosphere and social life*'. Reasons that students added for themselves included '*spreading the workload over the year*'. The questionnaire also showed that 40 per cent saw vocational courses in local universities as a realistic destination, contrasting with figures from the QCA which show that nationally, 54 per cent see HE as a realistic destination (Ecclestone and Hall, 2000). Lower rates of participation and achievement of qualifications in the north-east is likely to be a major reason for the discrepancy. In the light of discussion below about fluctuations in motivation, second-year students were more likely to say they were doing the GNVQ '*for the qualification*'.

In the interview sample, students chose a GNVQ because it was a 'good qualification' with progression to higher education, a vocational, 'real life' emphasis and continuous assessment. These reasons parallel those given by

900 students surveyed by the QCA (Ecclestone and Hall, 2000). None saw themselves as 'academic' students and for fourteen of the eighteen, GNVQ was a 'second chance' to overcome past low achievement. The goal of a good qualification, seen as essential for employment and vague notions of educational progression, enabled most students to survive setbacks during the course, discussed below.

Teachers in the sample had different roles and responsibilities on the GNVQ course, and different experience of vocational education before and in parallel with their GNVQ teaching. Nevertheless, they all believed strongly that 'good' qualifications were essential for students in a difficult context for jobs and progression to higher education. Eight saw their main aim as helping as many students as possible to achieve the GNVQ and to help students decide on, and achieve, realistic end goals. Six believed passionately that GNVQs should have parity of esteem with A-levels and were therefore positive about the political aim that GNVQs would improve national standards of achievement. In this respect, they valued GNVQ as more rigorous than its predecessor the BTEC National Diploma. In keeping with hopes for parity of esteem and the need to motivate students who might otherwise not achieve an advanced level qualification, eight teachers were positive that students had clear summative assessment targets with national status. These aims place them firmly in a tradition of vocational education in FE colleges going back to BTEC National Diplomas, as well as the CPVE and the BTEC First Diploma and discussed in the last chapter.

Although there were similarities in their overall aims for students, teachers' specific GNVQ roles affected whether they saw themselves as being directly responsible for helping students gain the qualification. Roles also affected the emphasis that teachers placed on different goals. Three of the sample were course leaders and this added a pressure to conform to national standards for grading set by QCA and awarding bodies. Some teachers were profoundly concerned about the pressures that all young people now face in gaining jobs or progressing to higher education. All believed that external pressures have changed the student cohort attracted to GNVQ. This led them to emphasise different goals for sustaining motivation:

> At this college, I feel that the students we attract onto the GNVQ course . . . come from poorer areas and quite often broken families which has led students in some cases having up to 3 part-time jobs and I'm sure that it's my personality but I feel as if I try to and help them and show that I care about their personal lives as well . . . They can talk to me and it will make them a better and more relaxed student in the classroom. Relaxed as though someone cares about them, not just how they are achieving academically.
>
> (Jo, Year 1 course leader, BS)

There was a perception amongst all teachers in the sample that social problems were increasingly affecting 'the type of students' that colleges increasingly cater for, particularly in relation to motivation and attitude. External pressures seemed to make teachers, particularly those in pastoral roles, strive hard to maintain motivation and to maximise achievement from a sense of responsibility to students facing difficult external circumstances: 'It's the very least we can do for them' (Mary, course leader HSC).

One effect of perceptions about pressures was that all teachers in the sample believed that, apart from a tiny majority, students were motivated primarily by external and introjected goals as opposed to intrinsic and interested motivation in a subject. Perhaps predictably, when students' motivation began to flag during Year 2, teachers emphasised external goals and, in particular, the persuasive power of credentialism:

> I have said to them: 'Think long term. What do you want in a few years' time? Do you want a good job with money, or do you want to be where you are now and stay where you are?'. I can't think of anything else. And they look at you and say 'No, I don't want to stay where I am'.
>
> (Barbara, personal and unit tutor, BS)

> The motivation is always encouraging them to do the best they can and if they do the best they can, they'll get so much more out of life. It's almost telling them to get their qualifications and get themselves to university and get yourself a better job. I try to motivate them to improve themselves.
>
> (Danny, unit tutor BS)

In the questionnaire sample, teachers were asked to select the 'most worthwhile aim for students in GNVQ': 47 per cent thought that students' ability to take more responsibility for managing and evaluating their work was the 'most worthwhile' aim, while 35 per cent thought that 'becoming independent learners' was the most worthwhile aim. Twenty teachers added their own 'most important' aim, and of these, ten prioritised motivation and skills for learning, three prioritised objectivity, rigour and fairness in grading, and four wanted as many students as possible to gain the qualification. In the fieldwork sample, six teachers prioritised motivation and skills for learning, two emphasised the importance of objective grades and gaining the qualification, and one prioritised critical engagement with the subject. Nonetheless, although there were different priorities, it is important to reiterate that each individual teacher had a mix of aims.

Useful learning

Notions of 'useful' learning varied between subjects and individual students and teachers. Student data show the iterative and fluctuating links between apparently extrinsic motives and deeper forms of engagement suggested by the typology in Chapter 2. There was, for example, evidence of intrinsic and interested motivation based on engagement with topics and subjects. The young women on the two HSC courses applied assignments on health, psychology and mental illness, child abuse and family problems to understand aspects of their own lives. Annette, a lively, articulate and enthusiastic student with a very strong preoccupation with her own individuality, used all the assignments to explore her life and personality and social issues she cared about. Her assignments were all written in the same creative, deeply personal 'stream of consciousness' style, interwoven erratically with ideas from reading:

> The case studies [for a psychology assignment] had to be 'chosen care settings',[1] not real ones. So I did one fictional one, right, and then I did me for the other one. Because I know loads about myself and I'm getting counselling, so that's a care setting . . . So I used extracts from my diary and analysed them and I highlighted different parts of the extracts which I thought were significant.
>
> (Annette, HSC, Year 1, Riverside)

Another of the confident, sparky young women who comprised all but one of the eight students in the Health and Social Care sample adapted the assignment brief in a similar way to Annette:

> I have done my case study on [my sister] and I am well into that because I have lived with [sister's condition] practically all my life . . . You have to do all the different approaches and I have worked out how to link my sister to those approaches by what the psychologists would say . . . I used to want to be a child psychologist but after seeing it in real life, it's just not worth it because they are not very good.
>
> (Britney, HSC Year 1, Riverside)

One of the most striking features of all students in the sample was their confidence, enthusiasm and their view that they were becoming independent young adults. Throughout two years of fieldwork, students engaged enthusiastically with the course, its teachers and the intrinsic interest of particular units or topics. They all wanted to produce good work. The comment below is typical:

> I did an assignment in the first week. My boyfriend was on backshift so I just did it for 12 hours a day and I just kept on doing it because I got stuck right into it . . . about hospitals in the 1840s and about the anaesthetics they had to use, and you just can't believe what it was like in those days.
>
> (Jane, HSC Year 2, Bridgeview)

In contrast to their less motivated peers, students in the study frequently carried textbooks and files of work and sometimes swapped books, passed on useful material or talked about work informally with friends. Enthusiasm and pride in their work seemed crucial to their self-image: they 'loved' being a student, they 'loved the assignments', the teachers were 'great'. They compared themselves to other less motivated students in their group and equated maturity with confidence in GNVQ assessment procedures, being well-organised and having good relationships with teachers.

Three of the eighteen were motivated predominantly by intrinsic challenges in assignments and the interested motivation of overcoming difficulties and gaining new ideas. As one of the six highest achieving students, Darren's stream of enthusiasm in interviews for his assignments was striking:

> John's [unit] has been the best one. A lot of people have found it hard and it is but I think it is the case of being challenging. It's a lot more challenging when you have to go out and find information . . . It was 'Business in the Economy', about supply and demand and stuff like that. It was pretty cool and I really enjoyed it. You had to do different graphs and stuff and it was all about theories and there was argumentative type passages as well. There was no right or wrong answer, it's a case of your . . . theme and your . . . explanation of the matter.
>
> (Darren, Year 1 BS, Riverside)

There was also a strong view amongst the Business students that assignments should be relevant to people and organisations in 'the real world' and to their future and current jobs. More introjected and identified ideas of relevance motivated students when they moved from GNVQ into work. In the second year of the study, Kevin and Lynda had found jobs. They saw some limited GNVQ subject knowledge, together with skills of being organised and confident as important for their new role; but the most transferable aspect of GNVQ model was that the assessment created the necessary introjected and identified motivation for accepting accountability, a finding that resonates with Bates' analysis of GNVQs (Bates, 1998a). As trainee manager for a furniture store, Kevin pointed out:

> They [GNVQ] would always ask you why you had done something. The way we have been training at work is that you always have to give reasons for doing anything. So if somebody phones up from Head Office and says 'why haven't you done this' and you haven't got a reason for it, that is when they get annoyed.
>
> (Kevin, BS, Riverside)

More specifically, he related instantly to a new assessment procedures in an NVQ introduced for staff training:

I just knew straight away because it's the same set-up and specification . . . the assessor didn't have to explain a thing: I just said 'I know what I have to do'.

Teachers showed a similar mix of views about what was relevant and important in the course. In keeping with traditions in the vocational FE curriculum, teachers combined goals for students' personal development and a second chance to achieve a good qualification with a belief that subjects must be directly applicable to real life. Apart from Neil and Caroline, teachers did not discuss the goal of cognitive depth within a subject. Teachers' ideas about relevance varied according to the content of units they taught and beliefs about the purposes of post-16 education. Three teachers were unit teachers and their aims were more strongly related to subject development and students' personal growth within it. In overtly vocational units, such as 'Planning a Health Campaign' or 'Communications', 'Planning a Business Activity', 'Human Resources', general life-skills and specific applications of knowledge and information to students' goals for careers were important. In 'Marketing' for example:

I like to give the students a context where they can relate whatever I'm teaching to that context . . . I try to make them think about their own lives and part-time jobs and I think that's important rather than just giving them theory.

(Jo, BS)

Other teachers had quite different views of relevance, sometimes challenging the official connections in the unit specifications between theory and work demands. In units such as 'Psychology' and 'Social Policy', the 1996 assessment criteria contained the contentious idea that theories apply directly to the aims of policy-makers and to the practice of care workers. Both teachers disagreed profoundly with this assumption of relevance but the official status of the criteria meant they had to promote it. Nevertheless, they played it down, emphasising instead the introduction of concepts and ideas as a basis for progression within a body of knowledge. For Neil, the flawed aims of the specifications were inferior to his passionate belief that sociology and social policy are inextricably linked to the purposes of education:

You want to educate people so that they can question what's going on here. Either in their own lives, within their family or within the UK . . . Okay, you can turn back and say they need the facts and it's pretty difficult to be critical without at least some of the historical information and seeing where we come from and understanding how things work. So you do need facts or factual knowledge because when you start looking at facts, they are so open to interpretation that the actual foundation of factual knowledge starts to splinter.

(Neil, HSC unit tutor)

From a different perspective, three teachers who were unit tutors without an official pastoral role, talked primarily about the subjects they themselves liked and the need to generate students' interest and confidence in them:

I always remember when I was a student, the teachers used to say 'pick an area that interests you and investigate that, do as much as you can – don't worry if you're not covering everything, but you are doing something that interests you.

(Danny, unit tutor BS)

It's the subject so I like teaching it and it also gives them an introduction to Psychology which is all the way through the course anyway, so they walk away this term with an idea of perspectives in psychology, a basic understanding and an interest in it. . . . There's two [students] who really do think about the stuff and . . . you can see them taking in what you're saying and trying to make sense, and when they understand it, yes, that's totally rewarding and they're asking questions as well, that's just great.

(Caroline, HSC unit tutor)

'People like me'

Subtle social dimensions to both identified and intrinsic forms of motivation also emerged. Students enjoyed the security of the GNVQ group and navigated between personal goals, the demands of the GNVQ assessment system and good relationships with peers and teachers. Although disdainful of other students' lack of engagement with the course, they maintained good social relationships with them. For confident students, an image of being motivated, being popular with peers, getting good marks were, far from being 'uncool' as I'd asked, all strong assets:

I play off it actually . . . You know Rick and Tim come in and say, 'Darren, how well have you done' and I say, 'well, I've done the whole assignment and I've just got to type it up'. . . . They say 'oh you've done that'. I like to go out and help them . . . and I think that's a major plus point. Like today, I was helping John and it was, like, all rolling off the top of my head and I've only basically learnt it this year but I say 'well you want to do it this way and that way' and I think 'like, how do I know all this'?

(Darren BS, Year 1, Riverside)

The most confident students who wanted to do well on the course managed being seen as a 'swot' by mixing friendships across the group:

> They all call me a swot, because I always bring my assignments in. They call me the posh one from Hexham because they're all really rough and geordie. But they joke and we're all really good friends . . . they know I want to do well and they are not bothered. They are open about it and we are not horrible to each other about it . . . Even though some of them can't be bothered, they will sit and talk among themselves and I will just get on and they know that I want to get on so they just leave me.
>
> (Britney, HSC Year 1, Riverside)

Some students took time to gain social and assignment-related confidence. For Annette, familiarity with the specifications combined with her growing realisation that, in contrast to her school experience, college gave her a new space to 'be herself' and a new status with peers. In Year 2, her social status, a creative approach to assignments, together with some pragmatic accommodation to the demands of the criteria, all contributed to her Distinction grades.

The central role of social factors in students' motivation are an important counter to assumptions in colleges and amongst policy-makers and their intermediaries that individuals want flexible access to education outside institutional and group structures. An important characteristic of social motivation was that students sought 'people like them' to work with. The six highest achieving and most confident students saw the importance of relationships within the group and with teachers and managed them strategically. Once Michael progressed from GNVQ to the first year of a degree, social motivation became paramount. Away from 'the totally cosy' GNVQ group, he found new peers to ease the transition to an unfamiliar community where there were new but implicit norms for engaging with teachers and assignments and no assessment specifications to help him work out the rules. He consolidated a coping strategy from his school experience:

> K: In terms of being a student, and the group you're in, is there a pressure on you not to be a 'good' student, to be a cool and laid-back student?
>
> M: Sometimes but not really the close group I'm in. It's those particular people outside the group but that was the same as some people on the GNVQ. Luckily, the people I know work hard . . . it's just like at school, all my friends were in the high groups and my aim is to keep in with the higher groups. This happened to my sister and she happened to go for the lower groups and she hasn't got as far as I did.

Other dimensions of motivation appeared in support from parents and external contacts. However, only the six highest achieving students drew on family and work colleagues for specialist help with assignments and seemed to be intrinsically motivated by social support to do well in assignments. For example:

> I work on a part-time basis and a lot of the contract lads who work part-time are at college or in education so we all confer on breaks and lunchtimes.
>
> (Darren, BS Year 2, Riverside)

External support could reinforce identified motivation. For Tracey, an apparently less confident, more serious student, this was a source of pride:[2]

> My manager at work motivates me a lot. If he knows I have homework, he will sit me down at one of the tables in the corner and make me do it.
>
> (Tracey, BS Year 2, Bridgeview)

For others, though, lack of knowledge amongst supportive families created another impetus:

> It makes me more independent and motivated to do more work because my mam and dad don't know anything about what I'm doing and I can't ask them . . . most of my family don't know what I'm doing either so I've got to do it myself.
>
> (Naomi, Year 2 BS, Riverside)

Naomi's close friendship with Louise, one of the six high achieving students in the sample, was a powerful motivator. But differential achievement could also have negative effects. By Year 2, as Louise gained a series of Distinctions and Naomi maintained Merit grades, the friendship waned and Naomi's motivation declined too. For all eighteen students, group motivation and social commitments were a crucial factor in enjoyment of college. Yet, by Year 2 in Riverside college, poor attendance for group projects eroded social motivation amongst Riverside students in the sample. Particular cultures within each learning group were therefore influential and lack of resentment over poor attendance and variable grades depended on good relationships. There was more friction and dissatisfaction over such factors at Riverside. Nevertheless, although social commitments fluctuated, the eighteen students in the sample cared that peers did well on the course. And, in contrast to teachers' view that comparing work meant copying, some compared grades to set new targets:

> You feel that if they got that grade you could have got that grade too . . . David got a distinction on his assignment and I got a pass and I think I

could have done the same and got a distinction so next time I'll work harder and I might get it.

(Stephen, BS Year 1, Bridgeview)

Access to the assessment specifications also met other social needs. Karen, for example, used them to communicate with teachers that, given her lack of confidence, would have been difficult otherwise. Unlike the rest of my sample, she had no clear end goal beyond the course. She worked hard for assignments but needed detailed feedback from teachers in numerous attempts to improve them. For her, the specifications 'make the teachers talk to you more, not just give the lesson' meant that she seemed less concerned about her status with peers than working with teachers to improve her understanding of the criteria. This had an impact similar to the one noted by Patricia Broadfoot about records of achievement:

> The opportunity for one to one discussion made an enormous impact on many students who had never before had the chance of an individual conversation with a teacher about their learning on a regular basis. An important element of these processes is their impact on students' views of themselves.
>
> (Broadfoot, 1999b: 105)

In contrast to the importance of social dimensions in students' perceptions of their motivation, teachers did not mention social factors. Instead, teachers saw themselves as minimising friction and managing tensions within the diverse groups they taught, including the Advanced GNVQ cohorts, rather than creating opportunities for social commitments. Some also worried that students 'helping each other' was plagiarism or cheating and saw discussion amongst students about assignments as unhelpful competition over grades. Indeed, as Chapter 7 shows, pressures on teachers to ensure reliable grading, combined with their views about the purposes of assessment within student groups, reinforced an individualistic approach to assessment and motivation which down-played the potentially demotivating effect of variable achievement of grades. In discussing this observation at a seminar towards the end of the study, teachers felt that they did not address the social dynamics of GNVQ groups. However, whilst this is partly a pedagogical problem, the structural barriers militating against social dynamics within colleges (discussed in the previous chapter) should not be under-estimated.

New spaces

In contrast to more confident students, the GNVQ sample also had a number of young people who might be said to have more fragile identities both as learners and also as peers within the group. Despite growing in confidence in leaps and bounds over the two years of the study, and often with sophisticated insights into the requirements of different units, Stephen was a quiet, conscientious young man who progressed from Intermediate GNVQ in college. Over three years, he was slowly transformed by a college atmosphere and the GNVQ itself. Yet, in spite of his growing confidence, he found it hard to negotiate the tension between peer approval and wanting to do well on the course:

> You like to get on with your friends but you also want to do the work so it's trying to find the right balance between the two. I don't think you can find the right balance.
>
> (Stephen, BS Year 2, Bridgeview)

The personal development of all students, but particularly the less confident ones such as Stephen, Tracey and Karen was of paramount importance for five of the nine teachers who had been immersed in vocational education for over ten years. For them, the goal of a 'second chance' for students within a close-knit group was intrinsically motivating for their own sense of professionalism:

> I do like vocational education, I like the students once we've had them for a few months and because they're a group you get to know them, and I just love them, I love being in a class with them . . . and because of the nature of the course, these students come in as 'no-hopers' and seeing themselves, it's written all over their faces 'I'm a failure' and it's so nice when you hear that they've gone on to university. Obviously, some can only go so far and achieve so much, but for some, they find their niche and they make a go of it.
>
> (Barbara, unit and personal tutor, BS)

Teachers' own professional motivation was a crucial factor in defining their goals for students. As discussion above indicated, their official role in the GNVQ teaching teams affected the priority they saw for students' motivation. Five teachers had a pastoral role and prioritised students' personal development, general lifeskills and confidence over subject knowledge or high grades, although the latter were undoubtedly important. Tutors were therefore committed to building students' personal confidence and motivation and the data show the strength of their commitment, illustrated again by Barbara:

> I just like the rapport I have with them. I like to be able to talk about their progress, I think it's important. I don't think it's enough just to deliver the curriculum. I care about the students because they come from an environment where they have been looked after and they are in a situation where sometimes they feel on their own and you can lose

a student if you don't feel attached to somebody. So I enjoy tutorials from that point of view.

(Barbara, unit and personal tutor, BS)

Actions to sustain motivation

Aiming low

Despite their obvious engagement, students' motivation fluctuated dramatically over two years and the specifications came to provide powerful reinforcement for introjected motivation amongst all eighteen students who used them to try to judge how hard to work for each assignment. Most students aimed for easily achievable grades and twelve students were amongst the 65 per cent of the questionnaire sample that 'never' or 'sometimes' aimed for Distinctions. Most students were therefore wary of Distinctions. The questionnaire sample was asked: 'How often do you aim for a Distinction?' A cross-tabulation between rates in each college showed that 47 per cent of Bridgeview students 'never' aimed for a Distinction compared to 8 per cent of Riverside students: 27 per cent of Riverside students 'often' aimed for a Distinction compared to 11 per cent of Bridgeview, and 30 per cent of Riverside students 'always' aimed for one compared to 6 per cent at Bridgeview. Although 40 per cent gave 'workload' as a reason not to aim for a Distinction, 36 per cent said that Distinction was 'too hard'. It is not clear why there was such a marked difference between the two colleges, although discussion about the 'comfort zone' in Chapter 7 may offer pointers. Group norms and confidence may have played a part since data from the teachers do not indicate any variables in expectations or support for students. In the teachers' questionnaire, 70 per cent agreed that the criteria were off-putting for all but the most motivated students. In the fieldwork sample, 24 per cent aimed for, and gained, Distinctions while the rest aimed for Merits or Passes. This is close to proportions within each group and to figures produced by the QCA. These show that, nationally, 27 per cent gained Distinctions in Business GNVQ and 26 per cent in HSC (QCA cited by Ecclestone and Hall, 2000).

All but six students in the fieldwork sample were cheerfully instrumental about doing less well for units or teachers they do not like or aiming high in 'easy' units, and low in 'hard' ones. The language of 'hard', 'easy', 'horrible', 'boring', 'interesting', 'irrelevant', 'uncomfortable', permeated students' appraisals of assignment requirements. A careful strategy allowed some, like Michael, to coast towards the end by aiming for Passes or Merits because, mid-way through Year 2, he had the overall Distinction grade needed for university. Apart from six who usually aimed for Distinctions, less confident students used the specifications to judge the content of each unit in advance in the light of their perceptions about their own strengths and weaknesses. Again, these comments are typical:

> Basically last year I only got a few merits and mostly passes. I thought I will just aim for the merit rather than aiming too high and being disappointed.
>
> (Wendy, Bridgeview BS)

> I always go for a Pass. I get the Pass out of the way and then I say 'did I find that easy or did I find that hard'? If I found it really hard, I probably just stick at a pass whereas if I find it easy or interesting enough, I think 'I might as well go on and try and see if I can get anything higher.'
>
> (Annastasia, HSC Year 2, Riverside)

> After a few months of doing it, you realise these can be your strengths and weaknesses.
>
> (Kevin, BS Year 2 Riverside)

Yet, this strategy could backfire and Kevin, using the 1995 model, interpreted his performance wrongly:

> I ended up after all that with just getting a merit . . . It was because of the way they assess it and . . . the information gathering and the problem handling and all that sort of thing . . . You have to fill up four blocks [the grading theme boxes on the feedback sheet used in the college] and I had three of them filled up completely with four distinctions in each and the other one I had two so I was just two short on that . . . By the end of the first year, teachers were saying to me 'you're pretty much guaranteed a distinction' and I thought I did keep going, but obviously I tripped up along the way.
>
> (Kevin, Year 2 BS, Riverside)

Meeting the requirements

In spite of limited goals for Distinctions, confidence with the criteria enabled students to internalise the official assessment language of GNVQs identically to teachers. Depending on which model they used, they referred constantly to the 'assessment specs', 'the PCs' [1995 performance criteria], 'the bullets' [nickname given to the grade criteria listed as bullet points in the Capey model], 'the grading themes', 'the evidence indicators' [1995 model headings], 'task by task assessment', unit numbers rather than subject titles or 'task 1, task 2, task 3' instead of assignment topics or activities. Direct quotes from the assignment briefs and the grading criteria also crept, frequently and unelicited, into interviews with students. Although not sharing other characteristics with higher achieving students, like them, Stephen was confidently familiar with the minutiae and logistics of the assessment system. In explaining how he approached an assignment, he quoted the brief *verbatim* and related his own interpretation of its remit to interpretation by his peers:

> It asks you to talk about the political, social, economic and legal characteristics of two countries in the EU. Talk about business and how the differences in those countries would compare to the business. Then it says 'take into consideration these following points underneath. I took that as meaning 'put those points in the bit above with the legal and all that' and other people have taken it and done the legal characteristics separately but that doesn't seem to explain it.
>
> (Stephen, BS Year 2, Bridgeview)

Confidence with official language enabled students to make their own sense of what was required. Similarly, when asked what getting a Distinction involved, all students could recall the language of the grading criteria. Those who gained Distinctions began to internalise what the criteria meant while others were uncertain about terms such as 'evaluate' and 'critically analyse'. By Year 2, Michael also internalised phrases from teachers' feedback as he worked on new assignments:

> The past couple of times I have talked about a subject and it's quite vague. So I have thought 'open that up a little more' to achieve the Distinction and then evaluate it.

The typology of autonomy and assessment practices, discussed in Chapter 2, identifies three views of knowledge that might underpin development of autonomy and motivation. These are reiterated briefly here and Chapter 7 explores in more detail the formative assessment activities that teachers and students engaged in.

- *transmission* of content, procedures and requirements, linked to assessment which tracks and checks that these are covered;
- *transaction* over content and processes, linked to discussion of assessment criteria and negotiation of appropriate evidence of achievement;
- *transformation* of ideas and knowledge, linked to robust, diagnostic questioning in class and tutorials, together with feedback and strategic uses of ipsative, self and peer assessment.

Depending on how teachers viewed their role and the effects of GNVQ assessment requirements, transmission of knowledge arose from the assessment specifications themselves or teachers' perceptions about the demands of their subject specialism. At the same time, teachers were committed to maximising students' chances of passing whilst maintaining the integrity of the grades they awarded. The two teachers most committed to the aims and structures of the GNVQ requirements talked of transmitting subject content and enthusing students to be interested in it, but appeared to prioritise 'drumming the demands' of the GNVQ system into students 'from day one' (Mary, course leader, HSC). In two observed lessons with Jo, for example, she adopted the same enthusiastic, coaxing approach to students compiling their portfolio for the impending visit of the awarding body's moderator as she did for engaging their interest in her unit subjects. Six teachers incorporated the assessment requirements in their teaching, referring frequently to the language of the criteria within lessons, as well as more generally to processes of 'tracking', 'covering', 'listing' and 'hitting the bullets'. Phrasing from the criteria also appeared in their written feedback on assignments.

Yet there were strong differences in structures and systems for helping (or making) students meet (or get through) the requirements and these seemed to reflect the attitudes of teachers towards them. Thus, in three of the four courses, tutorials were a compulsory part of the GNVQ, with pre-booked appointments, expectations of attendance, official recording systems and regular written reports to parents. In these courses, targets were set around the specifications and teaching and assessment activities emphasised their transmission. In contrast, the course leader for the 1995 model tried to interpret its spirit of independence as a voluntary, self-directed approach to booking tutorials and compiling evidence for the portfolio. But, at the end of Year 1, numerous notices appeared on the department's walls with managerial-style warnings and sanctions for compulsory review and portfolio-building sessions, letters home about non-attendance and a disappointed, directive tone in the two resulting, poorly attended sessions I observed.

In contrast to this extensive and intensive transmission of requirements, and formal systems to manage them, the 1993 GNVQ model aimed to allow students and teachers to negotiate assignments and to review achievement in relation to the criteria. As earlier chapters have shown, numerous problems with these aims produced the more directive, externally monitored model of the Capey pilot. Predictably, then, teachers' transaction in this study focused extensively on how to achieve the requirements or on the technical logistics of doing assignments. Of thirteen observed lessons for eight teachers, there was substantial negotiation in seven of them about the balance of time to be spent on an assignment in the lesson itself and about the specifications.

By Year 2, one college introduced new systems to raise levels of achievement, measured by grades. In Bridgeview, a system of 'learning managers' to bring students up to grades predicted from GSCE scores was introduced in the second year of the fieldwork as part of the second major restructuring of the college in three years, explained here by Danny:

> Dave came in and gave out [little pink slips] and said 'Right, you're going to see Bill Smith at a certain time next week' and they all ask

what the slips are for and Lisa sat there and said 'it's because we're all underachieving' and the rest were asking why they didn't have them, so it's picking out the underachievers.

K: Did she mind? Did she say it in a resentful or cross way?
D: I think more of a resigned way, that 'yes, I'm underachieving and if this what I've got to do then this is what I've got to do' . . . she has the attitude of 'I'm going to pass' whereas, based on the GSCE score, she comes out with a merit.

These emerging pressures on students to go beyond the minimal goals that some of them set for themselves led some to internalise the official language of 'underachievement' and to be resigned to other interventions:

We got told when you were 18 and over, everything got sent to you and Business Study teachers have written on the top 'parent or guardian'. I think they are trying to do that so that your parents will help motivate you.

(Stephen, Year 2, BS, Bridgeview)

Limits to motivation

Like any students, the students in this study fitted the demands of the course strategically around diverse commitments such as part-time jobs, a social life, relationships and doing other part-time qualifications, such as information processing. The questionnaire sample was asked to identify the 'two most important things that get in the way of your motivation to do your best work on the GNVQ'.

Bearing in mind the number of responses and the mean values, the most common obstacles were the heavy workload, work commitments and social life. Strong views about what constitutes an 'acceptable' workload are therefore an important caveat in any evaluation of students' motivation. Other research (Davies, 2000) confirms the extent to which post-16 students expect to work large numbers of hours alongside their courses and there is concern that this affects achievement:

Overwhelmingly, the motivation to mix work and study is to earn money . . . from a desire to maintain a preferred lifestyle rather than from financial hardship. There are therefore suggestions that work has negative effects on achievement.

(ibid.)

In the fieldwork, sixteen students had part-time jobs and four worked three full days a week, eroding a supposedly full-time course:

Table 5.1 What gets in the way of your motivation to do your best work in the GNVQ?

	N	Mean	SD
Social life	36	0.83	0.38
Too much workload in GNVQ	35	0.97	0.17
Work commitments	25	1.00	0.00
Family commitments	20	0.70	0.47
Boring work in GNVQ	17	0.71	0.47
Getting good grades is too hard	13	0.54	0.52

> I used to do four days of work and three days here . . . I still do my three days and I only do three days at Thorntons because I told them I had to do an extra day at college. And they said 'well you can work in the afternoon can't you' and I said 'I cannot'. So I get my Thursdays off now so I can try and get my work done.
>
> (Annastasia HSC Year 2, Riverside)

Students decided when to attend college and when to work at home or in the college's Independent Learning Centre and, in 15-hours per week formal contact, attendance appeared to be very variable, even in 'popular' lessons. Of eleven observed lessons, all seen half-way through terms,[3] only two had the whole group present and the other eight had less than 50 per cent attendance. In contrast, during fieldwork, Learning Centres were busy with students from different courses, combining study, and socialising, for long periods at a time. The attractive environment of the Learning Centre compared to the utilitarian classrooms was an additional temptation.

Being 'allowed to go outside college' or out of lessons to the Learning Centre were powerful motivators, symbolising escape from classroom boundaries and trust from teachers. A prevailing view amongst teachers and students, that 'autonomy' meant 'going off and doing things yourself', discussed in the next chapter, offered legitimate spaces to avoid difficult or boring parts of the course, 'nagging' and 'boring' teachers, and to compensate for poor time-management or a heavy workload. Other erosions of teaching time came from pressure to turn lessons over to 'catching up' or to work on current assignments. Resource constraints, such as pressures on full-time teaching contracts and the use of part-time teachers, eroded contact further.

Implicit and overt negotiation of 'acceptable' engagement fluctuated over the two-year course. Amongst questionnaire respondents, 'the qualification' was a more important goal in Year 1 than in Year 2 whilst amongst the fieldwork sample, initial certainty about goals became more tentative over the two years. At the end of the two-year course, nine of the eighteen students followed their initial goal. Four had their goal (nurse training) disrupted by having to wait a year for entry and five changed their mind about goals (see Appendix 2 for details).

Nevertheless, some students moved from introjected and identified motivation to intrinsic engagement on a fairly stable basis:

> It [motivation] was just external and now it's internal. I like most of the subjects and if I'm struggling [the teacher] will help me.
>
> (Tracey, BS Year 2)

Shifts in motivation occurred at points of transition. Once immersed enthusiastically in his new job, Kevin's disappointment with GNVQ at the end of Year 2 was replaced with retrospective enthusiasm and a philosophical evaluation of its benefits. As Michael worked out what forms of autonomy were implied by the norms of a university course, he drew on social acceptance with 'people like him' to sustain introjected and identified motivation until he could develop autonomy again. And, as she adjusted to the uncertainty of a temporary job, and her third change in idea for a career, Lynda's final interview, held in the college, combined nostalgia for the security of GNVQ and pride in her new but precarious independence. In these fluctuations, students echoed the often erratic adjustments of other young people to new decisions, setbacks and opportunities (see, for example, Ball, 2000; Bloomer, 2001; Hodkinson *et al.*, 1996).

Although introjected and identified motivation increased over the two years, students dealt stoically with negative fluctuations, particularly midway through Year 2 when a universal low point seemed to be prevalent in both colleges. These included: a heavy assignment workload; not getting expected grades; tensions in the group over treatment of those who met deadlines and those who did not; falling attendance and retention rates in Year 2 and a corresponding decline in social commitment to peers; having to defer a university place; being rejected by university. Students were particularly indignant about inconvenient timetables, where the 15 hours contact time was fragmented across days and also if favourite teachers no longer taught on the course in Year 2.

The highest achieving students sustained their self-reliance, as Darren's observation shows here:

> The first year we already laid the foundation, though, that was the thing, and so we're more than capable of going out and doing good work, regardless of whether the teaching ability or standards aren't up to the first year.
>
> (Darren, Year 2, BS, Riverside)

Despite fluctuations in all four courses, and, in Kevin's case, a lower final grade, there was no overt resentment. Instead, students were stoical, determined, and 'got through': it's just something you have to do . . . you just have to be able to get on with things (Kevin). These traits were more apparent amongst those who had progressed from Intermediate to Advanced:

> Doing a GNVQ, you expect [repetition] though, that's what a GNVQ is.
> (Louise, BS Year 2, Riverside)

Despite some teachers' reservations about the negative effects of GNVQ assessment, most accepted that students needed 'more hoops to jump through' because of the 'reality of the student intake'. However, there were mixed views about whether the quality of student intakes was declining in FE. The teacher, for example, who was enthusiastic about GNVQs, saw her groups, particularly when large numbers of students were, by 1998, progressing from Intermediate to Advanced GNVQ, as 'used to what's needed' and therefore 'better students'. Other teachers were much less positive about the calibre of students compared to the past and, outside the small sample of students chosen as motivated and autonomous, all but one teacher had fairly negative views about many of the students' attitudes and ability.

Teachers' expectations of what they could 'realistically' expect students to do in terms of assignments and general engagement were also influenced by students' expectations that GNVQ systems within college should fit around other commitments, particularly substantial part-time employment. These constraints were reinforced by resource pressures on time to prepare and 'get through' all the content and assignments, alongside managers' staffing allocations, designated teaching contact and 'learning time' for students to spend in the Learning Centres.

More subtle pressures on expectations arose when some students questioned a need to do more than meet the demands of 'the bullets', especially in units they found 'difficult' or 'irrelevant'. Despite his antipathy to what he saw as confused content and structure in the unit specifications, Neil continued in his attempts to introduce students to the wider context of social policy. By Year 2, his students overtly resisted any content not relevant to the assignment and would not wait for 'the bigger picture':

> That takes a bit of patience and I don't think GNVQ generates patience because they are dying to get out there and do the project, do the assignment. They can't wait to get some knowledge, they want to pick up the books and immediately find the bullet points.

In terms of student motivation, he saw the students responding to:

> things that are close to them, and that they can readily understand and see as being readily relevant. So when you look at something I've been teaching, none of these things seem to apply, apart from that it is part

of the qualification so they can't see the relevance of an overview of social policy.

It became easier for Neil to allow students to meet the requirements than to continue trying to motivate them to engage with difficult content. In the second year of the study, he therefore stopped teaching to the Distinction criteria and allowed students to opt out of lessons based on content unrelated to the topic they chose for their assignment. This was the only such incident in the study but, as the next chapter shows, it appeared to signify the potential fate of content, teachers or specific demands for autonomy that students might resist in a modular assessment system.

The highest achieving students

Of the eight cohorts in the fieldwork 24 per cent gained Distinctions, with six of the eighteen discussed in this chapter aiming for and gaining Distinctions consistently over two years. Since Distinctions were the main indicator of intrinsic motivation and personal autonomy in the GNVQ (and very fleeting indications of critical autonomy), some motivational characteristics of these six students are relevant here as a precursor to discussing autonomy in more depth in the next chapter. Michael progressed from GSCEs at school to the Business course at Bridgeview, Darren and Louise from Intermediate GNVQ to the Business course at Riverside. Annette progressed from GSCEs at school, and Britney from A-levels at school, to the HSC course at Riverside and Jacqui from Intermediate GNVQ in Bridgeview college to the Advanced HSC course. These students aimed for and achieved Distinctions, mastered the assessment system and were committed to its demands whilst being able to address their own interests. They had clear end goals that they saw as both credible and positive and could move from external to introjected and identified motivation to intrinsic and interested motivation in certain subjects, frequently with great enthusiasm. They also played strategically to their strengths. They sustained introjected motivation during periods of drift or fluctuation in engagement and drew on social motivation and good peer dynamics to get them through low times during the course.

Social motivation was central to their achievement. They were lively, confident students who were committed to positive group dynamics within the group, had good relationships with teachers and cared about the achievement of other students including, for Jacqui, lower achieving students outside her GNVQ group. They also drew on sources outside college for support and ideas in their assignments, although Louise and Jacqui did not appear to have the same parental support and interest for their course as the other four black swans. Despite being judgemental of peers' poor motivation and lack of engagement, they were confident with other students and proud of being role models. The black swans seemed comfortable with their identity, particularly as learners, and confident with 'outsiders' to the community, such as the researcher!

These students also enjoyed getting on well with teachers both informally and formally. Unlike other students who merely 'put up with' different values and formative assessment practices amongst teachers, they adapted to teachers' strengths and weaknesses and maximised opportunities to draw on expertise from teachers they rated highly. Soon after progressing to university, for example, Michael appreciated new styles of teaching and assessment, even if they were unfamiliar and initially unsettling. Again, he used social motivation to get him through this difficult transition. In addition, the higher achieving students internalised some of the cultural capital implied in the assessment specifications and in teachers' feedback, as opposed to articulating it by rote as other students did.

However, there were gender differences. During my analysis of transcripts and fieldwork notes, data relating to the two young men had more coding on 'cultural capital' and 'social dimensions' than on 'responses to requirements'. The young men were also more confident in asking teachers for help, in transforming the feedback into deeper learning and in talking at length in interviews for this study. In contrast, the young women tended to be more instrumental in their motivation and engagement (apart from Annette), focused more on personal and peer dimensions to learning and were less confident and talkative during fieldwork activities. Interestingly, and despite lower morale amongst students and teachers in Riverside college, noted earlier, four students were from Riverside. The sample size as a whole does not suggest that this might be generalisable and analysis in Chapter 7 of teachers' approaches to assessment during the GNVQ course does not shed light on this either. It may be because the student intake at Riverside is more diverse and cosmopolitan than at Bridgeview, giving students in this study some initial social confidence, or because they had other sources of confidence and autonomy in their lives.

Summary

For all eighteen students, GNVQs were an important second chance to gain a useful qualification in a conducive, reasonably cohesive community of friendship cliques and a small core of teachers with whom they had regular contact. Students with limited past success in formal qualifications were motivated by gaining command of the assessment procedures and language and achieving acceptable levels of performance. They all had their own meaningful ipsative targets and measures of progress and used the specifications to assess aspects of these, to gain confidence and motivation, and to shape their work in a context where resources, particularly contact time with teachers, were reduced. In particular, the assessment system reinforced security and sustained motivation for students progressing from Intermediate GNVQ. Command of the specifications also gave Intermediate students an important social status in the eyes of their peers.

Students showed a complex mix over two years of introjected, identified, intrinsic and interested motivation and parallel fluctuations in social motivation and individual self-reliance. All eighteen students had some characteristics of 'embedded learners' in other studies (Ball *et al.*, 2000) and confidence and personal development were bound up with a largely optimistic process of 'becoming somebody'. The image and reality of being a successful GNVQ student depended on good relationships with peers and teachers and a conscious move away from a school environment. This enabled them to develop successful studentship through being able to make the most of educational opportunities and setting small steps for ipsative measures of progress. In addition, the identity of GNVQ student depended on being able to fit GNVQ work around external commitments. It seemed that the six highest achieving students showed a fleeting potential to develop some characteristics of 'vocational transformers' (Fevre *et al.*, 1999) based on periodic but genuine intrinsic and interested engagement with subject content.

Nevertheless, by Year 2, introjected and identified motivation dominated students' attitudes to the course. Students internalised the external framework offered by the assessment procedures, saw less enjoyable activities as a means to an end and had strong ideas about relevance and usefulness. In addition to the demands of the course, some students dealt with profound changes in family life and in perceptions of their own identity. Dealing with fluctuations and transitions required students to sustain clear end goals, to have support at home and from peers they had respect for and to engage with subject content. The highest achieving students had good relationships within the group and with teachers.

Figures 5.1 and 5.2 are an attempt to capture the interactions of different forms of motivation and to locate the eighteen students within them. It adopts Martin Bloomer's notion of 'learning career', 'in which people's dispositions to those aspects of experience which bear upon their capacity to learn, endure or transform over time . . . shape their dispositions to learning over time' (Bloomer 2001, also 1997). This shows, as Bloomer argues, that 'drift' and 'engagement' within a programme are not distinct (Bloomer, 1999). Figure 5.2 summarises the main points when motivation fluctuated most obviously over the two years.

As the next chapter shows, motivation is bound up with the types of autonomy students think they gain from GNVQs, and with their perceptions of what is important.

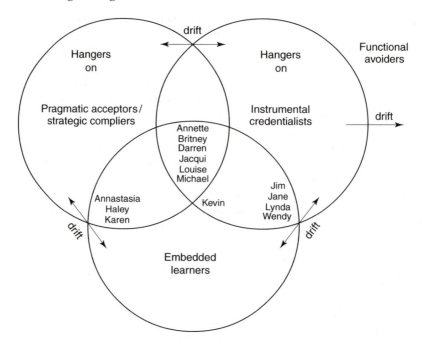

Figure 5.1 Motivation and 'drift' amongst GNVQ students. The categories draw upon work by Macrae *et al.* (1997), Bloomer and Hodkinson (1997, 1999), discussed in Chapter 3 and above.

YEAR 1

External/introjected motivation	Identified/Intrinsic/Interested motivation
Instrumental credentialism ⟶	Embedded learning/strategic compliance ⟶

Term One   **Term Two**   **Term Three**

YEAR 2

Introjected/identified motivation ⟶	Introjected/external motivation ⟶	External motivation
Strategic compliance	Strategic compliance/ hanging on	Instrumental credentialism

Figure 5.2 Types of motivation over two years of a GNVQ programme. The categories draw on the typology of motivation discussed in Chapter 3 and work cited above.

6   Doing it their way: autonomy in GNVQs

Introduction

Discussion about students' motivation in the previous chapter showed the extent to which teachers transmitted and transacted around subject content and the demands of the assessment specifications. There were some sporadic, tentative examples of students being able to internalise feedback from teachers about their work as the basis for beginning to understand their own learning processes and students' ability to use the language of the assessment specifications was motivating. Ultimately, however, this internalisation constrained the depth of engagement they could achieve. Specifications were especially important for less confident students who wanted a second chance to succeed in formal education and an outcome-based assessment model provided an initial prop, enabling students to resist peer pressure not to be a diligent student. For all students, access to the specifications provided a source for personal, achievable goals and was also a basis for the types of procedural autonomy discussed in this chapter. Command of the official language within the GNVQ community of practice was a foundation for internalising expected standards of achievement, particularly in the early stages of the course. If used imaginatively, specifications could, potentially, provide a springboard from extrinsic, target-led motivation to the deeper forms of self-determined motivation suggested by the typology. As Michael's experience of moving from GNVQs to university indicates in Chapter 7, it is important to explore ways of removing the prop so that students can develop deeper forms of autonomy and prioritise intrinsic forms of motivation.

It is clear, then, that different types of motivation offer varying foundations for developing types of autonomy within a formal programme. This chapter therefore explores students' autonomy during the course and the factors that influenced teachers' images of autonomy and their ability to encourage autonomy amongst students. Analysis here leads into a focus in Chapter 7 on the various formative assessment activities that both underpinned motivation and autonomy and responded to manifestations of these attributes. The first section explores dominant images of autonomy amongst teachers and students and the second section relates these images to the factors that appeared to constrain autonomy.

Images of autonomy

'On your own'

Throughout the fieldwork, students and teachers conflated autonomy with 'being on your own' or 'doing everything yourself'. From a group interview with Year 1 students at Bridgeview, for example:

> It [independence] means going off yourself and find out more yourself and getting it checked and then carry on;

> you like to do things on your own, you don't need any help, you don't rely on anybody else to do your work for you, you go and you do your research.

These views did not alter over the two years and, for some students, GNVQs appeared to suit existing dispositions:

> I just do things by myself . . . in class I always like getting involved in whatever the lecturer is saying where everyone else just sits there and says nowt . . . my assignments I just do my assignments myself and don't ask for help . . . like today, he [lecturer] is explaining the bullets[1] just to get a Pass and I've already done them. I'm always like that.
> (Jane, HSC Year 2, Bridgeview)

'Doing it yourself' had positive connotations for all the students in the sample. Becoming autonomous within the GNVQ was synonymous with growing up. For Jacqui, pride in her grades led to new confidence with peers and adults. Louise saw her mature approach to GNVQs as linked inextricably to moving out from her parents' house and getting her own flat. In a similar vein, Britney was proud of her independence:

> I don't let anyone bother me and I'm always on the go and don't really rely on anyone anymore. It's the same at home. I don't rely on my parents for anything, for money or help unless it's something serious. I usually get on and do things myself . . . Everyone has noticed how much I've changed. For someone who is only 18, from 16 to 18 I've had such a big jump and changed so much.
> (Britney, HSC Year 1, Riverside)

In addition to life-related notions of personal autonomy, most students saw a greater emphasis on procedural autonomy and were proud of their familiarity and self-reliance with the minutiae of the GNVQ system:

> The most tangible is the specifications; I think when everyone first started they couldn't understand the way they were worded but the more you do them, the more you seem to find out what they want because they use words like 'conclusion', 'evaluate' and 'compare'.
>
> (Stephen, Year 2 BS, Bridgeview)

As discussion below shows, a minority of students began to internalise what these criteria meant as a basis for critical autonomy.

Teachers who were more enthusiastic about GNVQs expressed fewer dilemmas about doing everything possible to get students through the requirements. For them, 'meeting the requirements' was itself an essential intrinsic goal, both as a motivator for cajoling students but also for the type of independence and self-reliance that GNVQ encouraged. In contrast, teachers who were more negative showed their own introjected and identified motivation associated with 'getting students through' or, in two cases, with minimising the impact of the requirements on their teaching and assessment practices. Neil wanted to rebel by subverting the assessment requirements by using his own criteria but, in practice, did not. As the previous chapter showed, students and eight teachers in the sample internalised the specific technical language of the assessment system, using it extensively in their everyday discussions about teaching, learning and assessment without any prompting at all. This was a strong indicator of the importance of the specifications. The two teachers most negative about GNVQ assessment hardly used the language at all: when they did, they qualified it as 'GNVQ-speak', thereby symbolising a separation from it.

Personal targets

Although students could more readily identify their procedural autonomy, most students seemed to be motivated more strongly by developing their own versions of personal autonomy. Annette, for example, initially saw the assessment procedures as an annoying hindrance. As her experience of Health and Care assignments showed in the previous chapter, she used the assignments to 'analyse herself' and to explore lives of young people she knew. By Year 2, and despite very erratic shifts between different forms of motivation, she eventually reconciled her personal interests and an idiosyncratic, creative approach to assignments with the grading criteria. Nonetheless, she remained more grudging about the need to gain procedural autonomy over requirements than did other students.

Data from interviews and the card sort activity showed the extent to which students valued different attributes and constructed their personal progress in precise, individual ways. These encompassed small and longer-term changes, based on informal, ipsative targets and their own haphazard assessments of progress.[2] For some, new targets were, initially, extremely daunting. Haley, for example, had to adapt to Advanced specifications in college from Intermediate ones at school. In her first assignment:

> I noticed that it was written more difficult, not just for you to understand but for you to really think about what you were having to answer . . . it wasn't that it was written down but you had to think of the whole meaning of what the question was. Whereas you were told exactly what to do in the Intermediate but you had to expand it in the Advanced.
>
> (Haley, BS Year 1, Bridgeview)

A plethora of transitions emerged that students saw as important are illustrated here by statements from group and individual interviews:

- becoming more organised;
- learning how to use the library;
- being open to anything people bring to me;
- going out and finding information;
- using a computer, using the Web;
- putting things from books into my own words;
- learning about things I've never heard of before;
- in Intermediate it was all done for you, whereas here you have to go out to the Learning Centre and do a lot more yourself.

Three students recognised changes in their approaches to learning. In responding to his card sort, Michael saw autonomy differently in the first term at university than he did in GNVQ and began to relate critical autonomy, tentatively, to his progress in getting to grips with issues and topics in different subjects:

> K: Which type [of autonomy] is your priority?
> M: (pointing to 'critical' statements) This one has an effect on the other two and I think they do need to be developed. Say this one [reads out statement]: 'I understand ethical issues in the subject'. One of the criteria might be about an ethical issue so if you don't understand the subject, you don't understand the issue and you're not going to be able to develop your work and understand the procedures for Pass, Merit and Distinction.

Students' personal autonomy was also an explicit goal for eight of the teachers. Yet, there were very different interpretations of how to promote this and teachers had different views about what personal autonomy meant and the impact of GNVQ assessment on its development. Thus, Jo, Barbara and Mary saw the development of students' awareness about their strengths and weaknesses within the course, and the ability to manage their lives around GNVQs, as part of a pastoral role as well as permeating their teaching of subject units. For them, personal autonomy focused on success in GNVQs, thereby intertwining personal with procedural autonomy.

In addition, just as students identified their own ipsative targets for progress, teachers were rewarded by very precise changes in individual students. All nine teachers showed a detailed awareness of individual students' progress, even in contexts where unit tutors only had intermittent contact with a group. Teachers valued small steps in students' personal autonomy, in examples of achievement or confidence in particular lessons or assignments:

> Tracey [student in the sample] is a quiet student and she'll struggle on without asking and she'll not ask if there's a big group and she'll not ask me while the rest are here, but the other day she caught me by myself in the Learning Centre and had a few things she wanted to ask me.
>
> (Danny, BS, unit tutor)

Another student designed a questionnaire for a unit on statistics and administered it in a supermarket:

> I didn't expect her to do that. I thought she would confine it to college or perhaps home and friends . . . she has gone out off her own bat, gone up to people and spoken to people. She wouldn't have been able to do that two years ago.
>
> (Barbara, unit and personal tutor, BS)

Signs of engagement and students' (very rare) confidence to ask subject-related questions or to challenge subject-related claims were rewards for Caroline and Neil. Two other teachers related personal development to confidence with the GNVQ requirements themselves. For Mary, a pastoral role to develop awareness of strengths and weaknesses was synonymous with meeting the precise demands of the assessment system:

> The tutorial part is getting them aware of what's expected in the GNVQ, how to perform within the GNVQ in their assignments because a lot of them have come from school and they are unaware of what is required in GNVQ, so we have done a lot of assessment at the

beginning . . . It's really linking everything up, it is like a pastoral role that we are doing for them.

None of the teachers related the idea of personal autonomy to a broader view of general education. And, although Neil did define it more generally, he saw numerous barriers to his professional role in developing it. In discussing the card sort activity of constructs relating to autonomy, he pointed out that:

> I wouldn't suggest I would go anywhere near personal autonomy. When I am taking two hours a week for one semester, that's a term and a bit. If I never met them before, and the chances are that I haven't, I don't even know them so I have got no chance of trying to understand who they are as people and then suggest and encourage ways of living which I think is what personal autonomy is about. It's about how you approach life. That never enters the consciousness.

From a narrower, course-related perspective, Danny recognised that students may set their own limits to achieving their best, but saw boundaries to his role:

> I feel as if it is the job to deliver the subject content and not really to dictate what they do in their lives. You do say things like 'well don't go out at the weekend' [when deadlines are looming!] but that's just a general comment. [Reads one of the card sort statements]: 'recognising strengths and weaknesses in all aspects of their lives': again, that's going beyond the subject area that I feel I'm trained in, and in terms of the time I've got, it's just beyond me being able to do that.

Lack of a broad view of personal autonomy was compounded in both colleges by the absence of an elective programme as well as by lack of contact time with students. Nevertheless, the drive for funding meant that colleges encouraged students to take additional certificated courses such as the Duke of Edinburgh award. Take-up of these opportunities varied greatly amongst the eight cohorts in the study.

New identities

Personal autonomy was also associated with deliberately seeking new learning identities from previous failures or low achievement. Students' progression, motivation and autonomy were bound up with forming new identities as successful learners. Four wanted to retrieve a failed attempt at A-levels while fourteen viewed college itself, as well as GNVQ, as another chance to succeed. Tracey, for example, was no longer motivated negatively by being 'worried about the deadlines, the teachers, the headmaster' at school. Annette used the 'more adult' atmosphere of college to work out her own identity and status with peers, free from bullying at school for 'being different': 'If I'd have been bullied here, I wouldn't feel confident enough to go to university'. Three students were consciously changing their self-image as learners from how they were at school and were therefore motivated by 'doing better than the teachers think you can'. All eighteen saw general confidence and social skills as crucial outcomes of GNVQ, as well as the benefit of being at college for two years:

> I can talk to more people now. Before I was a bit shy but now I'm not, I don't care really . . . I'm confident at work as well. I'm a barman at work so I'm more confident in making decisions.
>
> (Jim, BS Year 2, Bridgeview)

The development of personal autonomy continued after GNVQ. By the end of his second year at university, Michael was especially proud that he no longer relied on his parents for dealing with his bank manager or university tutors. Iterative links between personal and critical autonomy were also apparent when he related new confidence in questioning and improving practices in his part-time job at work to frustration that university tutors on his Business degree would not debate political and economic controversies, such as the UK's stance on the Euro. Nevertheless, echoing Stephen Brookfield's discussion of the difficult effects for adults of new identities created through educational experiences, cited in Chapter 2, he found his emerging critical autonomy unsettling: 'I don't think I like the person I'm turning into: I'm not the nice Michael you knew during the GNVQ'. He was worried that his desire to question things made him a 'trouble-maker' and this was not an image he liked.

In the GNVQ course, personal autonomy seemed essential to having the confidence to ask questions: the ability to do this about GNVQ procedures moved some students into seeking more sophisticated guidance:

> You have to say 'right, I'm not sure about that so what do I have to do and where am I going to get this from?' You have to say 'well can you help me'? and be able to speak up and tell people the situation because people aren't going to know unless you speak up.
>
> (Kevin, BS Year 2, Riverside)

For Darren, one of the six high achieving students, previous poor achievement at school had led to him leaving a job to come back to college to do Intermediate GNVQ, followed by Advanced. His infectious, confident enthusiasm for subjects and status with his peers derived from his new identity as a successful and popular student. This meant a sophisticated balance between the self-reliance that was important for status and his ability to seek out teachers in order to deepen his insights into subjects. He had worked out what he could realistically expect from this dialogue:

> All you have to do is go to them and say 'look, I'm having a bit of trouble with this, can you sort me out'? Now, I wouldn't expect them to give me the answer but I would expect them to give me some kind of example, kind of thing, which could later be accepted in terms of me going and finding out what it is.
>
> (Darren, Year 1 BS, Riverside)

An understanding of the rules of the GNVQ game, both unspoken and overt, had mixed effects. It enabled students to use the official cultural capital of an assessment community and offered an opportunity to internalise expected standards of achievement. This made some teachers discuss the qualities they associated with independence and confronted students with the different values, styles and practices of different teachers and their particular interpretations of the assessment criteria. Higher achieving students saw these differences as an advantage for making them more sophisticated as learners:

> In unit 6, he wouldn't say what was right or wrong or give advice until we got the assignment back and we had to find out where the error was . . . 'if you ask me for advice, you're not being independent', that's his attitude . . . It's good to have a mix of attitudes because then we've got to find out what we're doing wrong ourselves and put it right . . . If they don't give you the answers, you'll go and look for them yourselves and you'll think 'I *can* do it, it's not as hard as I thought it would be'.
>
> (Louise, Year 1 BS, Riverside, original emphasis)

Critical autonomy

Although procedural autonomy, ipsative targets and criteria for personal autonomy were evident, indicators of critical autonomy were much less apparent. A key indicator was whether students gained Distinction grades, since, as Chapter 3 revealed, some unit criteria required students to engage with knowledge and ideas, to generate broader subject-related questions, rather than procedural or personal ones, or to engage with moral or controversial issues. Yet, the motivation that students in the sample gained from aiming for low grades, discussed in the previous chapter, limited their potential to develop any critical autonomy on offer from engaging with Distinction criteria.

Students developed little more than very fleeting examples of critical thinking, not even the high achieving students discussed at the end of the previous chapter. Cursory and fleeting examples of critical engagement with issues appeared in some of the assignments I marked with teachers. In 'Social Policy', for example, students attempted to grapple with sociological perspectives. In 'Behaviour at Work', they evaluated the relevance of theories about management styles in the workplace. In 'Financial Transactions', they suggested improvements to companies' business plans and had to indicate ethical issues arising from such plans. Brief examples relating to a social, moral or political issue or a connection between different units also appeared occasionally in interviews when students mentioned something new they had learned. Examples here show that students' critical insights were precise, small-scale, subject-specific and erratic and not synthesised across the course as a whole.

For the six high achieving students, it is possible to infer the beginnings of critical autonomy as a form of meta-cognition from the ways that students internalised aspects of learning.[3] By the end of Year 2, three students had developed insights about the quality of their work:

> You have to be able to be critical of your own work. Not just saying 'I did this wrong and I did this wrong' but how well you did something as well. You have to be able to analyse your own work, I suppose like someone else would analyse your work without knowing what you'd say.
>
> (Michael, BS Year 2, Bridgeview)

He transferred this insight to the first year of university when he recognised he had to gain new forms of autonomy without assessment specifications to work from:

> You have to decide on how complicated you have to make it [the assignment] and, like, the boundaries for the assignment. It depends on how well you understand the technical language.

He also saw that he would have to be less instrumental and not, for example, wait until the assignment before 'having to read the books', because 'you have to read them to *understand* and develop your own knowledge'.

In GNVQ, Darren also noticed for himself precise opportunities where he had to become more discerning. During interviews, he often mentioned them, ranging across different subjects in the course. Here is one example:

> You've got to look at hundreds of different graphs about employment and stuff . . . and you've got to pick exactly which ones are relevant.

For some students, critical insights became obvious once in a full-time job:

> I can see both sides of an argument now and I understand why people think like that, it's pretty important in every aspect of life, whether at work or at home.
>
> (Kevin, Riverside)

As with the students, questions about what types of autonomy teachers valued in GNVQ elicited general notions such as 'students going off and doing their own work', 'going to the Learning Centre without being told', 'spreading their wings in the local community'.

And, as discussion about personal autonomy shows above, teachers valued a myriad of small and large steps towards autonomy. The occasional precise examples of goals for critical autonomy, and conditions affecting its development appeared in subjects where students' ability to think, question and challenge reflecting a particular critical, academic tradition which teachers themselves have experienced and internalised. The sociology and psychology examples above were therefore inextricably linked to the two teachers' personal commitment to particular educational goals and to their own induction into them. For them, critical autonomy is about students 'being able to think for themselves' and 'being wary of common-sense' or propaganda.

In other subjects, examples of the type of critical thinking and engagement with issues that might eventually lead to critical autonomy were much more precise:

> We have been doing the European unit and I think there is scope to look at current topical issues and I have asked them to try and think of some. Some have come back and they have had newspaper articles on the BSE and the Euro. So it's starting to work a little bit.
>
> (Barbara pastoral and unit tutor, BS)

> It's important to see both sides of the coin . . . it's something we touched on years ago in the teacher training, teaching controversial subjects and how to handle that. . . . It could be personal and social education as we did some different issues on flexible working and the problems with that and people being used on a flexible basis and asking 'is it good for them, and does it fit in with their lifestyle'?
>
> (Danny, unit tutor, BS)

Some teachers related possibilities for critical autonomy even more specifically to individual students and the topics that students choose for assignments:

> [Reading out a statement in the card sort]: 'able to challenge taken for granted assumptions'. Again, depending on what they're being taught and who they are, I would get them to challenge. I think it's very diffi-

cult for them to challenge assumptions if it's not in the news or not something that's happening at the moment . . . for example, the breast cancer campaign because private companies are now selling breast cancer awareness pens, t-shirts. That would be a taken-for-granted assumption, that they coin money in [from these activities].

(Mary, course leader HSC)

Despite some examples of broader forms of personal and critical autonomy, or perhaps, more precisely, the potential for them, there were a number of constraints on them being a realistic goal, discussed below.

Constraints on autonomy

'The bullets'

The detailed assessment specifications in GNVQs were discussed in Chapter 3. Importantly for discussion here, the grading criteria in the 1996 pilot model following the Capey Review in 1995 were referred to by all teachers and students in the fieldwork as 'the bullets' because of their presentation in bullet point lists as 'Pass', 'Merit' and 'Distinction' criteria. My own marking of fifty assignments over the two years of fieldwork showed that students with intrinsic enthusiasm for the topics, aiming for a Merit or Distinction, accumulated 'the bullets' by starting with the Pass criteria. This generated a volume of material that was extremely difficult to synthesise and analyse in the sophisticated ways needed for a Distinction. Whatever official guidance said, students treated viewed progression to higher grades as a linear, quantitative process. They treated criteria as separate tasks, calculating the work for each and highlighting precise points on the text where, in a telling phrase, they 'hit the bullets'. By Year 2, students' assignments had annotations showing 'P4' (pass criterion bullet point 4), 'M' (merit criterion bullet point 6) and so on. From a group interview, a Year 2 student explained:

> I always aim for a Distinction. I do the Passes and then the Merits and then I look at the Distinctions and see how much time I've got left to try and get the Distinctions. But in that assignment [Planning a Small Enterprise] there was too much and, to be honest, I'd had enough of it so I didn't bother doing the Distinctions.

When asked what depth was needed for evaluation to meet Distinction criteria, he added:

> You don't really know. It could be anything. I'd say that 2–3 sides [over and above the merit] would be quite in-depth.

Notions of quantity and coverage were prominent and some students talked about 'needing about 40 sides of writing to get a Distinction'. Splitting the Capey 'bullets' into further parts and then aiming at them erratically was also prevalent:

> In Task One, if there were bits of a Pass and bits of a Merit, I would still try to answer them both to see if it was easy, and if I could just add to the Pass bit, I would leave the Merit bit and move onto the next question. If there was a Pass/Merit/Distinction there, I would still try to answer them all. So I could get all the Passes or a few Merits and Distinctions and Passes. I just try to answer all the questions I can.
>
> (Student, BS Year 2)

Criteria in the 1996 model focused on procedural autonomy at Pass level. This enabled students aiming strategically for Passes and Merits to avoid critical autonomy altogether. A cumulative approach generated quantities of information that only the most persistent and motivated students could synthesise, let alone evaluate. The logical response was to produce compliant statements geared directly to each criterion and to resist extraneous or irrelevant work. Students also set limits to acceptable engagement, linked partly to perceptions of what was relevant, useful knowledge. The official status of 'the bullets' made five students, including four of the high achieving students, overtly minimalist in units they disliked:

> I do follow the bullet points but I find that the tutors want you to go into a lot more depth than it says in the book but yet the books have the points you have got to get to get a pass so why can't we just follow the points to pass and that will be it . . . [name of tutor] goes on and on and he gives you all this info and you think 'do we need this, it hasn't got it in the bullet points'.
>
> (Britney, Year1 HSC, Riverside)

In separate interviews, students complained about contradictions between teachers' assignment briefs and the specifications and there were pressures on some teachers to reduce expectations to covering the bullet points rather than doing a broader project. Three teachers in the sample adopted this approach.[4]

Self-reliance

Despite the importance of social motivation, students varied in whether they supported each other individually, in friendship cliques or across the group. Darren and Louise saw themselves as the most able in their group and helped each other extensively, while Michael, Jacqui and Darren helped students outside their immediate clique. The rest maintained a solitary approach, where autonomy meant 'not being dependent on anyone else, being independent on [*sic*] yourself' (Jane, HSC Year 2, Bridgeview). Despite good relationships with teachers and other students, the association of autonomy with 'doing things yourself' formed a strong aversion to asking for help, either from teachers or students, particularly for less confident students:

> Most people try to [do the work] themselves and then if they can't, they ask their friends first and the teachers after that.
>
> (Stephen, BS Year 2, Bridgeview)

> If I do some work, and I'm not happy with it, I can take it to someone and they can say 'it's brilliant' but I still think I have done it wrong. I have to be confident so that I can go and do something myself, whereas if I just take it to someone else, that is not being independent by getting someone else's opinion.
>
> (Wendy, BS Year 2, Bridgeview)

In difficult units like Social Policy, even enthusiastic students who wanted to do well were reluctant to ask for help:

> *Lynda*: The unit was hard and you had to keep asking [name of tutor] for help all the time so I felt like I wasn't achieving and that he was doing the assignment for me.
>
> *K*: So you had the idea that if you ask for help you weren't being independent?
>
> *L*: Yes.
>
> *K*: And did you get that idea from the course or was it your view?
>
> *L*: Just my view because in Intermediate [GNVQ] they said 'don't ask us all the time because you'll not get a very good grade' so that's what I picked up and took to the Advanced.

Lynda's apparent confidence with the GNVQ assessment system enhanced her status with peers but also formed a barrier to the help she needed to become critically autonomous. In the same assignment, she rejected ideas from the tutor about good books to use because 'you wanted your own evidence for the bibliography'.

A view that 'help' signified 'having problems' or being 'thick' reinforced self-reliance, especially when social acceptance within the group meant displaying the autonomy that was a source of pride and maturity for more confident peers. Even confident, popular students associated help from teachers with college work with other forms of dependency:

> I always feel stupid about asking for help or to borrow money . . . I feel like I have failed in some way . . . I would probably just try to do it

myself and then I might not do it very well and would have to settle for whatever mark I could get.

(Kevin BS, Year 2, Riverside)

Expectations of the level and type of engagement that students wanted were shaped by the requirements themselves, being in the same group for two years, limited formal contact with teachers and dispositions which students brought from past experience of assessment.

Old learning identities

Other norms arose from habits learned from school. Notions of 'making mistakes', 'getting it wrong', 'showing yourself up' appeared frequently in interviews and led most students to play safe:

> Nobody ever looks at anybody's work . . . we all just think 'that's what we've got, there's no point'. If they have got a Distinction, well done to them . . . I just hand it in really because I think if I've got all that right and it comes back, I would be 'oh well what have I done wrong because I thought I'd done that'. I just hope for the best.
>
> (Wendy, BS Year 2, Bridgeview)

Further reinforcement to a stoical self-reliance came from negative judgements about 'lazy' peers:

> If you have worked hard and the other person hasn't, they say 'I could do that and get a better mark' and I don't think that's fair, it's just laziness.
>
> (Annastasia, Riverside Year 2)

Some students' unwillingness to go beyond dispositions they brought from past experience of learning programmes could limit the autonomy they might gain from trying new things or engaging with feedback:

> I'm not a different person when I come to college; I have a definite way of doing things and they don't want it like that, it doesn't meet the way they want it.
>
> (Kevin, Year 2 BS, Riverside)

> I always feel I have to prove myself to a new teacher . . . if I've got a referral for instance, I find it hard to take what they are telling me to do . . . I've always been like that . . . So if I get a referral, I prefer just to get on with it rather than them taking me aside and telling me.
>
> (Annette, Year 1 HSC, Riverside)

'Good' teachers and students

Students related different types of autonomy to different teachers' skills and different subject demands. In the card sort exercise, nine students were asked to relate autonomy to the 'teacher you learn the most from'. All chose one who 'pushed them beyond what seems easy'. The six highest achieving students differentiated between such teachers and those with a more pragmatic approach. For example:

> [name of tutor] puts into perspective what you have to do but he doesn't motivate you to do the tasks, although he's a top bloke.
>
> (Darren, Year 2 BS, RS)

During the two years, students evaluated teachers according to their skills, motivation and adherence to the GNVQ requirements:

> A: Sometimes teachers want to do their own thing and give a broader aspect to the subject . . . whereas other teachers will just do the bullet points because that is what you need to get the Pass.
> K: Why do some do that and not others, do you think?
> A: I think some like teaching more than others. Sometimes they find it tedious to teach a subject so they just do it as quick as they can . . . It's like [name of tutor] is a psychologist and I find the way he teaches GNVQ is the way he would teach A-level . . . He goes into the subject in depth and he wants you to find out what's in the subject rather than you just doing the bullet points. I think he likes it.
>
> (Annastasia, HSC Year 2, RV)

Expectations of 'good' GNVQ teacher fluctuated over two years. As workload and identified motivation increased in Year 2, my last interview with Darren, Louise and Naomi produced an animated discussion between them about whether subject expertise, personality or knowing the GNVQ requirements was the main criterion for being a 'good' teacher. The latter won the day. In contrast, students who saw college as a space for trying out new ways to gain confidence and status with peers and teachers meant that good relationships with teachers was the most important aspect of GNVQ. For Annette, 'real' teachers were authentic, tolerant and challenging and brought aspects of themselves and their lives into their subject. She was dismissive of teachers who 'just stuck to' the assessment criteria: they 'depressed' her.

By the end of the course, then, most students came to see command of the GNVQ assessment procedures as the most important characteristic of a good teacher, even though other characteristics had been more significant earlier. It is also significant that 55 per cent of the sample, chosen by teachers at the start of the fieldwork as motivated and autonomous, came from Intermediate GNVQ. Given that Intermediate students comprised only 25 per cent of the cohort in the four groups represented by this study, this instinctive choice suggests that 'good' students were, in the main, those who were procedurally autonomous and able to work independently with the assessment specifications and processes. Yet, for teachers like Neil, there was a profound disjuncture between his views about what makes a 'good' student and the personal and learning attributes and traits that he saw GNVQs encouraging in the groups he taught.

Teachers' genuine respect and concern for students, intrinsic interest in their subject and, crucially, 'being a real GNVQ teacher', with command of the assessment system, were all important characteristics for students' confidence that they could develop autonomy. In the card sort, Lynda, for example, believed that she had the potential for attributes such as 'seeing different sides to an issue' or 'recognising controversial issues' but that some teachers saw this as unrealistic:

> [for social policy] I picked gender and he goes 'oh that's too complicated, you'll never pull it all together'. He doesn't think we can do it but I showed him and he goes 'oh you managed it, you pulled it together quite well'.
>
> (Lynda, HSC Year 2, Bridgeview)

Lynda was a striking example of quiet determination, consistent engagement and optimism and she was developing a new positive image of herself as able to overcome previous negative expectations. Usually, she saw this teacher as having high expectations of her, suggesting that his response here was a deliberate challenging tactic.[5]

Transitions and 'turning points' also shaped ideas about good teachers and assessment systems. For Michael, leaving the cohesive, tightly-knit group at Bridgeview meant learning, then negotiating, new norms in a university environment as well as new forms of cultural capital in relation to assessment:

> I've tried finding my personal tutor and my friends went to see him but we haven't been formally introduced. That's so different from GNVQ. It was totally cosy and now it's totally independent.

Michael's transition also suggests that, unless students can move beyond dispositions established or consolidated in GNVQ, their expectations of security and of continuing particular dispositions can result in drift.

Summary

GNVQ students influenced the shape and content of their course and enjoyed 'hunting and gathering' information (Bates, 1998a). Students' experiences also suggested that command of procedures, and confidence in using a common technical language, were essential for developing the confidence to try new things. Importantly, for some students confidence led to a willingness to discuss subject-related issues with teachers.

At one level, students seemed to bear out my initial proposition that procedural autonomy may be both a necessary pre- or co-requisite for other forms of autonomy. Each student had individual targets and precise indicators of her or his own progression, albeit *ad hoc* and erratic. In the light of the typology, some developed aspects of personal autonomy and occasional, fleeting aspects of critical autonomy. Individual teachers, the content of different units and different stages of the course all affected these characteristics. Students saw their emerging strengths and weaknesses as important and ten of the eighteen cited enthusiastically specific examples of how they came to see issues in different ways. There seemed to be potential to build upon the fluctuating, and sometimes precarious, intrinsic and interested motivation that all students showed, but only six seemed open to developing critical autonomy. Although procedural and personal forms of autonomy were important, there were more barriers to critical autonomy than robust indicators of it. This arose both from the specifications themselves and from students' responses to them.

Despite the potential for intrinsic, interested motivation and critical autonomy amongst the highest achieving students, there was no evidence of a transformatory approach to knowledge and subject content suggested by the typology in Chapter 2. The next chapter discusses how assessment practices in GNVQs both arose from problems of accumulation and coverage and reinforced them, but were also affected by other factors.

7 Biting the bullets: formative assessment in GNVQs

Introduction

The typology in Chapter 2 argued that students need to engage with implicit and explicit standards in an assessment community and to internalise assessment language and the implications of the criteria. These processes are integral to effective self-assessment and, potentially, a basis for deep engagement in the requirement for high grades. Notwithstanding the motivation that students gained from having and using the assessment specifications, there were indications in the previous chapter that the GNVQ assessment model exerted a powerful constraining influence on students' motivation and autonomy. Importantly, merely adopting others' language undermined opportunities and the inclination for teachers and learners to construct meanings together. More generally, introjected and identified adoption of external language and assessment structures trivialises what Black and Wiliam see as crucial social knowledge in assessment (Black and Wiliam, 1998a). To counter these effects, teachers would need to promote consciously a notion of collaborative dialogue to prevent students becoming stuck with the limited cultural capital created through the technical language and a particular mind-set about assessment that the GNVQ model imposed on their thinking. In turn, this conscious 'moving on' would need to encourage students to ask different types of questions of teachers.

Yet, analysis so far has highlighted diverse and complex factors that affect this apparently unproblematic theoretical notion of assessment communities committed to the achievement of all its members. At macro, meso and micro levels, diverse factors (ideological, epistemological, political, institutional and individual) all combined to influence constructions of motivation and autonomy amongst teachers and students in this book.

This chapter relates ideas and practices associated with autonomy and motivation discussed so far to the types of formative assessment that students and teachers in the fieldwork are engaged in. The first section explores old and new images of assessment that influenced students and teachers over the two years of the GNVQ programme. The second section examines the competing pressures that created a 'comfort zone'. This both shaped and reinforced norms and expectations about autonomy, motivation and formative assessment. The third section evaluates new forms of professionalism that seemed to be emerging amongst teachers in the fieldwork, influenced by GNVQ-related and non-GNVQ factors. The fourth section summarises the effects of factors discussed in the previous chapters based on college fieldwork on shifting values amongst FE teachers.

Images of assessment

'Tracking' and 'checking'

In addition to the impact of new images of assessment created by 'the bullets', discussed below, images of autonomy and motivation were both underpinned and reinforced by images of assessment from school. Students equated assessment with surveillance and external judgements. This view did not change over two years in the eight groups covered by this study, illustrated here by comments from two separate group interviews about the purpose of assessment:

- how you do your work and how you perform the tasks and criteria;
- how the lecturer looks at you and your assignment to see what they think your potential is;
- when someone looks at you and what you do and what your work is like;
- judging your attitude.

It seems reasonable to infer from such responses and from students' fears of aiming too high, that even if they experienced activities such as peer assessment and self-assessment, students would be unlikely to link them to learning and achievement. The questionnaire for this study also highlighted that: 72 per cent 'never' assess a friend's work and 62 per cent 'never' get someone else to assess their own work. Only 24 per cent always assessed their own work before handing it in while 34 per cent did not like to ask teachers for help or know what the higher grades require. Another study of attitudes to assessment amongst fifty well-motivated school and FE students in GCSEs, A-levels, GNVQs, BTEC National Diplomas and NVQs showed that very few students participate in peer assessment or engage deeply with self-assessment. Instead, students saw any assessment as the teachers' responsibility (Ecclestone and Hall, 1999). These findings resonate with teachers' questionnaire responses: 64 per cent said that students 'use the criteria to plan their work' while only 44 per cent said that they used them to 'evaluate their work'. However, although 50 per cent of teachers said that students 'use feedback to improve their work', 80 per cent felt that the criteria were 'off-putting for all but the most motivated of students'. No students in the fieldwork sample engaged in peer assessment, while self-assessment for fourteen of the eighteen involved checking their work against the bullets and using teachers' feedback to fill any gaps.

Students overlaid the particular demands of GNVQ with traditional images of assessment, such as 'scores' 'marks' 'right and wrong', bullets as 'marks' or 'points' (grades might be a 'few points off the higher one'). This encouraged the idea that gaining higher grades involved 'just doing more', 'just covering more bullets', 'going into more detail', 'just going off by yourself and then getting it checked'. 'Just' recurred very often in all the interviews and seemed to symbolise a straightforward, even easy, process. When combined with the cumulative approach to covering all the bullets, discussed in the previous chapter, students' images of assessment bore very little relation to the progressive theoretical notions outlined in the typology.

Further constraints on the type of transaction that was possible within GNVQ appeared when marking students' work. As Chapter 6 showed, students marked precise points where they 'hit' the individual criteria for Pass, Merit and Distinction. In marking the assignments, a logical response for teachers was to 'track and check', seeking out words and phrases that confirmed achievement. In marking a Psychology assignment, Caroline and I had problems with an assignment where a creative 'stream of consciousness' approach did not lend itself to this auditing approach:

> What I tend to do is mark these pass points, P1, P2, P3, P4 and P5 and then, as I'm going through, try to match up what [students] say with the bullet points but it doesn't allow for something which is in the air like this. I'm not saying she has not got it because I think when I read it, she did have, the same as you thought, but it is not easy to match to this.
>
> (Caroline, unit tutor, HSC)

We spent time discussing how Annette's work met the criteria but eventually referred it back so that she could relate achievement more explicitly to the criteria. I marked fifty assignments in total (five from each of ten units) and in each unit most students had to repeat parts of assignments more than once in order for them to meet the criteria for a Pass.

In our joint marking of Social Policy assignments, Neil contrasted his usual more holistic approach to a parody of marking to the 'logic' of GNVQs:

> Instead of doing it holistically, let's do it in the model of GNVQs. That is, let's go through and just check if she [student] has got all these things [the bullets]. They might assemble it by going through – 'I'll put that in, I'll put that in, that in'. *I'll* go through and check the same without reading it!

Gill also resented not being able to assess students' work holistically. Discussing her marking with me on another occasion led her to a particular view of how the marking system affected her assessment practices:

> As a result of our discussion last time, it made me realise why I was having major problems with the marking and feedback, so now I have accepted that it's just the bullets. So as a consequence, now I am conditioned. I still like to read to get the overview, but now I realise there isn't always an overview, and then just to look purely at the bullets, and if you haven't got the bullet, well, you have just got to do it.

Assessment activities

Given that personal and critical autonomy require students to engage actively with formative assessment, whether from oneself, from peers, teachers and, perhaps, family and workplace colleagues, I asked students to talk about how they used teachers' feedback on assignments and the feedback they valued. Students liked teachers to be clear and precise about how to fill gaps in criteria if work was referred, preferably face-to-face rather than through written comments. Students saw this type of feedback as the main characteristic of 'teachers they learn[ed] the most from':

> I like the way that [name of tutor] actually takes the time to type it up. He must have really read the assignments because he had every bit that you had to do, step by step and I thought it was brilliant.
>
> (Annastasia, HSC Year 2, Riverside)

Nevertheless, few GNVQ teachers wrote 'lots of comments to give you more ideas', and, Stephen, like Annastasia, regretted that GNVQs did not encourage teachers to be more flexible or to go beyond feedback about the criteria. However, he remembered a reason given by teachers:

> The guidelines are that strict that they can't mark differently. If they know what you mean but you don't say what you want then the external examiners can't pass you. A lot of the time, the teachers know you personally after seeing you for 2 years and they know what you are trying to say and people outside won't know what you are trying to say so they can't give us a pass.
>
> (Stephen, BS Year 2, Bridgeview)

This 'passing on' of official interpretations encouraged students to 'sign post' content to relevant criteria, since students were told: 'You have to write as if the examiner isn't very bright' (Stephen, Year 2 BS, Bridgeview).

High achieving students showed potential to use feedback on their work to boost intrinsic, and sometimes interested, motivation as a springboard for deeper forms of autonomy. There were also two good examples of observed lessons (Social Policy and Psychology) where Neil and Caroline both showed a robust, exploratory approach to questioning aimed to help students develop their understanding of the subject and to 'make them think'. But apart from these isolated incidents, and despite some examples of Distinction criteria that encouraged some critical engagement, marking assignments showed how hard it was, even for the most motivated students, to gain the depth and criticality demanded by the criteria. Problems in other assignments were exemplified in the Social Policy example here:

> It's the nature of GNVQ, it's the nature of this assignment that students think it's about gathering as much data as possible. It's the equivalent of going into an exam and writing all you know about something without structuring it. And you can get a pass at A-level with that. Just like you can get a pass at GNVQ. You don't have to be coherent to pass, so if you don't need to be coherent, you don't do it. They only do what they need to do.
>
> (Neil, unit tutor)

As a result of the complex GNVQ-related and external factors explored here, transmitting the requirements and transacting around them prevented any meaningful transformations of learning or knowledge (see also Bloomer, 1998; Boys, 2000).

Working in a 'comfort zone'

Terms of engagement

Access to the specifications enabled students in this study to move into an assessment community, but unlike other accounts of GNVQs (for example, Yeomans, 1999), teachers in this study did not 'protect' students from the specifications. Instead, students used them extensively. Ultimately, the uniformity and prominence of the specifications limited expectations of autonomy amongst all students in the sample. Whilst independent in 'finding out' information, they remained dependent in 'working out' solutions. Instead, students collected information for tasks set by teachers within units but did not set or test research questions (see also Boys, 2000). Teachers in my study taught units separately and divided work into tasks, and students liked the benefits of knowing what was expected of them. This approach enabled more students to pass but reduced the depth needed for Distinction grades. The specifications therefore both offered security and set boundaries to engagement. They also compensated for restricted contact time with teachers. More insidiously, they consolidated a view that autonomy meant solitary, compliant work and not needing 'help'. Since these attributes were both a source of pride and praise from teachers, less confident students and those who moved into a daunting situation or a difficult subject, found it difficult to ask for help. Reticence was reinforced by more confident peers appearing to 'just get on with the work' alone. This problem suggests that enabling less confident students to see how their confident peers really worked would help to communicate a more positive view of autonomy.

Making the assessment requirements more transparent encouraged a minority of students to mistrust how some teachers used the specifications. Students were particularly critical of what they saw as slip-shod skim marking and poor feedback:

> I look [over my work] first, just in case, 'cos they've got loads to mark and you can't really take their word for it . . . [in one assignment], I knew for a fact that I'd met the criteria for a merit and he was going 'you haven't done such and such' and I pointed to it and said 'there it is' and pulled it out, and I said 'this isn't on 'cos I've checked it off myself and went through it and through it again' and he'd taken them in all in one week and handed them back the next and you can't do that, not with all those assignments.
>
> (Jane, Year 2 HSC, Bridgeview)

In another animatedly indignant story, four students at Riverside had tested interpretations of grades by submitting exactly the same work for a resubmission as they had for the first and getting a higher mark! Yet, despite some challenges and criticism of feedback, there was very little overall negativity about assessment: students were sympathetic to teachers, seeing them as 'always rushing about' and 'having so many jobs to do'.

Whilst autonomy to challenge is important, mistrustful resistance raises broader tensions over whose expertise really counts in deciding what is useful or useless knowledge, difficult or simple work, or what criteria like 'critical analysis' really mean. These problems beg questions about the sophistication with which even the best students engaged with the criteria and suggest that GNVQs can lead students to make judgements about issues for which they may not be qualified (see also Bloomer, 1998).

The Pass criteria were an important benchmark for judging degrees of difficulty and making decisions about engagement. At the same time, the identical layouts and language of the assessment specifications implied that autonomy was the same in each subject and each year of the Advanced GNVQ. Familiarity with using a uniform set of specifications led confident students to a simplistic view of what was required, particularly for Distinction grades and, conversely, daunted less confident students. Further problems arose because the disparate design of each unit's specifications provided no explicit, or even implicit, coherence in the types of autonomy Advanced students could, potentially, develop over two years. In a unitised programme, students navigated parallel assignments, each demanding different types of autonomy that were obscured by the identical formats and vocabulary of the specifications. Distinction criteria shifted erratically, both within individual units and from Year 1 to Year 2 units, between procedural, personal and critical autonomy. This is likely to be problematic for students at *any* level of motivation or ability.

In unpopular or difficult units, these tendencies encouraged some students to judge in advance 'boring' or 'irrelevant' knowledge and learning activities and thereby to press teachers into reducing their expectations. Emphasis on procedural autonomy and resistance to 'difficult' forms of autonomy were reinforced by instrumental self and peer assessment. Students' responses here appear to resonate with young people's resistance to 'irrelevant' education in other studies (for example, Bates, 1989b). These GNVQ-related effects presented difficulties for teachers committed to broad pastoral interpretations of personal autonomy or to critical autonomy. Strong views about 'relevance' and 'usefulness', combined with aversion to difficult subjects, meant that the relevance of evaluating a health campaign was easier to sell to students, for example, than evaluating competing theories in social policy. The fate of Neil's critical goals in Social Policy is a salutary illustration of such pressures.

Students in the fieldwork also expected to manage GNVQs within pragmatic boundaries created by the logistics of their lives. These combined with their interpretations of the assessment specifications and perceptions of their ability to set expectations of acceptable workloads and legitimate degrees of difficulty demanded by assignments. Expectations were compounded by the many opportunities students had on the course for informal and non-formal learning. These undoubtedly provided invaluable and motivating support, especially in enabling and encouraging students to avoid 'looking stupid' if they asked teachers to help. There is therefore a strong sense that informal learning was essential to retaining many of the students on the course and it reinforced and justified the idea of autonomy as 'doing it yourself'. But less positively, it also seemed that *ad hoc* informal and non-formal learning consolidated low risk strategies and instrumental attitudes towards formative assessment. It also encouraged less confident students to maintain comfortable dispositions to learning, even when these hindered their achievement. Without a pedagogy for informal learning, alongside strategies to maximise its benefits and minimise possible disadvantages, it becomes difficult for colleges to balance demands for higher achievement with many students' expectations of low formal attendance and their preferences, instead, for informal learning. Lack of a strategy allows students to exert an undue influence on expectations and norms within particular assessment communities and widens the gap between high and low levels of achievement within learning groups.

The minimalist pedagogy created by these diverse GNVQ-related pressures and broader ones established a comfort zone. Students with high levels of autonomy and motivation could risk some discomfort in moving beyond an immediate, safe level of engagement. It is possible that the highest achieving, most motivated students could, potentially, act as magnets to draw their lower achieving peers towards better grades. Students with procedural autonomy and introjected and identified forms of motivation worked in a lower comfort zone. Some students, like Michael, aimed for Distinction grades but returned to an easier comfort zone to achieve Passes and Merits when he had the grades he needed. Others, like Wendy, ventured out of their comfort zone by aiming for higher grades initially but did not have the personal autonomy, confidence or social motivation necessary to stay there. Some, like Kevin, operated below their comfort zone but other opportunities, such as organising gigs for his soul band, enabled him to develop intrinsic and social motivation and autonomy outside the course and its assessment requirements. Annette fluctuated erratically between her intrinsic and interested motivation to work in a higher comfort zone and her desire for status with lower achieving, externally, or amotivated, peers. When operating above their comfort zone, Louise and Annette sometimes experienced overload.

The six students in the sample who consistently gained Distinctions, discussed earlier, went beyond procedural autonomy and haphazard ipsative measures of personal autonomy to achieve good grades through intrinsic engagement with assignments. They also developed some fleeting aspects of critical autonomy and a more considered approach to ipsative assessment.

Assessment for learning

In parallel to students' views about assessment as external, summative judgements of evidence, none of the teachers saw assessment explicitly shaping or affecting learning. Indeed, the most difficult questions to justify to them during fieldwork were related to my attempts to explore the activities they classed as 'assessment' and how they perceived the purpose of questions in class or tutorials. As one pointed out: 'You keep on referring to things as "assessment" that I see as "teaching".' Assessment was associated with marking assignments, collecting evidence of achievement and formal tests. Formative and diagnostic assessment, such as systematic classroom questioning where teachers constructed understanding by building on students' answers, and questions in a tutorial to encourage students to reflect on learning, were not associated with assessment. Data from all the fieldwork activities therefore bear out the prediction from other research on formative assessment, discussed in Chapter 2, that most teachers do not connect assessment with everyday formative and diagnostic activities that can enhance learning. This is not a GNVQ problem but, in this study, GNVQs reinforced it.

Instead, assessment for seven of the teachers in the sample was clearly a time-consuming, solitary and boring chore. Teachers' rooms were full of student files and portfolios and teachers carried a high and frequent marking load. As the next section shows, official scrutiny has made it a source of increasing anxiety for teachers. In response to my question about his approach to marking, Neil presented his view of a common professional attitude:

> Assessment is, I think for many teachers, probably the least thought about, the thing they find the least interesting. Everyone complains about marking, everyone. It doesn't matter if you are teaching A-level or GNVQ, anything, we all hate marking. It's no fun. You do it on your own, you are thinking 'what the hell are they on about, what have I taught them?' . . . So we hate it really and I don't think, as teachers, we give it enough thought. I certainly don't.

In keeping with this, teachers' written assessment comments were largely brief summative confirmations that students met or missed 'the bullets'. However, a key aim of the participant observation was to explore approaches to marking and feedback as indicators of teachers' ideas about the purposes of assessment and its implicit or overt links to ideas about learning. Although they did not see their feedback ticks and comments on work as 'assessment', six teachers provided detailed feedback to individuals in tutorials or while others worked on assignments in class. Three (Barbara, Gill and Jo) had educational rationales for their approach to feedback and hoped that students would respond to their written questions or queries on assignments. When we marked an assignment for an unconfident student who had made many mistakes, Gill explained her sparing written comments and her emphasis, instead, on one-to-one feedback:

> If I write everything [that's wrong] on here, it's soul-destroying and hence I tend to mark in pencil because I don't like to get things back covered in red ink myself.

She and Barbara had a similar precise approach: 'no crosses, always questions' and what I observed in notes made after a post-assessment interview as her 'precisely-placed wiggly lines, circles and straight lines' on specific parts of the text. Gill had a strong memory of her own experience as an adult student and saw the effects of feedback on students' identity as learners:

> I went through as a mature student and I know the things that had a big impact and I hated the very first piece of work I got with red ink on. And so consequently, I won't inflict it on anybody else. I think you can just as easily see that something is incorrect by the question mark. You can explain it but then once it's explained, that's it, it's not for the rest of the world to see that you did something wrong. . . . It's between

you and the student. And I think in many ways it builds up a relationship with the student and the student has confidence that you are wanting what's best for them rather than promoting their weaknesses.

For Gill, Barbara and Jo, feedback was an opportunity to convey their own educational goals to students and to build a relationship with them. Yet, this concern could also limit progression to more robust forms of feedback. If teachers prioritised goals of confidence and personal development, asking students too many questions in class or giving negative comments on their work harmed these goals. Gill's approach also showed the limits to meaning that can be conveyed without writing the dispiriting detail that she, and also Barbara, believed would be needed to help students understand what is wrong. They argued that a few written words made students believe they understood what might be wrong with their work when, in reality, they did not. In keeping with their commitment to students' personal progress and stage of development during the course, these three teachers tailored their comments carefully.

In contrast, lack of time for face-to-face feedback for tutors without a pastoral role made written comments necessary:

> I break each task down and if they haven't managed to achieve something under the evidence criteria, I explain to them because often you don't get a chance to explain one on one with them and say 'you need to do this and that' and I try to make it as detailed as possible.
>
> (Caroline)

More direct feedback on weaknesses, particularly for under-achieving students, arose from a good relationship rather than an overt strategy for giving feedback. In another marking exercise, I commented on Jo's approach:

> K: You have put here [points to Jo's written comment on a student's work] 'you have only scraped through!!' and . . . you have quite a personal way of saying things. . . . Is that a deliberate style on your part?
>
> Jo: No, that's just me. It's not something I've been taught, or something I've learned, it's just the way I am. I normally start with positive and if there's anything negative to say, sandwich that between two positive comments . . . I'm very careful based on the relationship with the student, because some students do take it the wrong way.

Another parallel to students' views about the purposes of assessment was teachers' own reluctance to use self-assessment, other than students 'checking the bullets' before handing work in. None of the teachers saw peer assessment or self-assessment as appropriate or possible. Although time constraints were a barrier, teachers also worried that unconfident students would be exposed: 'In terms of reading each other's work, I think it's too much to ask of the students' (Danny, unit tutor).

> I don't encourage students to look at each other's final grades because I think it might be de-motivating for them . . . especially if they are close friends. I have a situation like that in my 1st year, two girls that hang round together, one is a distinction and the other is pushing a pass . . . I think in cases like that it's de-motivating.
>
> (Jo, unit tutor)

In addition to a view that students were unsure of peer judgements about their work, some teachers saw students' views about the teacher's assessment role as the barrier:

> They would probably think 'I haven't done very well on that one and I don't want someone else criticising it because he is just one of my peers'. I think they look upon the tutor as the main person who can give the best feedback and they don't want a critical analysis here from someone they see on the same level.
>
> (Barbara, unit and personal tutor)

Discussion in Chapter 6 of constraints on autonomy showed the power of old habits and learning dispositions from school, where 'showing yourself up' or being seen to aim too high was something to be avoided at all costs. Limits to peer assessment and self-assessment were therefore powerfully held views amongst teachers and students in the sample. In addition, resource constraints in the form of limited time to build the right group dynamics made some teachers avoid peer assessment. Neil saw lack of maturity and underlying divisions within groups as a problem:

> I have never done [peer assessment]. In the groups I am with, there is a lot of animosity between them, and I think for some kids, it would simply be an excuse to have a go at another kid and some would not be able to stand it.
>
> (Neil, unit tutor)

New forms of professionalism

National standards of grading

The questionnaire showed mixed views about the effects of the GNVQ assessment criteria on teachers' assessment practices. Although 59 per cent of respondents said that the criteria had 'made them a better marker',

48 per cent said they did not provide comments to extend students' thinking into new areas of interest. This suggests, tentatively, that 'better marking' may mean more consistent in line with the criteria. In addition, there are strong hints of negative or at least neutral effects of GNVQs assessment on marking since 23.5 per cent 'strongly disagreed' and 17 per cent 'disagreed' that the criteria had made them better markers. However, the caveats above about 'shadow cast effects' and the limited insights gained from attempts to explore ideas and views through questionnaires obviously apply here.

The college-based fieldwork suggests reasons why extra feedback comments on students' work became superfluous although it does not reveal what type of comments teachers might have given before they assessed students' work in GNVQs. Nevertheless, seven of the sample felt that GNVQs had made their marking instrumental and more boring than before. Importantly, those who had developed personal approaches to feedback felt obliged to adopt a tracking and checking approach. It is not therefore surprising that, in a context where assessment is already overwhelmingly synonymous with summative evidence and judgements, and where motivation, commitment and ability vary greatly within student groups, teachers did not see self and peer assessment as potentially diagnostic or formative. And, although, as research cited in Chapter 2 indicated, this is likely to have been a view they held already, to teachers in this study, the GNVQ model implied another summative burden on students. Teachers' actions to maintain or enhance their goals for students' progress were therefore heavily influenced by the GNVQ requirements and students' responses to them.

But the most significant factor influencing teachers' responses to GNVQ assessment and its impact on their goals for students seemed to be the effect of new moves by QCA and awarding bodies to secure 'national standards' of grading. In the light of political discussion about 'standards' it is significant that anxiety to meet national standards was virtually absent amongst the two teachers using the 1995 model who never referred to, let alone used the phrase 'national standards', during two years of fieldwork. In contrast, six teachers using the Capey pilot model showed high levels of anxiety about meeting these standards and used the phrase 'national standards' often. As the examples of marking assignments showed above, attending QCA's regional Standards' Moderation meetings made teachers extremely nervous. In addition, a tradition where one awarding body moderator visited a team each year to review work and discuss ways of improving the course was replaced in 1996 by the QCA's requirement that awarding bodies must administer a complex and intensive 'scrutiny' programme based on national moderation of assignments.

In the 1996 pilot model, teachers could no longer establish what grades meant within their teams, taking into account the particular needs of their students, and then negotiate these with a visiting moderator. Indeed, as Chapter 3 argued, a crucial political dimension to a bid for parity of esteem with A-levels was that GNVQs had to move away from this 'soft' approach. In a research project for the QCA, it was apparent that for teachers in general vocational courses, this cultural shift was extremely unsettling (see Ecclestone and Hall, 1999). Nevertheless, it is important to relate these new monitoring processes to other 'micro disciplinary' practices associated with performativity, discussed in Chapter 4 and messages from awarding bodies about getting the grading 'wrong' had powerful parallels in the effects of college inspections or the visits to college by awarding body officials. Teachers symbolised distance by referring to external officials as 'The Moderator' or 'The Inspectors', often parodying them by adopting an ominous tone.

In the 1996 pilot model, GNVQ teachers' grades were graded for national conformity by the awarding body. After one year of using the pilot specifications, Barbara's team received a 'D' (low) grade from the national moderation exercise for the set assignment. This had a profoundly negative effect on teachers' confidence to trust their judgements about students' work and they were concerned to 'get it right' for the next exercise. Later that year, familiarity with grading gained the team an 'A' for the consistency of their grades and, therefore, their 'parity' with grades in other centres, and confidence returned. In the final year of the study, another visit by the moderator gained a low grade and indignation was again extreme. By 2000, grading of teachers had become a familiar experience. The FEFC inspection regime graded each subject area in colleges as well as cross-college functions and processes, while awarding bodies graded 'key skills' provision across colleges. Each external procedure required teachers to learn the official procedures, and different grading scales, to ensure consistency. The notion of 'consistency' dominated how teachers saw the purpose of these exercises. In GNVQs, consistency had to apply within the team when the moderator came to call and also stand up to exposure in a wider professional community at regional moderation meetings. The GNVQ grading exercise had a profound effect, as Danny's stream of indignation shows:

> It is upsetting when it comes back from somewhere way up high that you are a 'D' and you have been marking like this for many years. Here I am, a 'D', I know these students better than anyone else, I have seen them produce the work, I have gone through exactly the same criteria as anyone else, I got the D33 and D32, I didn't need them to do this but I got them[1] and all of a sudden, I am a 'D'. If they think that, then why don't they take it [marking] out of our hands completely?

But despite scepticism, anger and disappointment, such procedures had a resolute official status. Teachers were told at regional moderation meetings that Distinction grades were equivalent to an 'A' in A-levels. There was therefore pressure to raise achievements overall whilst keeping Distinction grades to acceptable levels. As Barbara and I marked assignments, she recalled a way of gaining consistency from a recent moderation meeting:

> We all sat round a table and the facilitator knew nothing about Business and that was the idea, he didn't want to sway us one way or another and we had to thrash it out around the table and come out with a pass, merit or distinction which we found very difficult to do . . . we just couldn't, and then we all started on about who had got the first grade [from the awarding body] and one centre had got an 'A' and everyone was 'how did you get an "A"?' . . . and what [the course leader] had done was taken every bullet point and wrote it down and gave it to the students separately and that's how they'd done it . . . and we said 'that's not the general idea'. . . . I don't think he let the students see the assignment, he just gave it to them a task at a time.

By Year 2 of the study, her team adopted this approach for some assignments to get students through them. Slowly, 'the general idea' that Barbara referred to above, namely a tradition in vocational education of designing what Danny, Barbara and Gill all referred to as 'nice assignments' (real-life projects based directly on students' interests and incorporating a number of themes and skills) was being eroded. Instead, teachers either broke up the assignment scenario around the bullet points or, in one unit, asked students simply to collect evidence against the bullets. Some teachers learnt from Standards' Moderation meetings that they could not help the students, that they must merely let them collect the evidence. This then produced confusion over whether this instruction applied to the QCA externally-set assignments or to all coursework.

The performative logic of conforming to this summative auditing process was therefore reinforced heavily by instructions from awarding body verifiers. The process was effective in transmitting requirements to teachers:

> K: What struck me when I was reading and then marking the assignments is that if you were to track the PCs [teachers' short-hand for performance criteria] into this, it would take you hours.
>
> C: [emphatically] *Hours*, and this is what they expect you to do. When I have been to Standards' Moderation, they expect you to track it and through to P1 etc. . . . they were saying 'well, where, show me where P2 is, where is the sentence?'. So in fact a student could write a sentence for this and get it.

The transmission of rules for marking tightened up interpretation of what individual criteria meant for the set assignments. Standardising grades became fairly straightforward with increasingly high levels of conformity and consistency in approaches to assignments. During a formal internal moderation of a set assignment for Health and Social Care with teachers on separate occasions in both colleges, three teachers from College B and I discussed whether students had met the criterion '*identify primary, secondary and tertiary aspects of the existing campaign*'. There was remarkable consistency in both colleges in relation to students' approaches to the tasks, the content and teachers' interpretation of grade criteria. This led to some precise regulation:

> *Jane*:   Do you think just a small sentence like that is enough? Some of the girls have done beautiful presentations on that aspect, but some of them have just put a sentence and that's it.
>
> *Mary*:   'To identify' is just a list. The Standards' Moderation that I went to, a list is six objects.

Similarly, Caroline in the other college had picked up the official line that 'identify' meant a list. She also experienced the difficulty indicated above about how much detail to accept:

> Every little thing has to be assessed, but, saying that, someone could put a sentence for each one of these [bullet points] and get a 'D'.

In keeping with this positivist precision, teachers were also directed how to differentiate 'identify', 'explain' and 'describe': for example, 'explain' had to be in prose but was more in-depth than 'describe'. The 'bottomless pit of absolute precision where verbal distinctions proliferate without end' that Richard Winter notes in competence-based systems (Winter, 1992) is confirmed here. Pressures to ensure consistency were reinforced by students' perceptions discussed in the previous chapters, that 'extra' dimensions to assignments were 'irrelevant'. Discussion of teachers' responses here also explains students' views of bullets as separate 'tasks', their cumulative approach to meeting the criteria and their resentment if asked to go beyond 'the bullets'. Nevertheless, as marking shows, if students did not closely follow the criteria, teachers had to refer work back to fill gaps.

Teachers responded in different ways. One team was anxious to conform to national consistency but was concerned about the effect that this had on students. In our joint marking of a 'Finance' assignment, Gill and I discussed how GNVQs affect students' responses to assessment. In the question below, I try to explore her views of the idea of GNVQ designers, that defining outcomes and requiring 100 per cent coverage, would raise standards of achievement:

> G: Well if it had been [BTEC] this assignment would still not have achieved . . . but I think, had it been the old system, there would have been a possibility that Joanne would have put greater emphasis

on her written bit, knowing that her [mathematical] ratios were the problem. But it wouldn't have retrieved it.

K: So in one way you can say that the GNVQ is forcing her to do the ratios to pass.[2]

G: [emphatically] Forcing her to *fail* . . . she would have still had to add to the ratios but she would have been in a stronger position . . . they just know they have got to pass all of these [bullet points] and so they look at it and think 'oh, horror story'.

Teachers were caught between wanting to allow students to develop confidence and skills around valid, relevant assignments where achievement could build up over a whole course, and the demotivating impact of resubmitting atomised bits of assignments in order to pass. The competing pressures outlined here led all seven teachers in the sample using the Capey model to break assignments into easily assessable tasks.

Different 'assessment communities'

Discussion in Chapter 2 of how teachers and students internalise notions of quality implied in assessment criteria showed that both parties need to see themselves as members of a 'community of practice' which can negotiate openly what the criteria mean, using a range of formative and diagnostic assessments. It is possible to see GNVQ groups as communities of practice since they are cohesive and shape students' expectations about learning in particular ways over the two years of a GNVQ. In contrast, examples above of marking assignments show that teachers were caught between loyalties to different communities. Those who taught diverse groups at different levels engaged with numerous communities in terms of student groups, teams of colleagues and contacts with different awarding bodies. And, apart from course leaders and personal tutors, unit tutors saw GNVQ students sporadically and for a short time over a term. Importantly, as well as negotiating the specific norms and expectations of each student 'community of practice', teachers had to relate to a wider professional community created by the emphasis on 'national standards' of grading in GNVQs.

In contrast to the strong organisational allegiances in the policy-based case study, organisational perspectives emerged amongst teachers, not as strong positive or even negative commitment to the college, but from competing smaller-scale allegiances. There was therefore a strong sense that the teachers were navigating new and old roles between different organisational cultures. Pedagogic commitments were particularly strong amongst teachers who had internalised values and beliefs from their experience of teaching and assessing in BTEC and A-levels. In Neil and Caroline's case, allegiance was strongly to a subject discipline. But teachers also had commitments to groups of students, colleagues in a course team, particularly in their shared staff rooms, and to their awarding body.

External interventions in teachers' familiar communities of practice, such as inspection and awarding body procedures, therefore affected teachers' perceptions of their professionalism. Effects varied, depending on traditions that teachers were familiar with. For teachers moving from an A-level moderation culture, being scrutinised was not problematic in itself, but being directly accountable to students for the grades they gave them was extremely threatening. As both Neil and Madeline pointed out, giving students a poor grade could make relationships with them very difficult: 'you have to live with the students for a year'. In contrast, external monitoring gave some teachers professional status and the chance to influence these processes. Mary, for example, was involved in external groups, such as subject advisory groups in NCVQ/QCA. For teachers enthusiastic about GNVQ, being in a wider community was professionally motivating. Nevertheless, gaining support for the decisions this networking brought was not easy and less enthusiastic colleagues back at college felt regulated and scrutinised.

A further dimension to negotiating new roles within a closely monitored assessment system was the power exerted by the specifications themselves. Four teachers questioned the way that unit writers have decided on content. In particular, Chapter 5 highlighted the example of assumptions written into the Social Policy and Psychology units that practitioners and policy-makers apply psychological and sociological theories to policy and practice in care and welfare sectors. As responses to the assessment criteria shown above, teachers could not use this disagreement as a basis for discussion with students and therefore had no room for manoeuvre. Nor did they have any avenue for professional discussion with specification writers.

Shifting values

Upheaval and restructuring in both the fieldwork colleges had disrupted old patterns of pedagogic allegiance as well as intensifying work conditions. At the same time, political intervention in regulation had introduced new communities for teachers to navigate. All but one of the nine teachers experienced dissonance in reconciling their values and beliefs with GNVQ requirements. The extent to which this happened, and teachers' explanations of reasons for it, depended, in part, on their experience of other educational traditions before GNVQs, but also on their sense of status within the college and the particular stage their individual professional careers had reached.

As the previous two chapters showed, teachers responded differently to the pressures they experienced. Neil, Caroline, Barbara and Gill struggled to transform the specifications to fit particular beliefs. Caroline and Neil aimed for students to achieve subject-based notions of critical autonomy as well as a firm footing in their subjects, and hopefully, some intrinsic interest in them. Gill and Barbara adapted their once-broader pastoral approach to personal autonomy in order to get students through the qualification and were highly conscientious about meeting official requirements. As Barbara became more confident with the criteria, she found new ways in the second year of the study to be more creative in her interpretations of their scope. Teachers who saw themselves as having a future career in FE, like Jo and Mary, were positive and enthusiastic in their transmission of the requirements but also transacted proactively in order to maximise student achievement in line with the specifications. Danny and Madeline appeared to transmit and transact pragmatically rather than enthusiastically to 'get students through'. Despite variation in values, beliefs and responses to GNVQs, all teachers in the sample showed high levels of commitment to student achievement in precarious local contexts of competition for good jobs and uncertain progression to higher education.

Some teachers in the fieldwork experienced profound role dilemmas when their creativity and goals were deflected from teaching and building rapport with students towards devising new strategies to cope with assessment. Neil and Jim were less compliant and had not internalised an official rationale for changing their practices. In their case study of change in two FE colleges, Ainley and Bailey (1997) argue that college managers often label such teachers as 'marginal performers' since they reject managerial or political rationales for change. Both Neil and Jim saw themselves as 'battling' for educational values in a context of hard-edged managerialism, but both felt they were losing. With some bitterness, Neil abandoned some of his strongly held views about critical autonomy in the face of student resistance to work that was 'too hard' or which did not meet the demands of the assessment criteria. Whilst this example supports an argument that outcome-based assessment models close down 'the space for generating alternative views and practices' (Edwards and Usher, 1994: 11), the study shows that they contribute to this problem rather than create it. Participation in the study also led Neil to view the current climate in FE with increasing incredulity and dismay, but also enabled him to understand his dilemmas. Nevertheless, a year after the study ended, he had not resurrected his goals for critical autonomy and was working pragmatically to the Pass criteria. In contrast, the two teachers who were positive about GNVQs enjoyed finding solutions to dilemmas created by change and pursued improvements enthusiastically.

New, more remote forms of regulation for moderation and assessment in GNVQs were especially influential on teachers' beliefs about autonomy, motivation and formative assessment. This was more evident when teachers did not experience other assessment systems with different underpinning principles. Although initially upset by an unfamiliar harder-edged approach by awarding bodies to moderating GNVQ assessment grades, after two years of the study teachers came to see an in-built logic to more guidance and standardisation. Eventually, they found ways to 'play the system'. In similar ways to the students, teachers developed strategic responses, such as being 'watertight' in complying with set, externally moderated assignments whilst loosening up in the internal ones. To offset some responsibility for what was required, teachers told students 'it's what the moderator/QCA wants'. In turn, awarding body moderators told teachers to complain to the QCA about problems with set assignments.

All seven teachers using the Capey model worked closely to the demands of the bullets. The political aim for reliable grading, and the diverse pressures on teachers and students discussed so far, made reductionism to achieve consistency in interpreting exact meanings of each criterion an entirely logical professional response. Writing 'nice assignments' or pushing students to 'think differently' became risky strategies and all but one teacher became anxious if students had not met the criteria. In part, this anxiety arose from concern about the demotivating effects on students having to resubmit work to 'fill the gaps', but also from a desire to 'get the assessment right' in terms of meeting the criteria. In contrast, and despite being more complex in its specifications and guidance, the 1995 model did not have the same standardising effects and the two teachers using it did not talk about 'compliance'.

In a context of increased external regulation and minimal, fragmented contact time with students, teachers balanced the pressures of student expectations and achieving 'national standards' with the risk that students might fail (see also Boys, 2000). Chapter 6 highlighted an increasingly popular strategy in FE colleges to alleviate the risk of failing or low achieving students, with the example of Bridgeview college's new regular monitoring and formal reviews. These used 'learning managers' to push students and teachers to achieve higher grades based on value-added predictions from GCSE scores. Yet, as political debates showed in Chapter 3, such strategies raise profound tensions over achieving 'national standards', simultaneously raising achievement at Pass or Merit level whilst adhering to very precise interpretations of criteria that keep Distinction grades (or their A-level equivalent) to an 'acceptable' level. Competing notions of 'standards' suggest that two of them, namely a loose, even spurious, reliability of grades between centres and bureaucratic approaches to standardising teachers' interpretations of the criteria, exerted a powerful influence on teachers in this study. All of them tried to reconcile these tensions with their own beliefs and goals for vocational education.

The strictures imposed by GNVQs therefore have strong parallels in other micro-disciplinary practices, discussed in Chapter 4, such as inspection, funding and quality assurance. These play a powerful role in instigating new technical processes and, through these, affecting the normative dimensions of college cultures by prioritising practices and discourses associated with 'checking', 'tracking', 'auditing' and 'evidencing'. More broadly, FE teachers' understanding of formative assessment has not been developed, making it perhaps predictable that the micro-disciplinary practices operating through the assessment model would infiltrate or replace existing formative assessment practices. Teachers and students viewed assessment as 'meeting the requirements' and not about deepening their learning. Yet, this view is widespread in National Curriculum assessment and replicated in official guidance for GNVQs.

These traits form powerful barriers to the possibility that teachers and students might view assessment as formative. Instead, analysis of the fieldwork data suggests that activities associated with formative assessment became little more than a pre-emptive extension of summative checking, tracking and evidencing. In the study, further pressures to adopt such approaches came from students' responses to the assessment requirements. Although there was no overt rebellion, there were subtle accommodations to specific criteria, shown in marking assignments during the fieldwork where it was difficult to resist a view that students had 'hit (or missed) the bullets'. Since teachers wanted students to pass and were scrutinised for their own compliance with national standards, the logical response was to provide formative feedback that indicates gaps in coverage. It rapidly became futile to offer ideas to students for other improvements, or to challenge viewpoints within topics or subjects or to encourage more depth in future. An auditing approach to feedback was therefore safer and less trouble.

Official guidance did not offer an alternative to this approach. None of the sample had read Jessup's early advice about formative feedback (1994) or his more widely known justification for the aims of an outcome-based assessment model (Jessup, 1991). Nor was there evidence in the study that staff development materials and support from bodies such as the FEDA had permeated the teams in the fieldwork. The fate of official guidance paralleled experience in schools:

> Guidance from [examination board] simply made the forms and purposes of, and the distinctions between teacher assessment, formative assessment and summative assessment more unclear. Instead, many schools, tired of receiving more and more documentation, filed these support packs and remained oblivious to there being a distinct definition or purpose of formative assessment.
>
> (Teacher cited in Pryor and Torrance, 1999)

Further problems arose from erratic communication of aims to teachers and other mediators of policy, such as awarding body moderators and inspectors. Except for one teacher who was active in GNVQ networks, teachers gained their interpretations of official aims for GNVQ assessment procedures from colleagues (what Neil called the 'rumour machine'), the specifications, visits by awarding body officials and FEFC inspectors, and from colleagues' interpretations of decisions from moderation meetings.

In the final year of the study, erratic, multi-layered and belated dissemination of policy aims and injunctions was evident in communication during June 2000 of the new assessment system being introduced for Vocational A-levels in September. In Riverside college, the two teams in the study involved in the Capey pilot, which formed the basis of the new model, were not consulted about their experience and middle managers leading dissemination meetings did not even know that there had been a three-year pilot in the college!

Summary

In evaluating the effects of these pressures on professionalism amongst FE teachers, the multiple perspectives used for analysis in this book show that three perspectives dominated teachers' views about autonomy, motivation and formative assessment. In contrast to policy-makers' rational accounts of developments in GNVQs from a cool, more remote perspective, all but one teacher highlighted the technical *irrationality* of the imperatives of the assessment system. The powerful symbolism of the official language that permeated teachers' interview accounts and informal discussion, without prompting, and their high levels of indignation at the pace and remoteness of change, both in GNVQs and in their colleges, highlighted a profoundly irrational situation which they all struggled to rationalise. A strange combination of technical irrationality and the powerful technical rationality of compliance and standardisation led to normative dilemmas over the purposes of vocational education. In particular, seven of the nine teachers had to reconstruct their ideas about desirable forms of motivation and autonomy. And, even if they did not use the concept of 'formative assessment' to describe their assessment activities, the assessment model had a strong impact on their feedback and assessment decisions. This resulted in an unsettling dissonance for those teachers who criticised the GNVQ model and its effects.

Interpretations of motivation, autonomy and formative assessment are therefore dimensions of FE teachers' professionalism. In this book, it seems that, like traditions of 'progressivism', such dimensions are 'subject to shifting justifications in response to political, social and educational factors' (Bates *et al.*, 1998: 110). In addition to the broader effects of performativity and micro-disciplinary practices within college cultures and systems, the assessment specifications and responses to them by GNVQ students in a comfort zone, also had a powerful but subtle effect on how these justifications manifested themselves in teaching and assessment practices. So too did awarding body processes designed to secure the consistency of grades demanded by the QCA.

8   Risking motivation and autonomy in lifelong learning

Introduction

There is now a widespread consensus that 'achievement' can be measured through attainment of qualifications, thereby motivating people for lifelong learning and preparing them for an increasingly competitive and temporary employment market. Yet, ideas about what count as realistic and desirable forms of autonomy, motivation and formative assessment are being reconstructed in the FE vocational curriculum. A case study of the Advanced GNVQ assessment model shows how diverse ideological, epistemological, political and professional pressures subverted the aims of its supporters. Theoretical and empirical explorations focused in this book on a 'policy trajectory' covering five levels: ideological constructions of risk in lifelong learning; theoretical constructions of motivation; autonomy and formative assessment; the aims and design of assessment policy; implementation of policy at institutional and individual levels. The ensuing analysis aimed to account for the ways in which a policy initiative evolves, changes and is interpreted over time. Capturing the interplay between factors operating at different levels avoids the danger of policy analysts, policy-makers and those on the receiving end of policy blaming a policy initiative, or teachers, for problems with students' autonomy and motivation. Conversely, it avoids portraying a policy initiative as having no effect on teachers and students at all.

'Risk' and 'risk aversion' have emerged as subtle but powerful themes in the book. The book shows that policy-makers came to see the radical aims of the GNVQ designers in the first assessment model as putting the public credibility of standards at risk. In addition, policy slippage in the remit given to NCVQ led the DfEE to gain control over the vocational curriculum, using an increasingly regulated GNVQ assessment regime as a way of ensuring consistency in national standards of attainment. In colleges, teachers worried about students' future prospects alongside meeting political demands for national standards while some students mistrusted teachers' uses of the assessment specifications and challenged their assessment practices. 'Performativity' encouraged summative tracking and checking so that any constructivist ideas of learning and transaction over content or process that might have been possible were almost entirely target driven. As a result, there was very little scope or space for personally meaningful targets other than those the students identified privately as important to them. Students did manage to carve ipsative goals out of the assignments and opportunities for non-formal learning. Nevertheless, the official targets led personal autonomy to become synonymous with procedural autonomy. And, in turn, any procedural autonomy evident in the study can be regarded as little more than performativity.

This chapter aims to draw out the final implications of arguments and analysis in the book so far. Since the sample is small and confined to one qualification, conclusions are written with a view to testing them with a wider audience of policy-makers, researchers and practitioners, as well as with mediators of policy such as awarding body officials and inspectors. The first section discusses the idea that the interplay of policy and implementation created an 'assessment regime' which, in turn, shaped students' 'assessment careers'. The second section explores the prognosis for academic researchers and other external constituencies interested in assessment policy being able to influence policy design and debate. The third section discusses strategies for improving formative assessment in FE colleges. Finally, the fourth section evaluates some implications of arguments in the book for the role of post-compulsory education in preparing young people for a life of creative and threatening risk.

Creating 'assessment regimes' and 'assessment careers'

It is possible to argue that policy-making in GNVQs, and the ways in which teachers, awarding body officials and students in colleges interpreted policy, created an 'assessment regime'. This notion draws on Foucault's concept of a 'regime of truth' applied to the outcome-based assessment system of NVQs by Richard Edwards and Robin Usher (1994). In NVQs, the emotive appeal to workplace 'competence', particularly for learners desperate to progress within, or to enter, the labour market, produces assessment practices, discourses and ideology that promise empowerment and work iteratively to control those who use and promote this form of assessment. Liberal humanism is inextricably bound up in such systems (ibid). In a similar vein, genuine concerns to offer something meaningful and high status to non-traditional learners underpinned a form of 'liberal vocationalism' as an ideological stance held by many of those who supported the aims of GNVQ inside policy processes and in colleges. At the same time, processes for developing what Ball calls 'policy texts' (Ball, 1994) set up new political mechanisms for specifying and regulating the detailed content of learning outcomes and assessment criteria. Political disputes over the assessment requirements of GNVQs created new processes through which policy-makers regulated the content of assessment specifications and the quality assurance and quality control processes that moderated and standardised assessment decisions.

Despite stronger regulation and attempts to secure understanding amongst teachers by loading more guidance into the specifications of the 1995 model, the regime that emerged in each of the three models between 1993 and 2000 was both complex and contradictory. Nevertheless, erratic communication, repeated change and multi-layered interpretation of policy aims did not prevent the GNVQ assessment regime encouraging a subtle, self-regulating acceptance of its purposes, practices and effects by all involved. As this chapter has argued, this happens in conjunction with other pressures to shape expectations, activities through 'the norms and net-works of (largely implicit) expectations and agreements that are evolved between teachers and students' (Black and Wiliam, 1998a: 56). Yet, it can be argued that all assessment systems, to a greater and lesser extent, create contracts that legitimate particular assessment practices. For example, if teachers' classroom questioning and assignment feedback has been limited to 'lower order' skills, such as adherence to correct procedures, students may well see questions about 'understanding' or 'application' as unfair, illegitimate or even meaningless (ibid.). This makes it important to explore the general and specific constructions and effects of different models in order to evaluate how the regime works in practice.

In GNVQs, the interplay between the assessment regime, practices and discourses within the college, and the comfort zone discussed above, formed what Hodkinson *et al.* (1996) drawing on Bourdieu, portray as 'horizons for action': young people and other individuals involved in their educational experiences operate within these. In the book, horizons for action produced embedded compliance and risk aversion from teachers and students alike as a *'pragmatically rational'* response to the conflicting pressures they were under, a notion drawn from Hodkinson *et al.*'s study of career-related decision-making (ibid.). Students' and teachers' discourses, responses and assessment practices in the book emerged from, and created, a community of practice implementing the assessment regime. The notion of 'culture' as the 'socially constructed and historically derived common base of knowledge, values and norms for action that people grow into and come to take as a natural way of life' (Hodkinson *et al.*, 1996: 148) is there-fore useful. The specific technical language of any assessment regime and its requirements, operating within the particular dynamics of learning groups within educational institutions form micro-cultures that legitimate certain knowledge, values and norms in learning and assessment activities.

Following this argument, it is possible to see the subsequent interplay of discourse, culture and practices and norms offered by, and shaped within, the GNVQ assessment regime as contributing to students' 'assessment careers'. The book has shown how engagement within any 'assessment community' occurs within largely tacit boundaries formed by expectations of students' ability, motivation, dispositions to learning and their prospects for progression into jobs or more education. Following Bloomer (1997, 2001) and Hodkinson *et al.* (1996), the two years of a GNVQ course created particular individual and group-based 'turning points', 'transformations' and 'horizons for action'. Young people also form, and experience, their own transformations and horizons. The notion of an 'assessment career' may therefore account for the socialising effects of an assessment regime in shaping learners' identities within a learning programme. It also enables researchers, qualification designers and teachers to relate learners' emerging identities and responses to other factors discussed in this book.

This idea draws on Bloomer's depiction of post-16 students' 'learning careers' (1997) where opportunities for types of motivation and autonomy are affected by the impact of schooling and life experiences on learners' identity, and social and individual commitments to learning. More specifically, it relates to Pollard and Filer's analysis of the formation of 'pupil careers' in primary schools where:

> 'pupil career' can be seen as a particular social product deriving from children's strategic action in school contexts [and] strongly influenced by cultural expectation.
>
> (Pollard and Filer, 1999: 22)

There is growing evidence that National Curriculum assessment exerts an extremely powerful influence on children's expectations about the purposes and formats of formative assessment such as feedback on their work, peer assessment and self-assessment and classroom questioning (see, for example, Reay and Wiliam, 1999; Torrance and Pryor, 1998). Also resonating with the picture of compliance and comfort built up in this study, Broadfoot and Pollard (2000) suggest that National Curriculum assessment increasingly encourages children to avoid challenge and to be intolerant of risk and ambiguity. Analysis in this study therefore suggests that GNVQ assessment continued to shape young people's perceptions of their own and their peers' identity, and, as a consequence, also shaped their views about desirable or acceptable involvement in formative assessment activities. This socialisation has implications for the ways in which students move between qualification pathways, especially when research already shows the instrumental impact of credentialism on post-16 students' choice of options for September 2000 (Spours and Hodgson, 2000). Further research could relate the typology developed in this book to a theory of 'assessment career', deriving from an exploration of Bourdieu's notion of 'habitus' and identity in different subject and qualification tracks and at different levels (Ecclestone and Pryor, 2001).

In the light of discussion of risk aversion and low expectations in Chapter 1, a useful dimension would be to incorporate these themes in autonomy and motivation through the type of structural analysis within local 'lived' education and job markets carried out by Ball *et al.*, 2000).

This could explore the effects of lifestyle in different regions and localities on young people's attitudes to learning programmes and assessment regimes. However, in a context of growing state incursion into moral and personal life in the name of 'risk aversion', noted also in Chapter 1, such research would raise new dilemmas about incursion into the increasingly blurred space between public and private spheres.

Finally, in considering the effects of assessment regimes and assessment careers on teachers' ideas about what being a good professional FE teacher means, it is important to recognise the impact on these ideas of new forms of political intervention and regulation. The previous chapter showed that teachers were navigating new communities of practice. Without strong organisational allegiances to a college or to a coherent curriculum tradition, they seemed to be caught between the direct influence of awarding bodies and inspectors as intermediaries of government policy and the norms and expectations of students' assessment and learning careers. This suggests that images and values within FE teachers' notions of professionalism are being squeezed in subtle ways by these influences.

Influencing assessment policy

Although some external constituencies working in policy development and implementation of the GNVQ assessment regime, represented in this book, were ardent supporters of the aims of GNVQs, they had great difficulty influencing policy developments. Categories to analyse different normative or ideological perspectives on education reform amongst policy-makers and teachers (see Ball, 1990; Hickox and Moore, 1995) help to show divisions over appropriate forms of assessment in the post-16 curriculum. An academic tradition, deriving from 'cultural restorationist' ideas about norm-referenced 'standards' rooted in subject knowledge, was represented by civil servants in the ex-DES and DfE, ministers, ex-SCAA officials and OFSTED inspectors. These constituencies were much more influential inside policy than the 'vocational modernisers' and 'liberal humanists' represented by civil servants in the ex-ED, officials in NCVQ, FEU and the awarding bodies, and the FEFC inspectorate. This 'side' of policy developments emphasised personal development and motivation rooted in a vocationally relevant, target-driven curriculum.

One interpretation of analysis in Chapter 3 and evaluation here is that conflicts between ideology and organisational interests have enabled the education side of the DfEE to gain extensive control of content, assessment models and quality assurance in the post-16 curriculum. This claim is supported by evaluation of developments in NVQs (Raggatt and Williams, 1999). An important dimension, shown in Chapter 3, is that instead of relying on technical experts as they had in the past, civil servants had to acquire new levels of detail in their assessment expertise that they had not hitherto needed. Researchers and other constituencies hoping to influence policy therefore need similarly extensive technical and conceptual knowledge about different assessment systems, insights into technically and politically fraught characteristics like reliability and validity, and appreciation of the impact of assessment on learning. Arguably, they also need to be realistic about what is politically and financially possible and to recognise that these dimensions to assessment policy are rarely played out explicitly (see, for example, West, 2000). In particular, awarding bodies have a key role in developing an authority and expertise in assessment issues that can contribute to a more robust push for involving other partners in policy-making. This requires a commitment to social partnership models of policy and curriculum design.

Yet, rather than arguing for better ways to identify legitimate experts and partners in these processes, interviewees from external constituencies believed that better control by the DfE (and then the DfEE), would have prevented NCVQ from running away with a larger remit than it was given or was capable of delivering. Analysis in this book suggests, instead, that external constituencies need robust insights into assessment issues, their associated technology and policy processes. Without this, it is difficult for these constituencies to contribute their expertise effectively and prevent central control from becoming hegemonic. This is especially important if QCA moves beyond the destructive turf wars seen in GNVQs by adopting high levels of central control in the name of 'consensus'.

Despite the need to understand and influence policy-making, it remains difficult for researchers and other constituencies to delve into the messy obscurity of policy processes for the vocational curriculum. In contrast to numerous policy studies of the National Curriculum, analysis in this book highlights the relative invisibility of individuals and constituencies in GNVQ debates, both inside policy processes and externally. This makes it important for researchers and other interested groups to understand more about the diverse constituencies and individuals that influence policy for vocational education and post-16 assessment policy as a whole. They also need insights into the organisational and normative perspectives swirling around debates in assessment and learning, alongside some acculturation into unfamiliar policy processes and alien organisational cultures whilst maintaining a critical distance. As Alison Wolf argues, opportunities for academics to work directly inside policy illuminate the peculiar pressures that policy-makers work under (see Ecclestone, 1999). It is also useful to know more about the 'epistemic communities' of expertise and knowledge that policy-makers draw on for their authority and credibility (see Hulme, 1998). Mapping policy initiatives and identifying the unofficial and official networks they create and use is, in itself, a useful exercise for researchers. As the post-16 education and training sector experiences yet another major restructuring under the national and local Learning and Skills Councils, understanding this policy and networks in this complex yet invisible sector becomes, yet again, more important.

Some practical issues arising from the fieldwork for this book may also be relevant for others who might want to research policy or become more involved with its complex processes and networks. For example, timing and focus were both crucial for gaining access to interviewees. The 'GNVQ story' had not been told from the perspective of its assessment policy and access took place at a pivotal moment of political and organisational upheaval, two months after the merger of SCAA and the NCVQ to form QCA in November 1997. Many NCVQ officials who had focused exclusively on GNVQs were moving into National Curriculum assessment policy and other research projects and NCVQ's unique organisational culture was dissolving into structures influenced strongly by assessment in the National Curriculum and by a SCAA-culture (see also Raggatt and Williams, 1999). All but two of the interviewees were at turning points in their careers and may have been less interested in an academic evaluation of policy once GNVQs had become well established in the QCA and key actors had moved on.

Research at moments of political transition and focusing on a controversial initiative means that researchers need to be aware constantly of different actors' diverse motives for taking part (Ball, 1994). These include records to set straight, scores to settle, reputations to defend, perhaps a career to rationalise, especially if someone was displaced or moved on, as well as contributions to be made public. Interviewees' and a researchers' motives are partly known to them, and partly tacit. Similarly, as Ball also points out, a researcher's own motives are partly known but partly tacit, requiring reflexive scrutiny during fieldwork and analysis (Ball, 1994). In particular, different constituencies or individuals might be defined as 'the powerful', on the grounds that they have considerable constitutional, legal and cultural resources that enable them to deflect or channel any research in which they are the object of enquiry (Walford, 1994; Halpin and Troyna, 1994). And, although attempting to place 'what might otherwise seem unconnected events in context, over time in relation to other policy initiatives is a proper task for researchers', policy analysts risk over-rationalising policy and presenting those involved as more dynamic and competent than might be the case (Edwards, 1993).

Such problems can lead to what Ball calls 'simple realism' (Ball, 1994) which presents rational, *post-hoc* justifications of policy both descriptively and unproblematically and reduces analysis to a series of individual decisions and key events. Research which relies on accounts rationalised long after the event therefore runs the risk of reinforcing individual and collective versions of 'espoused theories' (Arygris and Schon, 1974) which may, in turn, arise from collective organisational myths, and 'retrospective exculpations' to save careers or reputations. The simple realism Ball warns against is a particular trap in using illustrative quotes from the data. Nevertheless, limitations in policy accounts can be dealt with reflexively and by documenting particular contexts and organisational rules that govern what interviewees say, while multiple perspectives can enrich analysis and inject necessary scepticism.

It is also important to avoid the trap of 'policy science' where logistical issues dominate, alongside the distraction for researchers of 'policy busyness' (Whitty and Edwards, 1994). This was a particular problem in GNVQs where the sheer complexity of developments and their technical characteristics are not for the faint-hearted and where merely describing them can overwhelm analysis. In addition, the low status of vocational education policy and its relative invisibility to researchers meant that a snowballing approach to sampling had to unearth key individuals, build up a chronology of events and constituencies involved and facilitate access to those with high political or organisational status. Some interviewees agreed to take part once they knew someone else had either said they were 'essential' to the account or had been interviewed themselves. No one refused access and only two (civil servants) put explicit on/off the record boundaries on certain comments, allowing organisational, personal and normative perspectives to emerge.

Last, the case study shows the need to guard against a tendency for researchers critical of the effects of education policy to pathologise policy-makers and their intermediaries as 'powerful', instrumental or cynical and dominated by 'new Right' ideology. Despite arguments that GNVQ policy emanated from pervasive neo-liberal notions of market and consumer choice (for example, Bloomer, 1998; Hodkinson, 1998d), attributions of 'new Right' ideology did not apply to the complex, and passionately presented, educational beliefs held by most of the policy-makers in this book. Nor did attributes of 'powerful' or 'elite', commonly applied in the research literature to policy-makers, apply to all interviewees. Instead, normative themes in the data confirm analyses by Hickox and Moore (1995), Moore and Hickox (1999) of the contradictory and unstable ideologies that continue to permeate the vocational curriculum. It was important to recognise differential power and status and, surprisingly, to acknowledge that researchers do not merely trade in the 'broken dreams of practitioners' (Ball, 1997) as highlighted in the introduction. There were broken dreams of policy-makers to acknowledge in the GNVQ policy story too.

Improving formative assessment in FE colleges

Any suggestions for improving formative assessment have to take account of structural barriers to students' motivation and engagement with learning, and problems at political levels of debate and activity in the post-16 vocational curriculum. Nevertheless, there are strategies at the levels of epistemology and professional practice that might be pragmatically possible. These involve developing less prescriptive assessment regimes, considering the epistemology of learning embedded within them and promoting effective professional development in using formative assessment as part of a strategic approach to developing autonomy and motivation. Such strategies are discussed here.

Some theoretical and practical barriers to using formative assessment to enhance motivation and autonomy, highlighted in the book, were undoubtedly a direct result of the GNVQ assessment regime. There is therefore a clear need to rethink how formative assessment is presented officially to teachers and other mediators of policy, such as awarding body officials, inspectors and those supporting professional development such as the Learning and Skills Development Agency, colleges and universities. It is possible, for example, to include discussion of theories of learning and their implications for formative assessment in official guidance provided to teachers, inspectors, students and other bodies involved in developing and evaluating assessment regimes. Such discussion would need to explore the connections between autonomy, motivation and formative assessment and to highlight some of the tensions between constructivist and behaviourist approaches discussed in Chapter 2.

Dissemination through 'policy texts' (Ball, op. cit.) was woefully inadequate in GNVQs, making transformation rather than mere dissemination essential. In part, initial teacher education and professional development programmes can contribute to this but other strategies are also needed. Specific attention to disparate, erratic forms of autonomy embedded within assessment specifications and to different types of autonomy obscured by identical formats and vocabulary is another realistic improvement to presenting the assessment regimes in Vocational A-levels and GSCEs, and indeed, in their general education counterparts. More broadly, policy-makers and other agencies involved in implementing and evaluating assessment regimes need to commission and use more robust research evidence about how different assessment regimes encourage or discourage particular forms of autonomy and motivation. This proposal has implications for the role of inspection and curriculum development agencies as key mediators of the disjuncture between seeming to raise achievement and encouraging low risk, low level forms of learning and achievement.

Other factors lie outside the direct influence of any assessment regime. There is, for example, likely to be variation in the extent to which teachers themselves have experienced constructivist models of learning and personal and critical autonomy. There is also lack of professional awareness about the different purposes of assessment which is not addressed explicitly by FE teacher education programmes or by continuing professional development in FE colleges. Both forms of support have been seriously under-resourced and under-theorised, although new possibilities arise from the DfEE's current investment in professional development for FE teachers and managers. There is also scope within colleges to develop an institutional assessment policy, with specific emphasis on developing students' autonomy and motivation through more effective formative assessment. In addition, senior and curriculum managers can consider how to invest in staff development to help teachers develop their assessment skills. They might also evaluate whether putting too much emphasis on raising levels of achievement, measured solely by higher grades, discourages students' intrinsic motivation and critical autonomy.

Course teams could consider how students might progress more coherently and strategically from procedural autonomy to personal and critical autonomy during a course and to discuss the attributes that individual teachers believe to be necessary for personal and critical autonomy. This consideration would include the possibility that critical autonomy might not be desirable, necessary or possible in every unit of a course. Additional strategies could build the social motivation and commitment that were so important to students in this book and teachers could discuss their expectations of autonomy and different types of motivation with students at set points during a course. This might enable them to exploit the potential amongst students for intrinsic, interested and social forms of motivation and discourage an over-emphasis on introjected and identified goals that arise from 'getting through the course' and setting instrumental targets. It also means actively discouraging students from equating 'autonomy' with solitary work and not asking for help. Enabling less confident students to see how higher achieving students manage their learning through mentoring and peer review are obvious practical strategies for this. Last, a pedagogy for managing non-formal and informal learning, rather than leaving it to the mercy of students' norms and expectations, is also desirable. However, this would need to preserve the spontaneous and private aspects of such learning: the work of Michael Eraut and colleagues (Eraut *et al.*, op. cit.) on informal and non-formal learning may provide important pointers.

Better techniques are therefore important. But so too is a more robust understanding of political and epistemological barriers to using formative assessment effectively. Without this, simplistic and implicit theories of learning continue to be bound up in the rhetoric that surrounds assessment policy. This suggests that researchers need both to mediate both political and academic theorising and engage FE teachers and managers, and those involved in teacher training and professional development, with its implications. Just as policy texts are ineffective in changing practice, it is not enough merely to offer research evidence to all the diverse constituencies represented in this book. Instead, researchers need to find new ways to engage practitioners more deeply with issues raised by research. With support and resources, the book suggests that some aspects of formative assessment are within teachers' power to improve. Yet, low morale and intensification of work in FE colleges can tempt researchers and teachers themselves to see policy and its effects as the main cause of problems and themselves as powerless to influence policy. Suggesting improvements might be dismissed as merely another symptom of long-running political and media derision of teachers or as a tendency for university researchers to '*patronise*' FE practitioners (Ainley and Bailey, 1997: 1). Indeed, in a climate where policy-makers criticise college teachers for not achieving goals for lifelong learning (Coffield, 1999c), researchers' suggestions for improving assessment practice could well be dismissed by teachers as a 'theory too far'.

Despite barriers, current political emphasis on 'raising achievement' does open a space to renew debate about the quality of achievement and teaching, learning and assessment and the necessary professional development to support it. The book has also shown that, instead of generalised discussion about formative assessment, teachers responded positively to requests to reflect on specific learning or assessment 'episodes' or problems and on students' progress. This suggests the potential of problem-based action research to encourage reflection and changes to formative assessment (see Pryor and Torrance, 1999; Swann and Ecclestone, 1999; Swann and Arthurs, 1999 for discussion).

The final barrier to teachers' understanding of formative assessment arises from forms of quality assurance to regulate grading decisions that exerted such a powerful influence on teachers' beliefs and practices in this book. Change to regulation reflects pressures arising from an intensification of national and local requirements for summative recording, accountability and certification. In addition, the book has shown how attempts by the QCA to standardise assessment decisions became a political imperative in order to create a populist image of norm-referenced standards. In part, regulation raises issues about government control and lack of trust of teachers in an assessment system devolved largely to teachers (see also Wilmut, 1999). It also suggests that government agencies intend, probably implicitly, that burgeoning guidance and regulation will compensate for poor staff development and an absence of regular discussion of criteria and requirements amongst teachers, students and awarding bodies. Without such processes, it is difficult to gain professional commitment to securing 'standards' as opposed to cynical compliance with procedures to standardize decisions. Although it is an unlikely prospect, government agencies, awarding bodies and inspection agencies need to open up the fraught political and epistemological debate about 'standards' and the effects of different meanings on learning and on the forms of assessment that support it.

Preparing young people for a risky life

Safe and low risk assessment strategies became rational responses amongst teachers and students in this book, enabling them to reconcile diverse expectations and pressures arising from structural, political, epistemological, professional and institutional factors. Although the motivation and autonomy that students developed during their course had both positive and negative aspects, the strongest impression is of comfort and compliance. The study therefore raises some profoundly difficult political and professional questions about the nature of post-16 students' achievement and educational aspirations over what is likely to be a long life of increasingly formalised learning and assessment.

Arguments in the third section highlighted the importance of being more strategic and precise about where, how and why different types of autonomy and motivation are developed. It is not obvious, for example, that intrinsic motivation and critical autonomy in formal education are necessary at every level of study and in all units of a qualification. Instead, procedural autonomy or the most instrumental forms of introjected motivation might sometimes be sufficient, depending on stages and types of curricula. If so, it is not helpful to portray intrinsic motivation and critical autonomy as automatically and always a 'good thing' or the absence of 'emancipatory' knowledge in courses like GNVQs as a self-evident shortcoming (for example, Bloomer, 1998; Helsby *et al.*, 1998). Evidence from this book supports an argument that, if and when it occurs, critical autonomy is rooted firmly within specific, often quite precise, vocational contexts and subjects. Teachers had variable understanding of and commitment to critical autonomy and broad forms of personal autonomy, even within their own subject. They also appeared to see some students as ready and able to deal with critical autonomy and others as not. This too may be a more realistic caveat than blanket calls for it. Personal and critical autonomy were also side-tracked by concerns amongst students and teachers to maximise *ad hoc*, often implicit, goals for ipsative progress whilst meeting the formal requirements. Further pressures arose from credentialism, concerns about students' future goals, their immediate personal and social preoccupations and from resource pressures and the demands of the assessment regime.

Such complex pressures mean that old liberal humanist and Leftist ideas about intrinsic motivation or self-actualisation, and personal and critical autonomy as goals for all educational undertakings cannot simply be resurrected at this point. Nor can they be 'bolted on' to curricula and still be meaningful to students and teachers. Unless qualification designers, teachers and students see personal and critical autonomy, intrinsic and interested motivation, as genuinely relevant, calls to promote them will be regarded merely as irrelevant, vacuous academic drift, tacked on to narrow vocational curricula in order to appease their promoters. And, as Ann-Marie Bathmaker observes in her study of GNVQ, such calls can lead academic researchers to all-too-readily see teachers as the instrumental implementers or 'dupes' of impoverished government policy (Bathmaker, in progress). These arguments raise further difficult questions about the role of young people themselves in deciding what is 'critical' and 'relevant' in the post-16

curriculum and how far external constituencies and teachers themselves
should impose their own views of these attributes (see also Fielding, 1998;
White, 1997 for discussion). In addition, developing the radical and emancipatory forms of autonomy that are implicit in many academic calls for
critical intelligence requires teachers to have experienced it themselves in
their own learning. A context of upheaval and lack of staff development
makes it extremely unlikely that this happens in relation to considering
professional roles and responsibilities, let alone to debating broader values
about education.

At the same time, the end of visionary aspirations inside the QCA for the
vocational curriculum, together with uncertainty over which constituencies
have a legitimate role in designing qualifications, create further barriers to
involving teachers in developing a vocational curriculum that can foster
different types of autonomy and motivation. Leaving this to *ad hoc* invita-
tions for individuals, which sometimes included teachers, to help write
specifications for individual units within qualifications, shown in Chapter 3,
is not good enough. It is therefore difficult to make design and consultation
processes for determining content and assessment strategies in the post-16
vocational curriculum more coherent.

Calling for renewed debate and then citing numerous barriers to
achieving it is a depressingly familiar academic trait! Yet, the importance
of developing new ideas about what constitute desirable knowledge and
skills in post-compulsory education is all too apparent (see, for example,
Ainley, 1999; Bloomer, 1997). In spite of reservations, new spaces may
emerge over debates about what constitutes 'achievement' and over what
forms of autonomy and motivation might appear in a citizenship curriculum. Chapter 4 showed that such a space has not been evident in further
education for a long time. Perhaps a new focus from the two post-16 inspectorates on teaching, learning and achievement opens the first space.

Despite the enormity of the tasks highlighted here, the process of raising
questions about good assessment practice and factors hindering its development in FE colleges is merely the beginning of a long process of change.
Analysis offered in this book confirms the need to be more precise, and
then more strategic, about what types of autonomy can and should be fostered in different curricula at different levels. The typology developed and
tested in the study might provide a basis for evaluating how far any assessment system can develop different types of autonomy and motivation
within specific structural and institutional contexts. The book also offers
new insights about whether behaviourist and constructivist models of
assessment can be reconciled and suggests, tentatively, that the typology
might provide a basis for doing so.

Unsurprisingly, broader issues remain. A study of the GNVQ assessment regime has taken place when new political targets are being set for
higher rates of achievement in qualifications. Targets appear to signify

high expectations but arguments here suggest that these expectations are mainly technical ones based on instrumental formative assessment activities that ratchet up students' grades in formal programmes. If formative assessment becomes a mere technology, it will conceal increasingly low expectations about the *purposes* of learning or expected engagement with it and the very real danger that motivation, autonomy, formative assessment become empty dispositions and technical processes.

Instead of a post-compulsory system that aspires to foster voluntarism and intrinsic motivation, together with social and professional commitments to these attributes, subtle and self-regulating forms of compulsion and compliance could increasingly appear. Indeed, as concerns mount about the effects of non-participation in formal or purposeful education, noted in Chapter 1, increasingly judgemental views about appropriate behaviour for young people are emerging with new concerns and risks. The effects of paid work on their prospects for getting good grades, their reasons for leaving courses and not gaining good grades are just three examples of such concerns.

This suggests that performativity accompanied by a subtle ideology of 'risk' and 'risk aversion' not only produces a 'minimalist pedagogy' based on low expectations of learners' potential for intrinsic motivation or critical autonomy, amongst policy-makers and their intermediaries, institutional managers and teachers, and students themselves. Low expectations, combined with the micro-disciplinary practices associated with assessment and quality assurance regimes, lead to increased safety and compliance in learning activities. More subtly still, such trends begin to redefine what we see as a 'good life' for young people, reducing their horizons to those we have traditionally associated with children at school. In the absence of vision for the post-compulsory curriculum, fears that too many students will fail or leave with no qualifications leads to the safety of meeting targets rather than worrying about whether learning is useful and meaningful.

New notions of educational risk are therefore evident. Nevertheless, a regulated, low-trust, low risk version of autonomy is not overt, or deliberate since students, teachers, curriculum designers, policy intermediaries and researchers are not immune from new risks. It would also be an unintended effect if arguments here implied that the tension between concerns about the moralising and controlling effects of risk consciousness, and the very real risks of exclusion, unemployment and low skills, for many people is not a profoundly difficult one to resolve. In addition, students in this book needed and enjoyed a safe haven during their course and they achieved a qualification that they valued. Dangers of a critical researcher creating yet another moral highground are all too apparent in this chapter! Yet, without scrutiny of the tensions highlighted here, systems of learning, assessment and evaluation based on technical rationality shape social, professional and individual norms in new ways until, as Habermas observed, these become 'rational'. In education policy and practice, overt and implicit definitions of 'risk' require new responses that are increasingly codified and then regulated. In assessment and quality assurance systems, new layers of expertise then emerge to ensure that teachers and students use them properly. Not only do these produce increasingly formalised learning and assessment but also a circular logic of prescription, clarification and regulation that slowly confines space for innovation and creative risk.

One implication of arguments here is the need for a new dissenting perspective to those that currently characterise responses to policy for lifelong assessment. As I argued above, merely calling for more critical autonomy within the post-16 curriculum has an increasingly vacuous ring to it. Nor do such calls address the way that an increasingly incursive morality discussed in Chapter 1 may make more educators believe that people's lack of motivation affects the fate of others or that certain forms of learning and autonomy are 'irresponsible' or just too risky. Once risk comes to be seen as any transgressional behaviour, those who do not participate or achieve could come to be seen as deviant 'Others' and this changes educators' attitudes to them (see, for example, Bullen *et al.*, 2000; Colley, 2000). Risk aversion in a context of low expectations also implies that a tradition in adult education of 'starting where learners are' and using their desire to learn alongside 'people like them' also affects perceptions about desirable social capital. Instead of being a starting point for creative risk, such goals transmogrify all too easily into safety and security, both in pedagogy and aims for education. And once this takes hold, the old liberal mantra of 'starting where learners are' ends up leaving them there.

More insidiously, perceptions that almost any risk becomes a threat elide diverse educational and social problems. For example, illiteracy and functional illiteracy and poor achievement of formal qualifications are presented increasingly frequently as responsible for a litany of deep-seated social and personal problems. From this perspective, refusal amongst individuals and communities to address educational problems becomes something akin to a moral panic, eroding faith in human agency and voluntarism.

A concluding comment from Michael, one of the high achieving students in this book, illustrates the need to cut an academic, political and pedagogic path through the minefield of risk aversion that increasingly accompanies assessment regimes. Instead of offering an ultimately stultifying comfort zone, assessment regimes need to prepare students for a life of creative and threatening risk, and uncertainty. In his first term at university, Michael recognised both the risk and opportunity presented by having to wean himself off the security of the GNVQ criteria in a situation with much looser boundaries:

> M: [not having criteria] improves your autonomy. You have to decide what you want to put in and what you want to aim for, rather than doing this criteria and that.

KE: Even if they offered [detailed criteria] to you, would you feel reassured by that so when you came to university on day one, there it all was?

M: Yes, but that would be the easy way out . . . when you go out into the big bad world, there is no criteria is there? There is no set way to work so I think it's a way of encouraging you.

Appendices

Appendix 1 Policy-makers' sample

Coding for designation in Chapter 3 is highlighted in bold

the five NCVQ officials who set up GNVQs (**NCVQ officials**)

the two lead subject officers for Business and Health and Social Care in the NCVQ (**NCVQ officials**)

two NCVQ officials, one who managed the Capey Review in 1995, the other evaluating the 1996 pilot of new specifications (**NCVQ officials**)

John Hillier, chief executive of the NCVQ until 1996 (**NCVQ official**)

Gilbert Jessup, deputy chief executive and head of research and development in NCVQ from 1986–1995 (**NCVQ official**)

the current head of GNVQ policy in the QCA (**QCA official**)

a college lecturer who wrote specifications for Advanced GNVQ Business (**external official**)

three civil servants leading GNVQ policy inside the Employment Department and Department of Education between 1992 and 1997 (**civil servants**)

two inspectors for GNVQs in the Office for Standards in Education (**inspectors**)

the lead inspector for GNVQs in the Further Education Funding Council Inspectorate (**inspector**)

a test designer for BTEC Business between 1992–1995 (**awarding body official**)

the development in charge of for the DfEE-funded support programme for GNVQs run by the Further Education Development Agency (**external official**)

Tim Boswell, Minister for Further and Higher Education from 1992–1995

John Capey, chair of the NCVQ-commissioned review of GNVQ assessment and NCVQ council member

the head of the Further Education Unit from 1989–1994 (**external official**)

the chief executive of the RSA awarding body (**awarding body official**)

Appendix 2

College-based fieldwork (a): The teacher sample

Name	Subject	Units in GNVQ	College	Qualification	Experience in FE and GNVQ
Caroline	Psychology	• Communications in Care Settings • Psychology	Riverside	Certificate in Education MSC Psychology	Five, all in GNVQ, also teaches BTEC National, unit tutor in GNVQ
Madeline	Nursing	• Planning a Health Campaign	Riverside	Certificate in Education Nursing and midwifery qualification	Fourteen, BTEC National and other vocational courses, unit tutor in GNVQ
Mary	Nursing	• Communications in Care Settings • Planning a Health Campaign	Bridgeview	Certificate in Education Nursing qualification MA in Post-Compulsory Education	Five, all in GNVQ, course leader for GNVQ HSC, does not teach other courses
Neil	Sociology	• Sociology • Social Policy	Bridgeview	Degree in Sociology MA in Education	Fifteen, two years in GNVQ, previously A-levels, also teaches BTEC National courses, GNVQ unit tutor

Name	Subjects	Courses	Campus	Qualification	Experience
Barbara	Statistics European Policy	• Communication and Numeracy key skills • Statistics • European Policy	Bridgeview	Certificate in Education	Twenty, seven years in GNVQ, previously CPBE, BTEC First, BTEC National, personal and unit tutor, does not teach on other courses
Gill	Financial transactions	• Financial transactions	Bridgeview	Chartered surveyor qualification Certificate in Education	Twenty-five, seven years in GNVQ, previously A-level and BTEC National, does not teach on other courses, GNVQ course leader
Jim	Accountancy Management	• Behaviour and Motivation at Work • Financial transactions	Riverside	Chartered accountancy qualification Certificate in Education	Fifteen, six in GNVQ, previously HND and Management courses, BTEC National, GNVQ course leader
Jo	Business studies	• Marketing • Human Resources	Riverside	B.Ed. in Business Education	Five, teaches some BTEC National, GNVQ unit tutor

College-based fieldwork (b): The student sample

Incoming qualification	Student: course and duration of fieldwork	Aiming for university	Vocational training	Job	Final destination	Final grade	Aim for grade
A-level	Annastasia, HSC RS, Yr 1 and Yr 2	Possible		Not sure	More FE, job	M	P/M
A-level	Britney, HSC RS, Yr 1 and Yr 2	Possible	Nursing		HE – Health Studies	D	D
GCSE	Annette, HSC RS, Yr 1 and Yr 2	Psychology			HE – Psychology	D	D
Intermediate	Louise, HSC BV, Yr 2 and job	Yes	Nursing		Care home (job)	M	M
Intermediate	Jacky, HSC BV Yr 1 and Yr 2	Yes	Nursing		Nursing	D	M/D
Intermediate	Susan, HSC BV Yr 1 and Yr 2	Yes	Nursing		Nursing	D	M
Intermediate	Jane, HSC BV Yr 2 only	Yes	Nursing		Not known	M	M
Intermediate	Karen, HSC BV Yr 2 only	No		Not sure	Care home (part-time job)	P	P/M

GCSE	Jim, BS, Yr 2 only	No			M	M
GCSE	Michael, BS BV Yr 2 university	Business	Police	University degree	D	D
GCSE	Wendy, BS BV, Yr 2 only	No	Banking or accountancy	Not known	M	P/M
Intermediate	Stephen, BS BV, Yr 1 and Yr 2	Business (2nd choice)	Not sure	Not known	M	M
Intermediate	Tracey, BS BV Yr 1 and Yr 2	No	Banking	Not known	M	P/M
Intermediate	Haley, BS BV Yr 1	No		GNVQ Year 2	M	P/M
Intermediate	Darren, BS RS, Yr 1 and Yr 2	Possible (2nd choice)		Job building society	D	D
Intermediate	Louise, RS, Yr 1 and Yr 2	Law		HE Human Resources	D	D
Work	Kevin, BS RS, Yr and job	Business		Trainee manager	M	D
GCSE	Naomi, BS RS, Yr 1 and Yr 2	Law		Not known	M	M/D

College-based fieldwork (c): Sequence and scope of fieldwork activities with teachers

1. Post-teaching interviews	2. Participant observation	3. Post-assessment interviews	4. Card sort 'seminar' with 8 teachers	5. In-depth individual interviews about effects of GNVQ	6. Final seminar to discuss analysis of fieldwork and general findings	7. Questionnaire to 60 GNVQ teachers in FE and 6th form colleges in North-east
(Sept 1998-Jan 1999)	(Jan 1999–April 1999)	(Sept 1998–March 1999)	(June 1999)	(November 1999)	(June 2000)	(April 2000)
<ul><li>subject</li><li>aims</li><li>progress teachers want students to make, goals for progress during the session</li><li>factors affecting changes to goals and aims.</li></ul>	<ul><li>marking unit assignments (50 in total) using the official specifications</li><li>discussion with teachers (see activity 3)</li></ul>	<ul><li>aims for marking and comments</li><li>purposes of assessment: uses of assessment to motivate students</li><li>aspects of assessment that are important, reasons for approaches to feedback</li></ul>	<ul><li>individual ranking of statements about (a) autonomy (b) motivation (c) formative assessment practices</li><li>pair discussion of reasons for ranking</li><li>group discussion of issues</li></ul>	<ul><li>official GNVQ documents that have influenced their assessment practice</li><li>how GNVQ assessment has affected their teaching and assessment, (a) values and beliefs (b) practices</li><li>whether GNVQs have changed values, beliefs and practices for the worse/better</li></ul>	<ul><li>presentation by me of original questions and summaries of findings from student and teacher data</li><li>discussion of interpretations, ethical issues relating to 'labels' for teachers and students, burden and usefulness of research for participants</li></ul>	<ul><li>worthwhile/ realistic aims for GNVQ</li><li>best/worst features of GNVQ assessment</li><li>how teachers use criteria with students</li><li>motivators for GNVQ students</li><li>characteristics of autonomous learners</li></ul>

- aspects of their activity that they would characterise as assessment during the lesson
- whether classroom and/or tutorial questions are 'assessment'

- use of specifications and criteria
- whether they look for, and encourage, autonomy through feedback, discussion of criteria etc.
- purposes and types of formative feedback

- typed-up version of each individual's responses as basis for the final interview

---

- type(s) of autonomy (a) important to them and why (b) possible for them to develop in GNVQs and why/why not
- type of motivation (a) important to them and why (b) possible for them to develop in GNVQs and why/why not?
- Purpose of your feedback and assessment practices

- types of autonomy developed in GNVQs
- purposes of feedback
- students' uses of feedback

College-based fieldwork (d): Sequence and scope of fieldwork with students

1. Group interviews	2. Individual interviews	3. Questionnaire to 72 students in the four courses covered by the study	4. Card sort 'seminar' with 9 students	5. In-depth individual interviews
(Sept 1998–Jan 1999)	(Jan 1999–May 1999)	(June 1999)	(June 1999)	(November 1999–May 2000)
• reasons for being on GNVQs • whether students see themselves as motivated and autonomous learners • if so, the characteristics they associate with these attributes • advantages and disadvantages of the GNVQ assessment system	• discussion of feedback and grades for assignments that teachers and I marked • how they use the assessment criteria during the assignment, what they do with feedback • qualities associated with Distinction grades • views about self and peer assessment	• reasons for GNVQ • end goals • advantages and disadvantages of GNVQ assessment • views about self and peer assessment • uses of assessment criteria	• types of autonomy: (a) realistic to develop; (b) that their best teachers develop with them • what motivates them • how teachers assess their work • paired discussion, group discussion • typed-up version from each individual's card sort as basis for the last interview	• (based on issues arising from construct analysis) • how autonomy and motivation has changed or stayed the same since leaving Year 1 or Year 2 • impact of GNVQs on learning

Appendix 3

A typology of autonomy and motivation

Type	Purposes/aims	Nature of knowledge/ learning	Source of authority	Formative assessment
Procedural/ technical autonomy	Procedures to meet requirements. – student/teacher views – specifications awarding body guidance	Transmission teacher and/or test specifications. Emphasis on quantity and replication of pre-defined knowledge	Teacher/government/ institution	External assignments, tests, definitions of quality and standards
External and introjected motivation, individual motivation	Meet aims within boundaries	combined with some	combined with some	combined with some
	Begin to define aims *outside* boundaries	Transaction between learner, teacher, texts and official guidance	Institutional and teacher autonomy in designing assignments and activities for a local context	Teacher/student interpretation of choices within boundaries
	Decide procedures to achieve aims		Students accountable for meeting requirements	Formative and summative checking and limited, depersonalised feedback based on checking gaps
Personal (practical, as in own practice) autonomy	Insights into procedural strengths and weaknesses in the course	Transmission but emphasis on	Students responsible for own work within external boundaries	External standards but broader boundaries too. Portfolios
	Reflection on broader strengths/weaknesses			
Identified, intrinsic and some interested movivation, individual and some social motivation	Awareness of options, interests, possibilities for progression.	Transaction and negotiation over external requirements, learning strategies, what counts as knowledge and evidence.	Responsible for own learning and for setting targets	Ipsative assessment and some differentiated personalised feedback to individuals. Peer assessment

Critical autonomy	Self-management and self-direction (procedural and personal).	Greater degree of negotiation about outcomes, aims, processes etc.	Peer commitment to work of other learners	Negotiation of standards and evidence
	Some awareness of wider context and moral dilemmas			
	Ability to make judgements about subject content and growing expertise in it	Transformation	Community of learners where authority shifts from teacher	Combination of assessment but emphasis on self- and peer-assessment
		Knowledge is dynamic, changing and increasingly reconstructed by learner	Complexity, creativity and openness in learning content and processes	Negotiated external and ipsative standards
	Cognitive synthesis and evaluation	Knowing is contextual		Internalisation of what counts as external standard.
	Awareness of subject knowledge in a wider context	Formal and informal discourses in a community of learners (teacher/students/colleagues)	Transmitted knowledge is genuinely open to critique	'Critical conversation' between teacher and learners and amongst peers.
	Awareness of subject-related strengths and weaknesses	Opportunities for higher order questioning and self-generated questions from students	Intrinsic standards of rationality and communication are both implicit and explicit but become more tacit as expertise grows	Robust questioning, debriefing and reviews of learning
Intrinsic and interested motivation, social motivation	Social commitments and sense of responsibility to a community (professional or social)			Iindividualised feedback

Notes

Introduction

1 BTEC is the acronym of the Business and Technology Education Council, formed from a merger in 1984 of the Technical and Education Council and Business Education Council which were set up by the Department of Education and Science to run vocational programmes. BTEC was privatised as a commercial awarding body in 1992 in order to offer General National Vocational Qualifications (GNVQs) and merged with the University of London Examination Board in 1997 to form EdExcel.
2 An important example is the Further Education Unit, which became the Further Education Development Agency in 1994 and was re-launched as the Learning and Skills Development Agency in 2001. From 1994, it ran a £5 million programme to support GNVQ teachers in implementing policy, funded by the Department for Education and Employment. Its new remit as the LSDA is now much more closely tied to government policy for the post-16 sector than it was as the FEU.

1 Learning in a risk society: empowerment, care or control?

1 The moral panic that now surrounds a crisis in literacy and numeracy is fuelled by very different proclamations in policy about the extent of the problem. Arguments focus both on definitions of absolute and functional illiteracy and numeracy and on numbers which range from 7 million to 750,000 (Kingston, 2001).

2 Theorising autonomy, motivation and formative assessment

1 I am extremely grateful to John Vorhaus from the Learning and Skills Development Agency, and Joanna Swann and Dylan William at King's College for constructive insights about issues raised in an earlier paper on which this chapter is based (Ecclestone, 2000a).

3 Constructing GNVQ assessment policy

1 See Appendix 1 for a list of interviewees and Chapter 3 for a detailed chronology of events in developing the assessment model.
2 The NCVQ's General Policy Committee (GPC) comprised a diverse range of consitituencies and interests and was responsible for overall political direction and implementation. It was also the focus for much debate about principles underpinning the assessment model.

3 I am also grateful to John West for insightful and constructive comments on an earlier draft of this chapter and also to Jo-Ann Baird from the Assessment and Qualifications Alliance (AQA) awarding body for her similarly useful insights.
4 This refers to the complex discussions outlined earlier in the chapter about whether reliability can be secured, as many in NCVQ believed, through strenuous attempts to gain validity.
5 My interview with Tim Boswell was surprising for his detailed technical insight and enthusiasm for the complex issues raised by outcome-based assessment in GNVQs. Similarly, Raggatt and Williams show that his enthusiasm for vocational qualifications was rare: Tim Eggar and Jim Paice were similarly enthusiastic in their ministerial roles (Raggatt and Williams, 1999).
6 This would be an imporant focus for a further analysis of how the impact of key initiatives have affected the roles of educational civil servants.

4 Changing FE colleges

1 The DES became the Department for Education in 1988 and merged with the Employment Department in 1995 to form the Department for Education and Employment (DfEE) in 1995. The two departments were split in 2001 into the Department of Education and Skills and the Department of Work and Pensions.
2 This became the Further Education Development Agency (FEDA) in 1994 and was re-launched as the Learning and Skills Development Agency (LSDA) in 2000.
3 City & Guilds has since disentangled itself from GNVQs and Vocational A-levels, leaving them to the academic examining board that was merged with City & Guilds in 1997 as part of the DfEE's drive to blur the divide between academic and vocational qualifications and to avoid damaging turf wars.

5 Getting through: motivation in GNVQs

1 'Chosen care settings' is the precise phrase from the assignment brief for the QCA set assignment discussed in Chapter 3 as an example of assessment specifications.
2 It seems easier to use categories and descriptions for young people when they are positive. In keeping with earlier discussion about reflexivity and the danger of 'essentialising' depictions of participants, it is important to reiterate here that researchers gain fleeting impressions of people and their motives. My depictions here of Tracey and Karen are constructed from the artificial relationship of researcher and the researched.
3 Timing of research is an important variable. In this case, attendance is poorer at the end of terms and on Mondays and Fridays! Nevertheless, it is important not to over-generalise about poor or good attendance. More broadly, timing raises a methodological issue discussed by Ball (1993) who argues that qualitative researchers often fail to acknowledge how time of year, day or week affect participants' feelings and responses. At the seminar to discuss findings, teachers thought qualitative accounts of motivation were useful but they also pointed out the effects of fluctuation and timing.

6 Doing their way: autonomy in GNVQs

1 All students and staff in my sample using the post-Capey pilot specifications refer to the specifications that set out the criteria in bullet points under each grade as 'the bullets'.

2 As Chapter 2 shows, 'ipsative' is a powerful but often overlooked form of self-assessment. It requires students to set goals and criteria for assessing them. The criteria derive entirely from one's own previous performance and are not an imposed external measure.

3 However, this ability, and the inferences I'm making here, are influenced by factors such as confidence with interviews and the ability to talk about one's learning. This raises questions about how students' cultural capital influences researchers' perceptions of them. Three young men and one young woman were articulate and confident, while other students were much less confident and precise. There were also differences between colleges: transcripts show that Bridgeview students were generally less talkative and confident than Riverside students. This methodological problem implies the need for other forms of exploration and closer, regular examination of students' work and their responses to materials, teachers' feedback and questions.

4 This must have been a widespread phenomenon in the Capey pilot because awarding bodies told teachers that complete assignment scenarios must be used in the new Vocational A-levels.

5 My observation of his lessons and interviews with him suggest the latter and again shows the importance of finding ways in qualitative research to go beyond 'espoused theories'.

7 Biting the bullets: formative assessment in GNVQs

1 The ubiquitous 'D' units (D32, 33 and 34) are part of an NVQ in training and cover competence-based assessment requirements. The NCVQ's requirement that staff in NVQs and, for a short time, GNVQs, must acquire them absorbed much of colleges' staff development budgets between 1993 and 2000.

2 This question is trying to explore her views of the idea of GNVQ designers, that defining outcomes and requiring 100 per cent coverage would raise 'standards'.

References

Ainley, P. (1999) *Learning Policy: Towards the Certified Society* (Basingstoke, Macmillan Press).

Ainley, P. and Bailey, B. (1997) *The Business of Learning: Staff and Student Experiences of Further Education in the 1990s* (London, Cassell).

Anderson, D. and Mullen, P. (eds) (1998) *Faking It: the Sentimentalisation of Modern Society* (London, Penguin).

Argyris, C. and Schon, D. (1974) *Theory and Practice: Increasing Professional Effectiveness* (San Francisco, Jossey-Bass).

Arthur, J. (1998) Communitarianism: what are the implications for education?, *Educational Studies*, 24, 3, 353–68.

Avis, J. (1995) The validation of learner experience: a conservative practice?, *Studies in the Education of Adults*, 27, 2, 173–86.

Avis, J. (1996) The myth of the post-Fordist society, in Avis, J., Bloomer, M., Esland, G., Gleeson, D. and Hodkinson, P. (1996) *Knowledge and Nationhood: Education and the Transfer of Work* (London, Cassell).

Avis, J. (1998a) (Im)possible dream: post-fordism, stake-holding and post-compulsory education, *Journal of Education Policy*, 13, 2, 251–63.

Avis J., Bloomer M., Esland G., Gleeson D. and Hodkinson P. (1996) *Knowledge and Nationhood: Education and the Transfer of Work* (London, Cassell).

Baird, J., Cresswell, M. and Newton, P. (2000) Would the real gold standard please step forward?, *Research Papers in Education*, 15, 2, 213–29.

Ball, S.J. (1981) *Beachside Comprehensive: a Case Study of Secondary Schooling* (Cambridge, Cambridge University Press).

Ball, S.J. (1990) *Education Politics and Policy Making: Explorations in Policy Sociology* (London, Routledge).

Ball, S.J. (1993) Self-doubt and soft data: social and technical trajectories in ethnographic fieldwork, in Hammersley, M. (ed.) (1993) *Educational Research: Current Issues* (London, Open University Press/Paul Chapman).

Ball, S.J. (1994) *Education Reform: A Critical and Post-Structural Approach* (Buckingham, Open University Press).

Ball, S.J. (1995) Intellectuals or technicians?: the urgent case for educational theory, *British Journal of Educational Studies*, 43, 3, 255–71.

Ball, S.J. (1997) Policy social and critical social research: a personal review of recent education policy and policy research, *British Education Research Journal*, 23, 3, 257–74.

Ball, S.J. (1999) Labour, learning and the economy: a 'policy sociology' perspective, *Cambridge Journal of Education*, 29, 2, 195–206.

Ball, S.J. (2000) Performance and fabrications in the education economy: towards the performative society, *Australian Educational Researcher*, 27, 2, 1–24.

Ball, S.J., Macrae, S. and Maguire, M. (1999) Young lives, diverse choices and imagined futures in an education and training market, *International Journal of Inclusive Education*, 3, 3, 195–224.

Ball, S.J., Maguire, M. and Macrae, S. (2000) *Choices, Transitions and Pathways: new youth, new economies in the global city* (London, Falmer Press).

Barnes, D., Johnson, G., Jordan, S., Layton, D., Medway, P. and Yeomans, D. (1988) *A Second Report on the TVEI Curriculum: Courses for 14–16 year-olds in Twenty-six Schools* (Sheffield, Training Agency).

Barnett, R. (1994) *The Limits of Competence* (Buckingham, Open University Press).

Barnett, R. (1997a) Beyond competence, in Coffield, F. and Williamson, B. (1997) (eds) *Repositioning Higher Education* (Buckingham, Open University Press).

Barnett, R. (1997b) *Higher Education: A Critical Business* (Buckingham, Open University Press).

Barnett, R., Nixon, J., Rowland, S. (1999) Round table discussion of critical thinking in higher education, *Teaching and Learning in Higher Education*, 4, 4, 167–75.

Baron, S., Field, J. and Schuller, T. (2000) *Social Capital: critical perspectives* (Oxford, Oxford University Press).

Bates, I. (1984) From vocational guidance to life skills: historical perspectives on careers education, in Bates, I., Clarke, J., Cohen, P., Finn, D., Moore, R. and Willis, P. (1984) *Schooling for the Dole?: The New Vocationalism* (London, Macmillan).

Bates, I. (1989b) Versions of vocationalism: an analysis of some social and political influences on curriculum policy and practice, *British Journal of Sociology of Education*, 10, 2, 215–31.

Bates, I. (1991) Closely observed training: an exploration of links between social structures, training and identity, *International Studies in Sociology of Education*, 1, 225–43.

Bates, I. (1998a) The empowerment dimension in GNVQs: a critical exploration of discourse, pedagogic apparatus and school implementation, *Evaluation and Research in Education*, 12, 1, 7–22.

Bates, I. (1998b) Resisting 'empowerment' and realising power: an exploration of aspects of the GNVQ, *Journal of Education and Work*, 11, 2, 187–205.

Bates, I. and Dutson, J. (1993) A Bermuda triangle? A case study of the disappearance of competence based vocational training policy in the context of practice, *British Journal of Education and Work*, 8, 2, 41–59.

Bates, I. and Allatt, P. (1999) *Youth, Family and Education: the formation of the independent learner*, ESRC funded project within the ESRC Programme 'Youth, Citizenship and Social Change'.

Bates, I., Bloomer, M., Hodkinson, P., Yeomans, D. (1998) Progressivism and the GNVQ: context, ideology and practice, *Journal of Education and Work*, 11, 2, 109–27.

Bathmaker, A-M. (in progress) *Learners and Learning in GNVQs: PhD study*, University of Warwick.

Beck, U. (1992) *Risk Society: Towards a New Modernity* (London, Sage Publications).

Beck, U. (1999a) What is a 'risk (society)'?, *Prometheus*, Winter 1999, 75–9.

Beck, U. (1999b) Organised irresponsibility: a reply to Frank Furedi, *Prometheus*, Winter 1999, 83–4.

Bell, C. and Raffe, D. (1991) Working together? Research, policy and practice in Walford, G. (ed.) (1991) *Doing Educational Research* (London, Routledge).

Black, P. (1995) Ideology and evidence and the raising of standards, *Annual Education Lecture*, Kings College, London, 11 July 1995.

Black, P. and Wiliam, D. (1998) Assessment and classroom learning, *Assessment in Education: Principles, Policy and Practice*, 5, 1, 1–78.

Black, P., Harrison, C., Lee, C. and Wiliam, D. (2001) Theory and practice in the development of formative assessment. Paper presented to the American Education Research Association Conference, University of Seattle, April 2001.

Bleakley, A. (2000) Adrift without a lifebelt: reflective self-assessment in a postmodern age, *Teaching and Learning in Higher Education*, 5, 4, 405–19.

Bloom, B. (1956) *A Taxonomy of Cognitive Objectives* (New York, Mackay).

Bloomer, M. (1997) *Curriculum Making in Post-16 Education: The Social Conditions of Studentship* (London, Routledge).

Bloomer, M. (1998) 'They tell you what to do and then they let you get on with it': illusions of progressivism in GNVQ, *Journal of Education and Work*, 11, 2, 167–87.

Bloomer, M. (2001) Young lives, learning and transformations: some theoretical considerations, *Oxford Review of Education*, 27, 3, 429–49.

Bloomer, M. and Hodkinson, P. (1997) *Moving into FE: the Voice of the Learner* (London, Further Education Development Agency).

Bloomer, M. and Hodkinson, P. (1999) *College Life: the Voice of the Learner* (London, Further Education Development Agency).

Blunkett, D (2000) Speech to Economic and Social Science Research Council, 2 February 2000, *Research Intelligence*, 71, March 2000.

Boswell, T. (1998) Interview for the author's Ph.D, Palace of Westminster, London, May 1998.

Boud, D. (ed.) (1988) *Developing Student Autonomy in Learning* (London, Kogan Page).

Boys, C. (2000) *The GNVQ Experiment 1991–1996: Lost for Words?* Ph.D Thesis, (Sussex, University of Sussex).

Bridges, D. (1998) Research for sale: moral market or moral maze?, *British Educational Research Journal*, 24, 5, 593–607.

Brine, J. (1995) Educational and vocational policy and construction of the European Union, *International Studies in Sociology of Education*, 5, 2, 145–65.

Broadfoot, P. (ed.) (1986) *Profiles and Records of Achievement: a Review of Issues and Practice* (London, Holt, Reinehart and Winston).

Broadfoot, P. (1996) *Education, Assessment and Society* (Buckingham, Open University Press).

Broadfoot, P. (1998) Records of achievement and the learning society: a tale of two discourses, *Assessment in Education: Principles, Policy and Practice*, 5, 3, 413–47.

Broadfoot, P. (1999a) Empowerment or performativity? English assessment policy in the late 20th century. Paper given to the *British Educational Research Association Conference* (University of Sussex, 12–14 September 1999).

Broadfoot, P. (1999b) Liberating the learner through assessment, in Collins, J. and Cook, D. (eds) (1999) *Understanding Learning: influences and outcomes* (London, Paul Chapman Publishing/Open University).

Broadfoot, P. (2000) *Culture, Learning and Comparison: BERA Stenhouse Lecture 1999* (Nottingham, British Educational Research Association).

Broadfoot, P. and Pollard, A. (2000) The changing discourse of assessment policy: the case of English primary education, in Filer, A. (ed.) (2000) *Assessment: Social Process, Social Product* (London, Falmer Press).

Brookfield, S. (2000) Adult cognition as a dimension of lifelong learning, in Field, J. and Leicester, M. (eds) (2000) *Lifelong Learning* (London, Routledge/Falmer).

Brown, A. and Keep, E. (2001) *Review of Vocational Education and Training Research in the UK* (Brussels: European Commission).

Bruner, J. (1966) *The Culture of Education* (Cambridge, MA: Harvard University Press).

Bullen, E., Kenway, J. and Hay, V. (2000) New Labour, social exclusion and educational risk management: the case of 'gymslip mums', *British Journal of Educational Studies*, 26, 4, 441–57.

Burke, J. (ed.) (1995) *Outcomes Learning and the Curriculum: Implications for NVQs GNVQs and Other Qualifications* (London, Falmer Press).

Candy, P. (1998) On the attainment of subject-matter autonomy, in Boud, D. (ed.) *Developing Student Autonomy in Learning* (London, Kogan Page).

Carr, W. (1995) *For Education: Towards Critical Educational Inquiry* (Buckingham, Open University Press).

Carr, W. and Kemmis, S. (1986) *Becoming Critical: Education, Knowledge and Action Research* (London, Falmer Press).

Chisholm, L. (1997) Lifelong learning and learning organisations: twin pillars of the learning society, in Coffield, F. (ed.) (1997) *A National Strategy for Lifelong Learning* (Newcastle, University of Newcastle).

Coffield, F. (1997a) Introduction and overview: attempts to reclaim the concept of the learning society, *Journal of Education Policy*, 12, 6, 449–55.

Coffield, F. (1997b) Nine learning fallacies and their replacement by a national strategy for lifelong learning, in Coffield, F. (ed.) (1997) *A National Strategy for Lifelong Learning* (Newcastle, University of Newcastle).

Coffield, F. (1997c) *Can the UK Become A Learning Society?* King's College London, Annual Education Lecture, June 1997.

Coffield, F. (ed.) (1999a) *Lifelong learning as a new form of social control*, in Coffield, F. (ed.) (1999) *Why's the Beer Always Stronger Up North?: Studies of Lifelong Learning in Europe* (Bristol, The Policy Press/ESRC).

Coffield, F. (1999b) Breaking the consensus: lifelong learning as social control, *British Education Research Journal*, 25, 4, 479–99.

Coffield, F. (1999c) Past failures, present difficulties and possible futures for research, policy and practice, in Coffield, F. (ed.) (1999) *Speaking Truth to Power: Research and Policy on Lifelong Learning* (Bristol, The Policy Press/ESRC).

Coffield, F. (2000a) A critical analysis of the concept of a 'learning society', in Coffield, F. (ed.) (2000) *Differing Visions of a Learning Society: Research Findings Volume 1* (Bristol, The Policy Press/ESRC).

Coffield, F. (2000b) Introduction: past failures, present differences and possible futures for research, policy and practice, in Coffield, F. (ed.) (2000) *Speaking*

Truth to Power: Research and Policy in Lifelong Learning (Bristol, The Policy Press/ESRC).

Coffield, F., Borrill, C. and Marshall, S. (1986) *Growing Up at the Margins: Young Adults in the North East* (Buckingham, Open University Press).

Coffield, F. and Williamson, B. (1997) The challenges facing higher education, in Coffield, F. and Williamson, B. (eds) (1997) *The Repositioning of Higher Education* (Buckingham, Open University Press).

Colley, H. (2000) What do we think we're doing?: how mentors' beliefs about disaffection influence the process of mentoring disaffected young people. Paper presented to the *British Educational Research Association Post-16 Special Interest Group*, Milton Keynes, 17 May 2000.

Colley, H. (2001) *Unravelling myths of mentor: power dynamics of mentoring relationships with disaffected young people*, Unpublished PhD thesis (Manchester, Manchester Metropolitan University).

Dale, R., Harris, D., Loveys, M., Moore, R., Shilling, C., Sikes, P., Taylor, M., Trevitt, J. and Valsecchi, J. (1989) *The TVEI Story: Policy, Practice and Preparation for the Workforce* (Buckingham, Open University Press).

Davies, P. (2000) *Learning and Earning: the Impact of Paid Employment on Young People in Full-Time Education* (London, Further Education Development Agency).

Department of Education and Employment/Further Education Development Agency (1998) *Improving GNVQ Retention and Completion*, (London, FEDA).

Department of Education and Employment (2000) Press Release on announcement of reforms to A-levels and GNVQs for September 2000 (London, DfEE).

Department of Education and Science (1988) *Advancing A Levels (The Higginson Report)* (London, HMSO).

Department for Education and Science/Employment Department (DES/ED) (1991) *Education and Training for the Twenty First Century* (London, HMSO).

Department for Education and Employment (1996) *Review of 16–19 Qualifications* (London, DfEE).

Department for Education and Employment (1998) *The Learning Age: a Renaissance for Britain*, Green Paper (London, DfEE).

Department for Education and Employment (1999) *Learning to Succeed*. White Paper (London, DfEE).

Dweck, C.S. (2000) *Self-Theories: Their Role in Motivation, Personality and Development* (Philadelphia: Taylor & Francis/Psychology Press).

Ecclestone, K. (1993) *Understanding Accreditation: Ways of Recognising Achievement* (London, Further Education Development Unit).

Ecclestone, K. (1994) *Understanding Assessment* (Leicester, National Institute for Adult and Continuing Education).

Ecclestone, K. (1996a) *How to Assess the Vocational Curriculum* (London, Kogan Page).

Ecclestone, K. (1996b) The reflective practitioner: mantra or a model of emancipation?, *Studies in the Education of Adults*, 49, 3, 1–23.

Ecclestone, K. (1997) On the frontline or at the margins?: research in post-compulsory education' *Research Issues in Post-Compulsory Education*, 2, 3, 319–31.

Ecclestone, K. (1998) Euston Road and the ivory towers: the impact of the GNVQ research industry, *Journal of Education Policy*, 13, 6, 679–97.

Ecclestone, K. (1999a) Ensnaring or empowering?: the implications of outcome-based assessment in higher education, *Higher Education Quarterly*, 53, 1, 29–49.

Ecclestone, K. (1999b) Care or control?: defining learners' needs for lifelong learning, *British Journal of Educational Studies*, 47, 4, 332–46.

Ecclestone, K. (2000) Bewitched, bothered and bewildered: a policy analysis of the GNVQ assessment regime, *Journal of Education Policy* 15, 5, 539–558.

Ecclestone, K. (2000b) Assessment and autonomy in post-compulsory education in the UK, *Journal of Education and Work* 13, 2, 141–63.

Ecclestone, K. (2001) 'I know a 2:1 when I see it': how lecturers learn degree standards in franchised programmes, *Journal of Further and Higher Education*, 25, 3, 317–29.

Ecclestone, K. and Hall, I. (1999) *Quality Assurance and Quality Control for Internal Assessment across Diverse Qualifications*, Report for the Qualifications and Curriculum Authority (Newcastle, University of Newcastle).

Ecclestone, K. and Hall, E. (2000) *An Analysis of Advanced GNVQ Assessment 1992–2000*, Report for the Qualifications and Curriculum Authority (Newcastle, University of Newcastle).

Ecclestone, K. and Field, J. (2001) Promoting social capital in a 'risk society': a new approach to emancipatory learning or a new moral authoritarianism?. Paper presented to the *European Conference of Educational Research*, University of Lille, 5–8 September 2001.

Ecclestone, K. and Swann, J. (1999) Litigation and learning: tensions in improving university lecturers' assessment practice, *Assessment in Education: Principles, Policy and Practice* 6, 3, 377–89.

Ecclestone, K. and Pryor, J. (2001) Assessment regimes and assessment careers. Paper presented to *the British Educational Research Association Conference, University of Leeds*, September 2001.

Ecclestone, K. and Tuckett, A. (2000) Moral authoritarianism in lifelong learning: a discussion, *College Research Journal*, Summer 2000.

Edwards, T. (1993) Researching a controversial policy, *Evaluation and Research*, 7, 1, 11–23.

Edwards, R. (1997) *Changing Places? Flexibility, Lifelong Learning and a Learning Society* (London, Routledge).

Edwards, R. and Usher, R. (1994) Disciplining the subject: the power of competence, *Studies in the Education of Adults*, 26, 1, 1–15.

Edwards, R. and Usher, R. (1996) *Post-Modernism in Education* (London, Routledge).

Edwards, T. and Whitty, G. (1994) Researching Thatcherite education policy, in Walford, G. (ed.) (1994) *Researching the Powerful in Education* (London, University College London).

Edwards, T., Fitzgibbon, C., Hardman, F., Haywood, R. and Meagher, N (1997) *Separate but Equal?: A-levels and General National Vocational Qualifications* (London, Routledge).

Eggar, T. (1991) Briefing letter to the NCVQ, setting up GNVQs.

Elliott, J., Hufton, N. Hildreth, A. and Illushin, L. (1999) Factors influencing educational motivation: a study of attitudes, expectations and behaviour of children in Sunderland, Kentucky and St. Petersburg, *British Educational Research Journal*, 25, 1, 75–95.

Eraut, M. (1997) Curriculum assumptions and frameworks in 14–19 education, *Research Issues in Post-Compulsory Education*, 2, 3, 302–19.

Eraut, M. (2000) Informal learning, implicit learning and tacit knowledge in professional work in, Coffield, F. (ed.) (2000) *The Necessity of Informal Learning* (Bristol, The Policy Press/ESRC).

Evans, K., Hodkinson, P., Keep, E., Senger, P. and Unwin, L. (1997) *Working to Learn: a Work-Based Route to Learning for Young People* (London, Institute of Personnel Development).

Fevre, R., Gorard, S. and Rees, G. (2000) Necessary and unnecessary learning: the acquisition of knowledge and skills in and outside employment in South Wales in the twentieth century, in Coffield, F. (ed.) (2000) *The Necessity of Informal Learning* (Bristol, The Policy Press/ESRC).

Fevre, R., Rees, G., and Gorard, S (1999) Some sociological alternatives to human capital theory and their implications for research on post-compulsory education and training, *Journal of Education and Work*, 12, 2, 117–40.

Field, J. (1991) Competency and the pedagogy of labour, *Studies in the Education of Adults*, 23, 1, 41–52.

Field, J. (2000) *Lifelong Learning and the New Educational Order*, Trentham Books, Stoke on Trent, 2000.

Field, J. (2001) Ambivalent identities: the role of risk and contingency in adults' descriptions of participation in education and training, *Journal of Adult and Continuing Education*, 7, 1, 94–100.

Fielding, M. (1998) Empowerment: emancipation or enervation? *Journal of Education Policy*, 11, 2, 399–417.

Fitz, J. and Halpin, D. (1994) Ministers and mandarins: educational research in elite settings, in Walford, G. (ed.) (1994) *Researching the Powerful in Education* (London, University College London).

Fryer, B. (1997) Learning for the 21st Century, *Report of the National Advisory Group for Continuing Education and Lifelong Learning* (London, DfEE).

Fullan, M. (1991) *The New Meaning of Educational Change* (London, Cassell).

Fullan, M. (1993) *Change Forces: Probing the Depths of Educational Reform* (London, Falmer Press).

Furedi, F. (1997) *The Culture of Fear: Risk Taking and the Morality of Low Expectation* (London, Cassell).

Furedi, F. (1999a) The fear of risk, *Prometheus*, Winter 1999, 69–73.

Furedi, F. (1999b) Beyond the dramatic: a reply to Ulrich Beck, *Prometheus*, Winter 1999, 81–3.

Furedi, F. (2001) *Paranoid Parenting* (London, Penguin).

Further Education Funding Council (1994) *GNVQs in the Further Education Sector in England* (Coventry, FEFC).

Further Education Funding Council (1995) *'College B': Report from the Inspectorate* (Coventry, FEFC).

Further Education Funding Council (1996a) *GNVQs in the Further Education Sector in England* (Coventry, FEFC).

Further Education Funding Council (1996b) *'College A' : Report from the Inspectorate* (Coventry, FEFC).

Further Education Funding Council (1997) *GNVQs in the Further Education Sector in England* (Coventry, FEFC).

Further Education Funding Council (1998a) *'The Learning Age': response from the FEFC* (Coventry, FEFC).

Further Education Funding Council (1998b) Press release for new inspection handbook, August 1998 (Coventry, FEFC).

Further Education Funding Council (1999a) *Inspectors' Statistical Handbook: Version 6* (Coventry, FEFC).

Further Education Funding Council (1999b) *'College A': Report from the Inspectorate* (Coventry, FEFC).

Further Education Funding Council (1999c) *'College B': Report from the Inspectorate* (Coventry, FEFC).

Further Education Funding Council (1999d) *Professional Development in Further Education* (Coventry, FEFC).

Further Education Funding Council (2000a) *Staff Statistics 1996–1997 and 1997–1998: Further Education Colleges in England* (Coventry, FEFC).

Further Education Funding Council (2000b) *Curriculum 2000: Video Briefing for Colleges* (Coventry, FEFC).

Further Education Unit (1982) *A Basis for Choice* (London, FEU).

Further Education Unit (1995) *A Framework for Credit* (London, FEU).

Gipps, C. (1994) *Beyond Testing: Towards a Theory of Educational Assessment* (London, Falmer Press).

Gleeson, D. and Hodkinson, P. (1999) Ideology and curriculum policy: GNVQs and mass post-compulsory education in England and Wales, in Flude, M. and Simenski, S. (eds) (1999) *Education, Training and the Future of Work: developments in vocational education and training* (London/Routledge/Open University).

Gleeson, D. (2001) Style and substance in education leadership: further education as a case in point, *Journal of Education Policy*, 16, 3, 181–97.

Gleeson, D. and Shain, F. (1998) Managing ambiguity: between markets and managerialism – a case study of 'middle' managers in FE, *Sociological Review*, 46, 4, 461–90.

Goff, P. (1996) *GNVQ Scrutiny Programme 1995–1996: Summary of the Main Findings* (London, NCVQ).

Grace, G. (1994) Education as scholarship: on the need to resist policy science. Paper for *Standing Conference on Research in Education* (London, RSA, 4 November 1994).

Graham, R. (1998) *Taking Each Other Seriously: Experiences in Teaching and Learning* (Durham, Fieldhouse Press).

Halliday, J. (2000) Critical thinking and the academic/vocational divide, *Curriculum Journal*, 11, 2, 159–75.

Halpin, D. and Troyna, B. (eds) (1994) *Researching Education Policy: Ethical and methodological issues* (London, Falmer Press).

Hammersley, M. (1993) (ed.) *Social Research: Philosophy, Politics and Practice* London, Sage/Open University Press.

Hammersley, M. (1994) Ethnography, policy-making and practice in education, in Halpin, D. and Troyna, B. (eds) (1994) *Researching Education Policy: Ethical and Methodological Issues* (London, Falmer Press).

Hammersley, M. (1998) Get real! A defence of realism in Hodkinson, P. (ed.) (1998) *The Nature of Educational Research: realism, relativism or post-modernism* (Crewe, Manchester Metropolitan University).

Hammersley, M. (2000) The sky is never blue for modernisers: the threat posed by David Blunkett's offer of 'partnership' to social science. *Research Intelligence* 72, June 2000, 12–13.

Hargreaves, A. (1989) *Curriculum and Assessment Reform* (Buckingham, Open University Press).

Harkin, J. (1999) Book review of Bloomer, M. and Hodkinson, P. (1997) *Moving into FE: the Voice of the Learner*, in *Journal of Education and Work*, 12, 2, 65–72.

Harlen, W. (1995) *Enhancing Quality in Assessment* (London, Paul Chapman).

Haywood, R. (1997) Links between learning styles, teaching methods and course requirements, in Edwards, T., Fitzgibbon, C., Hardman, F., Haywood, R. and Meagher, N. (1997) *Separate but Equal?: GNVQs and A-levels* (London, Routledge).

Helsby, G. (1999) *Changing Teachers' Work* (Buckingham, Open University Press).

Helsby, G., Knight, P., and Saunders, M. (1998) Preparing students for the new work order: the case of Advanced General National Vocational Qualifications, *British Educational Research Journal* 24, 1, 63–78.

Hickox, R. and Moore, M. (1995) Liberal humanist education: the vocationalist challenge, *Curriculum Studies*, 3, 1, 45–61.

Hill, D., McLaren, P., Cole, M. and Rikowski, G. (eds) (1999) *Postmodernism in Education Theory: Education and the Politics of Human Resistance*, London: Tufnell Press.

Hillier, J. (1996) *Introduction to the GNVQ Research Conference*, National Council for Vocational Qualifications, 11 December, Royal Institute of British Architects, London.

Hodgson, A. and Spours, K. (eds) (1997) *Dearing and Beyond: 14–19 Qualifications and Frameworks*, London, Kogan Page.

Hodkinson, P. (1989) Crossing the academic/vocational divide: personal effectiveness and autonomy as an integrating theme in post-16 education, *British Journal of Educational Studies*, 37, 4, 369–83.

Hodkinson, P. (1992) Alternative models of competence in vocational education and training. *Journal of Further and Higher Education*, 16, 2, 30–9.

Hodkinson, P. (1994) Empowerment as an entitlement in the post-16 curriculum, *Journal of Curriculum Studies*, 25 (5) 391–508.

Hodkinson, P. (1998) Technicism, teachers and teaching, *Journal of Vocational Education and Training*, 50, 2, 193–209.

Hodkinson, P. (1998c) The origins of a theory of career decision-making: a case study of hermeneutical research, *British Educational Research Journal*, 24, 5, 557–72.

Hodkinson, P. (1998d) Choosing GNVQ, *Journal of Education and Work*, 11, 2, 151–65.

Hodkinson, P. and Bloomer, M. (2000) Stockingham Sixth Form College: Institutional culture and dispositions to learning, *British Journal of Sociology of Education*, 21, 2, 187–202.

Hodkinson, P. and Sparkes, A. (1997) Careership: a sociological theory of career decision making, *British Journal of Sociology of Education*, 18, 1, 29–44.

Hodkinson, P., Sparkes, A.C. and Hodkinson, H. (1996) *Triumphs and Tears: Young People, Markets and the Transition from School to Work* (London: David Fulton).

Hopson, B. and Scally, M. (1982) *Teaching Lifeskills Programme: Volumes 1 and 2* (Leeds, Careers Counselling and Development Unit/University of Leeds).

Howieson, C., Raffe, D., Spours, K. and Young, M. (1997), Unifying adademic and vocational learning: the state of the debate in England and Scotland, *Journal of Education and Work*, 10, 1, 5–35.

Hulme, R. (1998) Transferring education policy: the case of post-compulsory education in England and Wales in the 1980s and 1990s. Paper given to *British Educational Research Association Conference* (Queen's University, Belfast 27–30 August 1998).

Hyland, T. (1994) *Competence, Education and NVQs* London: Cassell.

Jessup, G. (1991) *Outcomes: NVQs and the Emerging Model of Education and Training*, London, Falmer.

Jessup, G. (1994) Grading themes in GNVQs, London: National Council for Vocational Qualifications.

Jessup, G. (1995) Outcome-based qualifications and the implications for learning, in Burke, J. (ed.) (1995) *Outcomes, Learning and the Curriculum*, London, Falmer Press.

Jessup, G. (1998) Interview for author's PhD research at the Qualifications and Curriculum Authority, 11 February 1998.

Johansson, J. (2002, in press) Qualified education in Sweden: a new form of post-secondary education, in COSTA11 Action (2000) *Best Practice in Assessment of Evaluation* (Brussels: European Commission).

Jones, I. (2001) Presentation from research at the Centre for Urban and Regional Studies, University of Newcastle, to a seminar for chief executives of local Learning and Skills Councils, University of Newcastle, March 2001.

Keep, E. (1997) 'There's no such thing as society . . .': some problems with an individual approach to creating a learning society, *Journal of Educational Policy*, 12, 6, 457–71.

Keep, E and Mayhew, K (1998) 'Was Ratner Right' Produce Market and Competitive Strategies and their Links with Skills and Knowledge', *Economic Policy Institute Paper, Economic Report*, 12, 3, April.

Kelly, P. (1999) Wild and tame zones: regulating the transitions of youth at risk, *Journal of Youth Studies*, 2, 2, 193–211.

Kennedy, H (1997) Learning Works: how to widen participation, *Further Education Funding Council*, Coventry.

Kingston, P. (2001) 'It just doesn't add up', *Education Guardian*, Tuesday 12 June 2001, p. 53.

Lave, J. (1997) The culture of acquisition and the practice of understanding, in Kirshner, D. and Whitson, J.A. (1997) *Situated Cognition: Social, Semiotic and Psychological Perspectives* (New Jersey, Lawrence Erlbaum).

Lave, J. and Wenger, E. (1991) *Situated Learning: Legitimate Peripheral Participation* (Cambridge, Cambridge University Press).

Law, B. (1992) Autonomy and learning about work, in Young, R.A. and Collin, A. (eds) (1992) *Interpreting Career* (London, Praeger).

Macrae, S., Maguire, M., Ball, S.J. (1997) Whose learning society?: a tentative deconstruction, *Journal of Education Policy*, 12, 9, 499–507.

Malen, B. and Knapp, M. (1997) Rethinking the multiple perspectives approach to education policy analysis: implications for policy–practice connections, *Journal of Education Policy*, 12, 5. 419–45.

Mills, C.W. (1970) *The Sociological Imagination* (London, Penguin).

McNair, S. (1995) Outcomes and autonomy, in Burke, J. (ed.) (1995) *Outcomes, Learning and the Curriculum: Implications for NVQs, GNVQs and Other Qualifications* (London, Falmer Press).

Moore, R. and Hickox, M. (1999) Vocationalism and educational change, in Flude, M. and Simenski, S. (eds) *Education, Training and the Future of Work II: Developments in Education and Training* (London, Routledge/Open University).

Morgan, N. and Saxton, J. (1991) *Teaching, Questioning and Learning* (London, Routledge).

National Commission of Inquiry into Higher Education (1997) *Higher Education in the Learning Society*, Norwich: HMSO.

National Council for Vocational Qualifications (1995) *GNVQ Briefing: Information on the Form, Development and Implementation of GNVQs* (London, NCVQ).

National Institute of Adult and Continuing Education (1993) *Accreditation of Prior Learning for Overseas Candidates*. Unpublished report for the Department for Employment (Leicester, NIACE).

National Skills Task Force (2001) *Skills for All: Proposals for a National Skills Agenda, Final Report* (London, Department for Education and Employment).

Newton, D. (2000) *Teaching for Understanding* (London, Falmer Press).

NICATs (Northern Ireland Credit Accumulation and Transfer System) (1998) *Proposed Level Descriptors* (Belfast, Northern Ireland Office).

Oates, T. (1997) Assessment and achievement, in Hodgson, A. and Spours, K. (eds) (1997) *Dearing and Beyond: 14–19 Qualifications, Frameworks and Systems* (London, Kogan Page).

Oates, T. (2000) New research paradigms for the new millennium, *College Research Journal*, 3, 3, 20–2.

Oates, T. and Harkin, J. (1995) From design to delivery: the implementation of cores skills units, in Burke, J. (1995) *Outcomes, Learning and the Curriculum: the Implications for NVQs, GNVQs and Other Qualifications* (London, Falmer Press).

Office for Standards in Education (1995) *Assessment of GNVQs in Schools* (London, OFSTED).

Office for Standards in Education (1997) *Part One GNVQs – Pilot Interim Report* (London, OFSTED).

Office for Standards in Education/Further Education Funding Council (1999) *GNVQs: Evaluation of the Pilot of the New Assessment Model 1997–1999: a joint report by OFSTED and the FEFC Inspectorate* (Coventry, FEFC).

Office for Standards in Education (2000) *Newcastle-Upon-Tyne: 16–19 Area-Wide Inspection* (London, OFSTED).

Otter, S. (1995) Assessing competence: the experience of the Enterprise in Higher Education initiative, in Knight, P. and Edwards, A. (eds) (1995) *Assessing Competence in Higher Education* (London, Kogan Page).

Perry, A. (1999) Performance Indicators: Measure for Measure or a comedy of errors?. Paper for FEDA Research Conference, Cambridge, 9 December 1999.

Pilger, J. (1998) *Hidden Agendas* (London, Hodder & Stoughton).

Pollard, A. and Filer, A. (1999) *The Social World of Pupil Career: strategic biographies through primary school* (London, Cassell).

Power, M. (1997) *The Audit Society: the Rituals of Verification* (Oxford, Oxford University Press).

Prenzel, M., Kramer, K. and Dreschel, B. (2000) Self-determined and interested learning in vocational education. Paper delivered at *final colloquium of the DFG Research Programme 'Teaching – learning formal processes in initial business training', Gusta Stresmann Institute* (Bonn, Germany, 29 June–1 July 2000).

Pring R. (1994) *Closing the Gap: Liberal Education and Vocational Preparation* (London, Hodder and Stoughton).

Pryor, J. and Torrance, H. (1999) Investigating and developing formative teacher assessment. Paper given to *British Educational Research Association Conference*, University of Sussex, 13–15 September 1999.

Qualifications and Curriculum Authority (1997) *Mandatory units for GNVQs: Guidance Booklet* (London, QCA).

Qualifications and Curriculum Authority (1998) *GNVQ Assessment: Your Questions Answered* (London, QCA).

Radnor, H., Ball, S. and Burrell, R. (1989) The CPVE, in Hargreaves, A. and Reynolds, D. (eds) (1989) *Education Controversies and Critiques* (London, Falmer Press).

Raffe, D., Howieson, C., Spours, K. and Young, M. (1998) The unification of post-compulsory education: towards a conceptual framework, *British Journal of Educational Studies*, 46, 2, 169–87.

Raggatt, P. and Williams, S. (1999) *Government, Markets and Vocational Qualifications: an anatomy of policy* (London, Falmer Press).

Reay, D. and Wiliam, D. (1999) 'I'll be a nothing': structure, agency and the construction of identity through assessment, *British Educational Research Journal*, 25, 3, 343–55.

Rees, G., Fevre, R. and Gorrard, S. (1997) History, place and the learning society: towards a sociology of lifetime learning, *Journal of Education Policy*, 12, 6, 485–98.

Rogers, C. (1983) *Freedom to Learn for the 1980s* (New York, Merrill and Company).

Ross, C. (1995) Seizing the quality initiative: regeneration and the radical project, in Mayo, M. and Thompson, J. (eds) (1995) *Adult Learning, Critical Intelligence and Social Change* (Leicester, National Institute of Adult and Continuing Education).

Schuller, T. (1997) Relations between human and social capital, in Coffield, F. (ed.) (1997) *A National Strategy for Lifelong Learning* (Newcastle, University of Newcastle).

Schuller, T. and Field, J. (1998) Social capital, human capital and the learning society, *International Journal of Lifelong Learning*, 17, 4, 226–35.

Seddon, T. (1998) Steering futures: practices and possibilities of institutional re-design in Australian education and training. Paper for *British Educational Research Association Conference* (Queen's University Belfast, 28–31 August 1998).

Sharp, P. (1998) The beginning of GNVQs: an analysis of key determining events and factors, *Journal of Education and Work*, 11, 3, 293–310.

Smithers, A. (1994) *All Our Futures* (Channel Four, 'Dispatches').

Spours, K. (1997) GNVQs and the future of broad vocational qualifications, in Hodgson, A. and Spours, K. (eds) (1997) *Dearing and Beyond, 14–19 Qualifications, Frameworks and Systems* (London, Kogan Page).

Spours, K. and Hodgson, A. (2000) Seminar on proposed changes to the Advanced level curriculum: interim findings from DfEE research project, *Newcastle LEA* (Pendower House, Newcastle, June 2000).

Stanton, G. (1997) Unitization: developing a common language for describing achievement, in Hodgson, A. and Spours, K. (eds) (1997) *Dearing and Beyond, 14–19 Qualifications, Frameworks and Systems* (London, Kogan Page).

Stanton, G. (1998) Patterns in development, in Tomlinson, S. (ed.) (1998) *Education 14–19: Critical Perspectives* (London, Athlone Press).

Strauss, A.L. (1987) *Qualitative Analysis for Social Scientists*, Cambridge: Cambridge University Press.

Strauss, A.L. and Corbin, J. (1990) *Basics of Qualitative Research: Grounded Theory. Procedures and Techniques* (London, Sage Publications).

Stuart, N. (1997) The policy of UK government on lifelong learning, in Coffield, F. (ed.) (1997) *A National Strategy for Lifelong Learning* (Newcastle, University of Newcastle).

Sultana, R. (1995) A uniting Europe, a dividing education?: Euro-centrism and the curriculum, *International Studies in Sociology of Education*, 2, 2, 115–45.

Swann, J. (1999) Pursuing truth: a science of education, in Swann, J. and Pratt, J. (eds) (1999) *Improving Education: Realist Approaches to Method and Research* (London, Cassell).

Swann, J. and Arthurs, J. (1999) Empowering lecturers: a problem-based approach to improve assessment practice, *Higher Education Review*, 31, 2, 50–74.

Swann, J. and Brown, S. (1997) Teachers' thinking in the Scottish National Curriculum, *Research Papers in Education*, 12, 1, 91–114.

Swann, J. and Ecclestone, K. (1999) Improving lecturers' assessment practice in Pratt, J. and Swann, J. (eds) (1999) *Improving Education: Realist Approaches to Method and Research*, London, Falmer Press.

Tate, N. (1998) *Authority in the Modern World, Carmel Macallespie Annual Memorial Lecture* (University of Brighton, 3 March 1998).

Tight, M. (1998a) Education, education, education! The vision of lifelong learning in the Kennedy, Dearing and Fryer reports, *Oxford Review of Education*, 24, 4, 251–63.

Tight, M. (1998b) Lifelong learning: opportunity or compulsion?, *British Journal of Educational Studies*, 46, 3, 251–63.

Tooley, J. (1997) 'On school choice and social class: a response to Ball, Bowe and Gerwitz, *British Journal of Sociology in Education*, 18, 2, 217–30.

Tooley, J. (1998) *Educational Research: a Critique* (London, Office for Standards in Education).

Tooley, J. (2000) *Reclaiming Education* (London, Cassell).

Torrance, H. (1993) Formative assessment: some theoretical problems and empirical questions, *Cambridge Journal of Education*, 23, 3, 333–43.

Torrance, H. (2000) Post-modernism and educational assessment, in Filer, A. (ed.) (2000) *Assessment: Social Process, Social Product* (London, Falmer Press).

Torrance, H. and Pryor, J. (1998) *Investigating Formative Assessment* (Buckingham, Open University Press).

Trow, M. (1998) The Dearing Review: a transatlantic view, *Higher Education Quarterly*, 52, 1, 93–117.

Tuckett, A. (1998) Recruits conscripted for the learning age, *Times Educational Education Supplement*, FE Focus, 22 May, 1999.

Tunstall, P. and Gipps, C. (1995) How does your teacher make your work better?: Children's understanding of formative assessment, *The Curriculum Journal*, 2, 2, 65–87.

Unit for Development of Adult and Continuing Education (1992) *Learning Outcomes in Higher Education* (London, Further Education Unit).

Unit for Development of Adult and Continuing Education (1994) *Learning Outcomes in Higher Education* (London, Further Education Unit).

Walford, G. (1994) (ed.) *Researching the Powerful* (London, University College London Press).

West, J. (2000) *Validity and Reliability in Qualifications: technical and political considerations.* Unpublished MA dissertation (Sheffield, University of Sheffield).

West, L. (1995) Beyond fragments: adults, motivation and higher education *Studies in the Education of Adults*, 27, 1, 133–57.

White, J. (1997) Philosophy and the aims of higher education, *Studies in Higher Education*, 22, 1, 7–19.

Whitty, G. and Edwards, T. (1994) Researching the Assisted Places Scheme, in Walford, G (ed.) (1994) *Researching the Powerful in Education* (London, University College London).

Wilmut, J. (1999) *Internal Assessment* (London, Qualifications and Curriculum Authority).

Williams, R. (1983) *Keywords: a Vocabulary of Culture and Society* (London, Fontana Press).

Williams, S. (1997) The development of NVQs in the UK: an institutional analysis of policy failure in vocational education and training. Paper presented to the *Journal of Vocational Education and Training 2nd International Conference* (University of Huddersfield, 16–18 July, 1998).

Williams, S. (1999) Policy tensions in vocational education and training: the origins of General National Vocational Qualifications, *Journal of Education Policy*, 14, 2, 151–166.

Winter, R (1992) Quality management or the education work place: alternative versions of comp based education, *Journal for Higher Education*, 16, 100–15.

Winter, R. and Maisch, R. (1996) *Professional Competence in Higher Education* (London, Falmer Press).

Wolf, A. (1995) *Competence-based Assessment* (Buckingham: Open University Press).

Wolf, A. (1997a) *Evolution of GNVQs: Enrolment and Delivery Patterns and their Policy Implications* (London, Nuffield Fourndation/Further Education Development Agency).

Wolf, A. (1997b) Growth stocks and lemons: diplomas in the English market-place, 1976–1996, *Assessment in Education: Principles, Policy and Practice*, 4, 1, 33–59.

Wolf, A. (1998) Portfolio assessment as national policy, *Assessment in Education: Policy, Principles and Practice*, 5, 3, 413–47.

Wolf, A., Burgess, R., Stott, H. and Veasey, J. (1994) *GNVQ Assessment Review Report* (Sheffield, Employment Department).

Wright Mills, C. (1970) *The Sociological Imagination* (London, Penguin).

Yeomans, D. (1998) Constructing vocational education: from TVEI to GNVQ, *Journal of Education and Work*, 11, 2, 127–49.

Yeomans, D. (1999) Exploring student-centred learning in GNVQs: case studies of classroom practice, *The Curriculum Journal*, 10, 3, 361–84.

Young, D. (1990) *The Enterprise Years* (London, Headline Books).

Young, M. (ed.) (1971) *Knowledge and Control: new directions for the sociology of education* (London, Collier-Macmillan).

Young, M. (1998) *The Curriculum of the Future* (London, Falmer Press).

Zukas, M. and Malcom, J. (2000) Pedagogies for lifelong learning: building bridges or building walls?. Paper given to *Supporting Lifelong Learning Colloquium* (London, University of East London, 4 July 2000).

Author index

Subject index

A-levels 69, 70, 74, 75, 81
assessment: Assessment/accreditation of
Prior Learning 2, 85; *'assessment
career'* 170–173; *'assessment regime'*
169, 170–171, 173, 177, 183;
*criterion-referenced assessment,
norm-referencing* 2, 58, 69; *formative
assessment, feedback* 4,
11–12, 28–29, 35, 40–41, 51, 92, 97,
148–157–159, 176–179; *norm-
referenced assessment, norm-
referencing* 2, 48, 49, 69, 74, 75,
179; *ipsative assessment* 38, 134,
135, 138, 155, 170, 195; *outcome-
based assessment* 2, 5, 29, 36, 47,
48–50, 58, 59, 70–71, 75; *peer
assessment* 157–158; *reliability in
assessment* 69, 74, 75, 166, 173;
validity in assessment 70–71, 173
autonomy 2, 4, 11–13, 17–18, 25, 26,
27, 33–40, 47, 81, 165, 172;
constructs inside policy 53–69;
*constructs in further education
curriculum* 92, 97; *amongst GNVQ
students* 131–147, 153; *enhancing
autonomy in further education*
177–178, 180; *procedural autonomy*
36–37, 127, 132, 142, 147, 170,
177; *personal autonomy* 37–38, 127,
132, 135–136, 147, 154, 165, 170,
177, 180; *critical autonomy* 38–40,
127, 143, 147, 151, 154, 137–140,
164, 165, 177, 180

behaviourism, behaviourist learning 11,
28, 29, 32, 33, 40, 43, 44, 49, 181
Business and Technology Education
Council (BTEC) 1, 61, 70, 95, 99,
104, 109

Certificate in Pre-Vocational Education
(CPVE) 1, 49, 70, 82, 85, 93–95, 99,
104, 109,
City and Guilds awarding body 84,
95
communities of practice 3, 41, 42, 44,
162, 164, 171
constructivism, constructivist learning
3, 11, 28, 37, 40, 41, 43, 44, 49,
169, 177, 181
credentialism 20
cultural capital 138, 148

Department for Education and Science
(DES) 3, 22, 67, 68, 69, 76, 77, 79,
85, 94, 95, 173
Department for Education (DfE) 71, 77,
79, 80, 173, 174
Department of Education and
Employment (DfEE) 95, 169, 173,
174, 177
Department for Education and Skills
(DfES) 96

Eggar, Tim 68, 97
equal opportunities 18

Further Education Funding Council
(FEFC) 22, 64, 65, 66, 82, 83, 98,
100
FEFC inspectors/inspectorate 71, 72,
78, 97, 101, 102, 104, 167, 173
Further Education Development Agency
(FEDA) 65, 67, 68, 78, 79, 97, 98,
167
Further Education Unit (FEU) 61, 72,
78, 79, 84, 173

general education 85